Ronnie Knight

Living
Dangerously

Ronnie Knight
with Peter Gerrard

BLAKE

This edition published in Great Britain in 2000 by
Blake Publishing Ltd
3 Bramber Court
2 Bramber Road
London W14 9PB

A CIP catalogue for this book
is available from the British Library

ISBN 185782 3524

Typeset in Great Britain by BCP

Printed and bound in Finland by WS Bookwell

3 5 7 9 10 8 6 4 2

To Edie and Poochie Massey —
Genuine Friends

ACKNOWLEDGEMENTS

My thanks to my friends Peter and Shirley Gerrard. Shirley for her many hours of typing and editing, and Peter for making sense of my scribblings. And thanks to Bobbie Dixie and his wife, Sheila, who supported me throughout my years in prison.

CONTENTS

1.
HMP Send

I WALKED BACK from the Governor's office after being congratulated by him for my good behaviour while doing my time. Down to that he told me I had earned my category D. Three years it took. Three long years since I was forced to put my hand up to handling stolen money from Security Express. Three years since I was given a seven and bunged on 'A' cat, which meant I was watched day and night, strip-searched before and after every visit and escorted everywhere I went – even in the yard.

When I was on nine months' remand I expected that sort of treatment. But once I was sentenced and shipped off to Parkhurst I thought they would have shown a bit more leniency when you consider I gave myself up to the law in the first place. By coming back to face my accusers obviously I wanted to clean the slate and start afresh. But somebody up there must have had it in for me. It wasn't to be, so I had to swallow what I was handed out.

Still, all that was behind me now. And sitting in the prison gardens by the fish pond with the smell of new cut grass, flowers, warm sun and birdsong, I could close my eyes and imagine I was anywhere. If this sounds like I had myself a nice little berth to pass the time away in, or a better quality of life than many unfortunates outside, don't kid yourself. There's no similarity to a holiday camp when you're banged up in prison.

It's not the surroundings that make or break you, it's the fact that you are away from all the people you love. Away from familiar surroundings and the taken-for-granted luxury of being able to do whatever you feel like doing, whenever you feel like doing it. On top of that you completely lose control of that part of your life that's left outside the wire.

My father-in-law Bob died. He was a good man and I had the greatest respect for him. Yet I never got the chance to say goodbye to him or comfort the family outside. My favourite dog, RJ had to be put down, and to me and my wife Sue that was the same as losing a child. Worst of all I lost my Mum. She was suffering from Parkinson's disease and Alzheimer's, so she was being cared for in a nursing home. Once she was too ill to come out to Spain obviously I couldn't visit her and by the nature of her illness couldn't speak to her on the telephone. But I spoke to the nurses regularly to find out how she was getting on. I rang up the home from Littlehey prison and was told she was dead. As plain as that. No warning, no time to prepare myself. In fact she had died three days before, and nobody had let me know.

To say I was upset would be an understatement, especially as it was so unexpected. One of the reasons I had come home was to see that lovely woman who I thought the world of. And now all I'd be able to do when I'd served my time would be to say a little prayer beside a commemorative rose. As if losing her wasn't heartbreaking enough, I wasn't allowed to attend her funeral. Even Reggie and Ronnie Kray were shown compassion when their Mum died, and it would be stretching it a bit to suggest I was ever in their league. But the system had it in for me from way back, so I should never have been surprised that they couldn't resist the opportunity to twist the knife.

Compared to places like the Scrubs or Littlehey, HMP Send in Home Counties' Surrey sounds very nice. But this doesn't mean the authorities have gone soft. Me and every one of the other inmates there had to earn the privilege the hard way. Years of knuckling down to whatever was thrown at us. Of accepting that we were nothing but a number with no say in what went on in our daily lives. Of good behaviour in our efforts to gain that magic 'D' cat, when all we really wanted to do was smash the place up in frustration.

Believe me, I've been in some piss holes, and there were times when I thought I couldn't get through it. The hours creep past and you feel like you've done five years. You look at the calendar with the scribbles over every day you've done and your stomach knots up when you see it's only been five months. Quick bit of arithmetic and you work out, with good behaviour, another thousand days. One thousand fucking days and one thousand nights. Just try to encompass that length of time and your head feels like it's going to burst and you want to kick the door down.

I managed to keep it all inside though it wasn't always easy. Other cons must have looked at me and thought, good old Ronnie, he knows how to do easy time. But honest to God I'd never want to do those early months over again. What helped me to keep it together were the fellas I mixed with, the best bunch of mates you could wish for.

Every one of them were rascals, same as me, or we wouldn't have been in prison together. When we were messing about and having a good laugh I couldn't help thinking about the contrast between that place and some of the other prisons I'd been in. Particularly a place up Cambridge way: HMP Littlehey. I was looking for a move from Parkhurst so when I saw Cambridgeshire on the form I thought that'll do me because when I was a kid I spent a bit of time there and had nice memories of the woods and fields. Not that I'd be wandering through either but just knowing they were only outside the wire would be a nice thought. So I put myself up for it.

Two minutes inside the gate and I knew I didn't

like it – five and I hated the place. There was a funny atmosphere I couldn't put my finger on, but I knew it didn't feel right. Straight off the screws took a dislike to me. I suppose they thought, Here comes the famous Ronnie Knight – flash bastard. All wrong really. I'm just another bloke trying to do his time. It's the papers that keep putting my name up, mainly because of Barbara Windsor. Having been married to her for over 20 years there's no chance that even now we're divorced they'll leave me alone.

There were a few good blokes in that nick but what I found after a few days was that I was getting pulled up by some of them. They'd be saying, ''Ere, Ronnie, what you doing talking to this one or that one?'

Me, I'll talk to anyone so I've got to say, 'Well, why shouldn't I?' Then I'm put straight. 'That dirty bastard gets it off with little boys and him over there rapes babies then cuts them up.' Fuck me, I'm surrounded by pervs and nonces. I know I said I'll talk to anybody, but I meant whether they're a dustmen or a duchess – doesn't matter to me. But all that other business makes me feel sick. They want shooting. What they need is branding on the forehead with a red hot poker, then decent rascals would know to blank them. Without that there's no way of telling who's who, so I just made sure that I was very careful who I spoke to.

The boys I did time with at Send were as far removed from that scum as you could get. Every one of them off the top of the pile. Seven of us shared a dormitory. One side had bars all along like you see in

American prison films, except ours was only locked up at night. We had a bed each, cupboards for our bits and pieces, chairs, tables, a television in the corner and a bit of music.

During the day I worked in the gardens, and I loved it but by early evening I couldn't wait to get back in with the boys because we had such a great time. That's what I mean about good mates keeping you going. Everything turned into a joke. We gee each other up and take the piss, but without it you wouldn't last five minutes.

When your category changes the system has a rule that you must move to a different prison. They give you a short list of choices and for your own reasons you choose one of them. If your face doesn't fit those that make the final decision can make some excuse then send you to the opposite end of the country from your choice. But if you've kept your nose clean you're OK. I put Send on my application because Tony O'Brien, a friend of mine, was already there, and he reckoned it was, in his words, 'the dog's bollocks'.

Now my other five mates there were Frank Simms, John Lloyd, Paul Kidd, Big John Wheatley and the youngest, Danny Ho. Danny was a good kid, and though he's Chinese, one of your own. Trouble was in the six and a half years he'd been going round the system he'd made life hard for the screws, which means he'd been making it tough for himself. I think in his mind doing what he was told and just getting on with it went against the grain. Every opportunity he got he'd slip into the PO's office and wreck the place. No one wanted him so he was moved and moved, and finally he ended up in with us.

I'd known him for about two years because wherever I went he was either there first or followed me soon after. I could talk to him so I put him straight. 'Danny,' I said, 'keep your head down. It won't make you any less of a man. Behave like we do and see what happens.' Did I give him good advice or what? Six weeks later he got home leave – first time in nearly seven years.

Now Frank was a double live wire. He was born in Stratford, and was half a dozen years younger than me. In his youth he was a very tasty boxer, and when he was 11 won himself a medal at the centenary of Alexandra Palace. A few years later he turned professional with great success. Teaming up with his mate Jimmy Tibbs, a good man from a well-known family, they used to organise great boxing shows and between the two of them have trained some of the best boxers in the country. Where business is concerned Frank is a very serious man, but faced with adversity like he had been, while serving his long prison sentence, he'd risen above what the system has tried to do to him by his own humour and zest for life.

Frank was given an eleven. He never stops laughing, and he's always singing. He would talk to the plants when we were working, and he got me talking to them as well. He used to drive me and all the other boys mad and one of these days he'll drive himself up the wall. Sometimes I wished they'd just let him out so we could all get some peace.

I've known him for years, going right back to the seventies when he used to come into my club in London, The Artistes and Repertoire. It was there one night after he'd had a good drink that he said, 'Ronnie, I'm shooting off.' Away he goes, and a bit later I find he hasn't paid us for his last round. Came to £4.00. Next thing I hear he's got himself sent down for 15 years, so my four quid's out of the window.

Frankie and Jimmy Tibbs have always worked tirelessly for charity, and when they were in the fight game made sure that a percentage of the gate money from their promotions always went to a good cause. Years and years pass and I'm doing my bit of exile in Spain. Then who walks on to the field of a charity football match my wife Sue was organising but Frankie and Jimmy Tibbs. They had both flown a long way just to support Sue. Great guys! It was lovely to see them again even though it gave me a touch of home sickness. Match over, I took them both back to my villa. I gave them a few drinks and a nice barbecue, then bang! they're on the plane and gone. Frankie never once mentioned that four quid though!

Years passed again. Things happened in my life that led to me being banged up, and while I'm doing my time I hear on the grapevine that Frankie's back in the system. It seemed like it didn't matter what nick I was sent to, as soon as I got there different people I knew would tell me, 'You've just missed Frankie – ghosted out last week.' I think he heard I was coming and got himself a move in case he had to put his hand in his pocket.

I was having a chat with Johnny Lloyd one night when he mentioned Frankie – seems that his wife was a friend of Frankie's wife. Frankie's missus was seriously ill, which was upsetting Frankie as he'd never had home leave in six and a half of his 11-year sentence. I said to John, 'We've got to try and get him here to help him and his missus.' We had a word with one of the officers – decent sort – and though it didn't happen overnight a few strings were pulled and out of the blue in walks Frankie. He's a happier man these days. Drives us all crackers, but he still hasn't come across with that four quid. The interest must be about £4000 now.

Johnny Lloyd and Paul Kidd are another two friends from way back. I didn't see too much of Paul in the old days, but Johnny has been a good mate ever since A & R days. It was years since I'd seen him last, and after he'd greeted me when I arrived I said, 'Fuck me, Johnny, you look about 40 years old.' I knew he was 58, but he didn't look it. He told me he worked out in the gym every day to keep fit, but added, 'Ronnie mate, if you'd seen me a few years ago when Jean was doing time, I looked about 70.'

It was terrible. John's wife Jean had been convicted of laundering money from the £25 million Brinks-Mat robbery that had been carried out in 1983 at Heathrow Airport. It was gold bars and diamonds that were stolen, but once they had been sold on the resulting cash had to be cleaned up. For involvement in that Jean got five years hard time and had her parole turned down twice. As John remarked, the only thing that kept him strong through those years were their daughters and grandchildren.

'Imagine', he said, 'Christmas time – with all the family and kids over for dinner and Jean stuck in prison. Now it's the other way round. I'm doing five, and she's waiting for me.' He made me laugh when he added, 'You don't have to tell me what you've been up to, Ron. I only had to pick up a paper, and there you were.'

I mustn't leave out John Wheatley, or, at six foot two and built like an athlete, 'Big John'. He's only young but well respected. We'd all be lying about watching telly, and he'd ask, 'Shall I make a cup of tea?' and all us old geezers are saying, 'Yeah, go on then, son' and next minute he's handing mugs round. We didn't treat him as a gofer, he's just that sort of bloke – polite, quiet and respectful, which is why he gets respect himself.

If all those years ago somebody had said one day you lot will be sharing a cell together, we'd have chucked him out the window. But there we were. Certainly a lot older and definitely a lot wiser.

So that was the family. Seems a funny word to use, but while were in there that's what they seemed like. We lived together, and we looked out for each other. Because of these good friends my bird went so fast I couldn't believe it. Unlike the early part of my time, I looked forward to starting every new day. I suppose I was on a high. Like I'd come through a very dark tunnel and suddenly burst into the light. Every minute that ticked by was one closer to a freedom that I could almost touch.

Before it was so out of sight I couldn't even think of walking through the gates. It was too painful. But now I was with good friends, the sun was shining, and I knew nothing could stop me going home very soon. I won't dwell on the negative side of those years inside. I'd find it too depressing to think about. All the ins and outs of why I was doing that sentence is a story in itself for later on, but while I'm on about prison I'll run through all the places I've been in.

First off I'm sent to Brixton as an 'A' man. That's the category that determines the level of security you're under, and believe me 'A' is the tops. I get nicely settled in, get to know a few people, then bomp! 'Knight, you've got to move, we don't keep "As" here,' I'm told. I think whoever is running the show don't know their arse from their earhole, but I can't say anything – I'm just a number. So it's in the van and off to Wormwood Scrubs. Everything's over the top on the 'As'. Somebody on the security side must have worked out that it takes three weeks to dig a tunnel out of a cell, because every fortnight you've got to move to another gaff.

Just got the pictures on the wall when the key rattles in the door, and it's 'Move, move.' Could be upstairs or downstairs. But wherever, not only are there bars on the windows but they're also all covered in a fine mesh so nothing can be passed in or out. In the early stage of my sentence I couldn't get my head round the terrible situation I'd found myself in. But if nothing else I could look forward to a few visitors to break up the monotony. Though as if you're not fucked up enough already even that's made difficult on the 'As'.

If you want somebody to visit you all their details have to be put down on a form so that the police can check them out. If it suits them they can drag out their inquiries for ages. On top of that all visits are at first what they call closed. So instead of sitting round a nice table with a cup of tea they stick you behind glass. You're looking through at the visitors, and they're staring back at you. It's difficult to hear them very well and the same the other way round. In the end it gives everybody the arsehole and makes you wonder if it's worth the effort.

Two people who were acceptable to the prison and the police to come in and see me straight away were Jim and Joy Lumley, lovely people and great friends. I'd known Jimmy for donkey's years. I first met him through an old school pal, Siddy Smith, when we all used to meet up and go round the clubs and pubs. Like often happens with young mates we lost touch for years. Then it was a sad time that brought us back together again.

All I'll say for the moment is, when I came back to face the music in 1994 Jim and his wife Joy were there for me a hundred per cent. If he wasn't already a Freeman of the City of London I'd have put his name forward myself for what he'd done for me. Never missed a visit since and spent all his spare time helping to straighten my affairs. In fact he did so much it would take another book to list everything. On top of that he never earned one single penny out of me, unlike a lot of people who lined their pockets at my expense.

Five months I had to put up with being behind glass on 'A' cat. I kept complaining, but nothing was happening. Then I spoke to one of the Governors, and he allowed me an occasional Sunday open visit. He was doing me a favour, perhaps because he thought I wasn't being treated right.

Another thing 'As' are not allowed are phone cards. You can phone out, but you have to tell them what the number is and who you are ringing. Then they record your conversations. One bonus with this system is you get priority in the queues. There might be a dozen fellas lining up, but all you have to do is wait for the first one to put the phone down, then you walk down the line and make your call. Of course you can hear the newcomers mumbling behind you: 'What's his fucking game?' and all that, until one of the others straightens him: 'He's an "A" man, he's entitled.' No argument after that.

I'm in the Scrubs for about ten months when a screw says, 'You're for the off tomorrow.' 'What do you mean the off?' I ask. 'You're going somewhere where there's loads of water,' he replies, then he laughs and walks off. Now I know where there is a lot of water, and that's in Spain, but I doubt I'm being sent back to my villa. Back in my cell one of the boys says, 'Sounds like Parkhurst, Ronnie.' Bloody hell! I've heard all the stories about Parkhurst and Dartmoor, terrible places. I'd read in the paper that the day before there had been a lot of prisoners gone over the wall. So I can expect we'll be banged up 24 hours a day and get loads of aggravation from the screws. So what chance have I got for a quiet life?

We set off early, and it was hours before we pulled on to the Isle of Wight ferry. It was a terrible day, pouring with rain, and the boat was going up and down. I'm not a lover of sailing at the best of times, and what with being cuffed up and stuck inside the van I'm starting to feel a bit queasy. Then the two screws escorting me decide to go off for a cup of tea. 'Oi,' I remind them, 'What about me?' 'What about you?' asks one of them. 'Well,' I reply, 'what if there's an accident and the boat goes down?' What comfort do they give me? 'It never has before.' Bastards!

Eventually I got safely into reception, and I couldn't believe it. There was only one officer checking things out and no locked doors like in the Scrubs. Ten minutes and I'm booked into 'A' wing, well on paper anyway. Just as I'm walking out of reception another screw who I got to know as Charlie came in. 'Hello, mate,' he said, then he looked at me. 'Oh, it's Knighty. Where have they put you down for?' When I told him 'A' wing he said, 'Nah, can't have that. It's full of young kids, they'll drive you up the wall.' So he phones 'D' wing – Can you take him? Yes – all done. Good man, Charlie.

Right away I meet faces from the old club days. I didn't remember all the names, but suddenly I've got tea bags, sugar, biscuits – you name it – coming from everywhere. I'd brought plenty of gear with me that I'd bought with my pay-off wages from the last nick, but these boys wanted to give me everything. That's when you find out who your friends are.

After a few days one of the fellas said, 'You're in the papers again, Ronnie.' Sure enough somebody had been making themselves busy by phoning the press to earn a few quid. I forget the headline, probably something insulting like KNIGHT NOT SO BIG NOW or KNIGHT GETS ROUGH RECEPTION.

What it said was that as soon as I got there one of the screws stuck a bucket and brush in my hand and said, 'Get in the piss house and start scrubbing.' They couldn't have been further from the truth because straight away I was put on the garden party, and it was lovely. In fact I stayed in the gardens the whole time I was in Parkhurst. I couldn't have been there too many weeks before I'm in the news again. This time they had me down as winning a prize for growing the best onions in the prison. Where that came from I can't imagine but they must have been the fastest growing onions in the world.

I worked with an old lifer called Dick. Been doing the gardens for years, and there was nothing he didn't know about growing things so I learnt a lot from him. He'd say, 'Come on, Ron, we've got to feed the bees.' There were four hives, and of course once you've taken the honey you have to replace it with sugar water for them to live on. He told me, 'Don't fling your arms about, and they won't hurt you.' And he was right. You could let them settle on your hands without worrying about being stung.

To tell you the truth I wasn't nervous anyway because in the Scrubs I used to have them fly in my window early in the morning. I'd put a few sweets down, and they'd feed for ages. They were fascinating, and it gave me a bit of interest. And, let's face it, there's not much going on in these places. All the boys used to look round the door and go, 'Cor, sodding hell, Ronnie's got his cell filled with wasps.' None of them dared to come in while they were there.

Never mind my emotional state and other problems I had to put up with, what with being outside all day and generally mixing with a lot of good blokes, Parkhurst wasn't a bad nick. Certainly nowhere as bad as I'd imagined. Then some bright spark decided that the whole place was to be turned into a category 'B', which meant 'As' and 'Cs' had to move on. By this time I'm a 'C', so I put in my application for Littlehey. Apart from remembering Cambridge as a nice part of the world, my Sue's mum, Marge, lived there as well as my sister-in-law and kids. So getting a visit from them would be nice.

So much for being near family though. When I'd first got to Littlehey Jim had informed me, 'Ronnie, d'you know they all ride bicycles up here in Cambridge?' 'Yeah,' I replied, 'so I've heard.' 'Well,' he continued, 'listen out, and if you hear pedals squeaking nice and steady you'll know it's your mother-in-law coming to visit, and she's in a good mood. But ... if the pedals are going squeak-squeak-

squeak dead fast that'll be old Marge got the hump with you and coming up to bollock you.' Well, she must have got the hump over something because I only ever got the one visit from her.

Unless you're sick or disabled in some way, the system insists that you work. So as soon as I arrived at Littlehey I filled in an application for garden detail. I'm experienced at it so I think they won't be able to wait to get me sorting out their vegetable plot.

A few days after settling in I'm being escorted to work. After walking through corridor after corridor for a while I asked the screw, 'Are your gardens inside, then?' He looked at me a bit strange and said, 'No. What do you mean?' 'Because I put in for the gardens, and we haven't gone outside yet,' I answered. He looked at his sheet and shook his head: 'Nope, plain enough, you're down for the machine shop.' When I've kicked up a fuss he's told me that governor number four, a woman by the name of McAllister, had refused my application. This was the first time I'd heard of her, and it wouldn't be the last.

In the machine shop they made all sorts of items of clothing – slippers, shirts and underwear. So straight off they show me how to use an overlocking machine and get me stitching up collars and all kinds of bits and pieces. I hated it.

End of the day I put in a complaint that all the dust fibres were getting on my chest. Truth is I did have a bit of a cough, but I laid it on a bit heavy so they'd have to put me in the garden. OK, they said, report to the doctor first thing. To strengthen my case I put myself about and got hold of one of those inhaler gadgets just to prove I already had a medical condition.

My examination was going beautifully what with me coughing like a good-un. Until I put my ace on the desk: the inhaler. I could see by the Doc's face that he'd have me in the gardens for the afternoon shift. There's all bits and pieces with it, so he's picked them up and asked, 'How often do you have to use this?' 'Well, sir, since being in the machine shop it must be every ten minutes.' He's rocked himself back on his chair, made a steeple of his fingers and looked at me, looked at the inhaler and dry as you like said, 'I haven't seen one as old as this for a very long time – show me how you put it together.' What does he mean put it together? I thought all the odd bits were spare parts. I'd blown it. He knew I was pulling a stroke, and before I know it I'm back in the shop stitching gussets with 'Medical complaint not supported' stuck in my file.

As usual I'd applied for and sent off a visiting order for Jim. I was looking forward to his visit because he's so full of fun it doesn't matter what trouble I have he sets me up for another week. Anyway come the Saturday he turned up with another good friend of mine, George Massey, though ever since we were little kids he's been called 'Poochie'. That was down to an aunt of his who reckoned he looked like a little friendly puppy what with his blond hair and little face.

As soon as Jim brought the teas and chocolate

biscuits over to the table he told me there were loads of reporters and snappers outside the gates. They were all pushing and shoving around every car that came in to be first to interview Joanna Lumley when she turned up. It must have been one of the screws that phoned the papers and told them that J. Lumley was on my VO so the screw earns himself 50 quid for a phone call, and the papers get a little story. Never mind that she didn't turn up and was never going to – it made a nice headline. So that got us laughing hysterically even before we'd sat down.

On the next table an Indian kid was having a visit from his mum, and she'd brought him in a birthday cake. He was only young, and he was crying. I said to the other two, 'Look, they're having a bit of a party over there,' and Poochie looks and says, 'Yeah, but why's he crying?' Quick as a flash Jim comes back with, 'Well, it's his chapati, and he'll cry if he wants to.' Bit of a joke on that song from the sixties. We just fell about. In fact we laughed so loud even the Indian kid joined in, and he didn't know what the joke was. I think what it was, we were ready to laugh. That's how it is with us. Didn't matter how bad the jokes were we pissed ourselves. None of us will ever see 60 again yet we were like silly schoolboys, and I loved every minute of it.

Funnily enough that birthday cake was to get me into a bit of trouble. Jim pointed out that if the woman next to us could bring in food it must mean anybody can, so he said, 'Ronnie, next week I'm going to bring you in a couple of beef sandwiches.' All the following week I was like a kid waiting for Christmas because if there's one thing I'm mad about it's beef – something that seldom comes up on a prison menu.

I telephone Jim every day and have done ever since I've been inside. So on the Saturday before he leaves home I'm in the phone queue at eight o'clock. I'm a 'C' cat now so have to get in line like everybody else. When he answered he said, 'Funnily enough Joy's in the kitchen right now doing your sandwiches. Do you want mustard or horseradish?' I'm just about dribbling down the mouthpiece as I settle for radish. I can't wait.

You're not body searched at Littlehey. All they give you is a quick flick up and down with the metal detector, and you're in. When Jim sat down he says to me, 'I've got the beef in my pocket. But just in case we've made a wrong move what I've done is put each one into a Walkers crisp bag.'

Why he'd done that was because Walkers was the brand they sold in the canteen so no one's going to twig on that he's maybe pulling a stroke. He passes a bag over, and I dug the sandwich out. I've just taken a bite – and it's bloody marvellous – when I look up, and there's a woman standing beside me. Now I'm used to visitors coming up to me, shaking my hand and wanting my autograph. So when she asked, 'Are you enjoying that?' I just smiled and said, 'Lovely.'

She sort of puffed up like a frog and said, 'I'm Governor McAllister. What are you eating?' It was pretty obvious. I've got a full round of bread in my hand, so I just give her an innocent look and politely answer, 'Crisps, Ma'am.' 'Hand it to me at once,' she demanded. So I took another quick bite and passed it over. 'Now spit out what's in your mouth.' She's opened the sandwich, seen the white horseradish and thinks maybe I'm on beef with a dressing of coke.

She's gone flying off to the officer in charge, but I don't think he took a lot of notice what with people coming and going. Me, Jim and Poochie just sat looking at each other waiting for something to go off. But nothing happened. The visit wasn't cancelled, and she never came back either, but I knew that wasn't the end of it. Jim said, 'Sorry for dropping you in it, Ronnie,' but I just said, 'Fuck her, she never found the other sandwich.'

Eight o'clock next morning I'm nicked and up in front of the Governor. She wouldn't even look at me. Fourteen days loss of remission and three months closed visits. That was going to put the block on my weekly laughs with Jim. It would be just like being back on 'A' cat.

When Jim came up to visit me as usual we sat looking at one another through this bit of wood and glass they'd cobbled together in a hurry. No shelves, no nothing. Just a chair. We can see all the other boys and their visitors laughing and drinking tea, and we're stuck in a corner. After about 20 minutes I cracked. 'Sorry, mate,' I said, 'but I can't stand this. We'll have to call it a day.' 'Don't worry,' he replied, 'I understand.' He'd driven 50 miles for 20 minutes. Anybody else would have got the hump but not Jim. As long as I was all right he was happy.

The weeks are slipping by, and I'm still

complaining about working in the machine shop. But I'm told I have to stay in whatever job that's been allocated for at least three months. As a matter of principle I carried on making a fuss, but I was just ignored. So, near to the time when I could officially demand a change, I applied to the gardens and thought I'd got a result at last, because they've said, 'No problem – we'll pass your application through to the labour people.' But who looks after that department? Miss McAllister. So I was turned down.

One of the screws suggested I try for the hotplates, which is considered a good job. Bang – same result. It was put on my form though that I could move to the bricks, a course to teach bricklaying: Just what I needed at my age – to learn a trade. There'd be a lot of dust and that, but at least it would get me outside. Was I wrong or what? It is held inside.

After a while I got a bit handy at putting a few bricks down and built a wall about ten foot long. I was dead proud and full of it when I told Jim how competent I was. The next time he came up he said he'd told Joy about the wall. She'd said to tell me that next time I built one I should put a big hole in it, and then I could come and go as I liked. I'm looking for a pat on the back, and all I get is piss-taking.

To be honest I felt I was being victimised over the work detail. So I got Jim to ring up my solicitor and instruct him to write a formal letter to the Governor. Two weeks later back came a reply from one of the under Governors: 'Mr Knight can complain as loud and as long as he likes. But he will not get garden detail as long as I have a hole in my arse.'

Can you believe that? This was on official paper, signed and everything. Me and Jim argued over and over about this letter. He reckoned the last line read 'Until the cows come home,' but old Jim did love his wind-up.

I'm still backwards and forwards to the doctor, but he's having none of it. Completely unsympathetic. On the way out from my last examination I got chatting to the nurse, and she happened to say that as far as she could see I would only get a move when I actually collapsed on the job.

By some strange coincidence two days later they found me lying across the bricks with my head in a pile of cement. The nurse was brought quickly. She gave me some tests and then wrote a report saying I couldn't work the bricks anymore. It had taken a long while, but I'd cracked it at last. Or at least I thought I had until McAllister heard about it.

She kicked up a fuss with the nurse, and she kicked up a fuss with the doctor, insisting I was put back in the shop. Now I'm pissed off so I refused to work. 'Right,' she said, 'lock him in.' 'Hold up', I insisted, 'I'm entitled to walk round and get a bit of fresh air if I can't work.' All she said was 'Knight, it's not that you can't work, it's that you won't. So until you co-operate you'll be locked in.'

Next morning two officers turned up and gave my cell a spin. What she told them to look for I don't know, but they came up with a handful of phone cards worth about £50, when regulations said £6 or £7 worth maximum. I was taken in front of her again and told the matter would be dealt with on the following day. I just said, 'Excuse me, will I be in front of you when it comes up? Cos if I am I don't stand a chance.' She didn't answer, just ordered, 'Take him out.'

As it turned out I was brought up in front of Governor number three. Though I couldn't have been any worse off if I'd stuck with McAllister because the other Governor gave me 14 days loss of remission, took away my 'C' cat and put me on the 'Bs'. Then made an order for me to be shipped out. After the way I'd been messed about I didn't give a monkey's where they put me. Wherever it was couldn't be any worse.

* * *

Next stop Bedford Prison. I'm unpacking my gear, and I heard the name McAllister mentioned, so I asked the screw, 'Are you talking about the woman from my last nick?' 'No,' he replied, 'I'm talking about the Governor here – he's the husband of the one you're thinking of.' Here we go again I thought nothing like keeping me in the family. I know just what will happen – they'll be in bed, and she'll say to him, 'Now don't forget, love, make sure you keep an eye on Ronnie Knight when you get to work tomorrow.'

So that things would be nicely out in the open, I make my mind up that the first time I meet the new Governor I'm going to give him a pull and ask him what's up with his missus and why she always seemed to have the needle with me. But I never did meet him as I was in and out of Bedford within two weeks.

I was looking forward to this move because I'd heard that Blundestone up in Norfolk was quite a nice prison. I felt a bit sorry for Jim as it would mean him making a journey three times as long as before though he'd never complain. The only thing that got me down a bit was the fact that I'd lost my 'C' cat, specially over something that I thought was trivial. So now I was going to have to suffer that setback.

Blundeston was similar to Parkhurst. You got a bit of respect and weren't surrounded by nonces and silly people. I didn't get into the gardens, but I managed to get myself a decent job sweeping the landings, and as that didn't take five minutes I had plenty of time to myself.

I was only there a few days when I got a little result that proved to me that I hadn't been imagining unfair treatment at Littlehey. I was told to report to the Governor. But instead of getting a lecture about behaving better in his nick than the last one I got a pleasant surprise. He'd looked through my record and disagreed with the punishment I had received. Right there in the office he reinstated my lost remission and better than that, gave me back my 'C' cat. With that straightened up I felt a lot easier and settled down to sit my time out.

There was one little incident that cropped up which afterwards I thought I could gain a bit of mileage from. Out of the blue I'm suddenly up and down all night going to the toilet for a pee. I thought nothing of it until one of the boys suggested I got it checked out by the doctor. You've got to remember that everybody inside is either an expert on the law or the medical profession. If you've got a problem you can bet your life one of the inmates will have an answer to it. Most of the time all the answers are different, but never mind that.

I booked myself in to see the doctor. He checked me all over, and I waited for my tablets – or so I thought. Instead he puts on one rubber glove and asks me to lie on the couch. Need I say more? He wasn't getting gloved up to check my tonsils. Everything seemed clear enough, and I did end up with a few pills, and that was the end of it, until I arrived at Send.

Shortly after I moved in they started to build some new huts to extend the prison. They were only pre-fabs, but who cares because inside there would be single rooms with en-suite toilet and shower. Well, not quite en-suite but five star compared to crapping in a bucket in some of the other prisons.

No disrespect to the other lads. But being a very private person it was going to be marvellous to be on my own when I wanted to be. One bonus was that I'd be able to pull faces at myself in the mirror without the comments and piss-taking I had to put up with. Years ago my Mum said, 'Ronnie, just because you're a man doesn't mean you shouldn't look after yourself.' She said I should do facial exercises and rub cream in every night – so that's what I do. I might be older, but I'd pass for 60 anywhere.

Now I just had to have one of the single rooms

there. Obviously not everyone can have one so what are they going to do with a bloke who is backwards and forwards all night disturbing the other boys? Put him on his own naturally. So I need some insurance.

I book in for the doctor again, and this time I make sure he knows I've had this problem for ages. In fact got treated for it in Blundestone, which he knows anyway because my papers are in front of him. He didn't examine me, but he did ask if the tablets I had been given eased the problem, so I've answered, 'Well, yes and no. I used to get up about seven times a night, but with the pills I've got it down to five or four.' In the end he sent me to the local hospital outside. It was arranged that I go with one of the screws that I got on well with, and he promised me I wouldn't have to be handcuffed. Which was a relief as it could be embarrassing in public, especially as most people know my face.

When it's time to go, who turns up as escort but this little stuck up bastard who dislikes me as much as I do him. But I don't get any choice in the matter. Unlike the other fella, this one goes by the book and keeps me in handcuffs all the time. Did he think I was going to do a runner after more than three years and me with going home just round the corner?

I'm sitting in the waiting room and trying to keep my sleeves down over the cuffs but gave up in the end because it was a waste of time. What was nice, though, after all those years behind bars, was rubbing shoulders with ordinary people going about their business and seeing pretty young mums with their babies. It felt like I was a bit more normal myself.

Then it's my turn. I'm hardly through the door when the doctor starts pulling on that single glove again. I've told him, 'No need for all that lark, I've already had the two-finger job in Blundestone.' I might as well have saved my breath, for he just pointed out that medical conditions can change overnight, so would I please just co-operate and lie down.

I've got Dr Cold Finger probing me, that miserable screw smirking to himself and two young nurses wandering about. I don't know why they didn't just wheel me out to reception and let everybody have a look. Next, so they could check the capacity of my bladder I have to drink a jug of water, wait a bit, then piss into another jug so they can measure the difference in quantities. There must have been about three pints in this jug, and it was hard going getting it down. I commented that if it was lager I'd swallow it in one, but none of them even cracked a smile.

An hour later I'm bursting. I'm put into a cubicle, still with the bloody screw acting my shadow, and I start filling a jug. I can't stop. One's filled to the brim, and I'm half way up another one. The screw's looking at me with his eyes popping out of his head. 'How the fuck do you do that, Knight? You got twice as much out as you put in?' 'Look,' I replied, 'I don't need any of your clever banter – I could have a very serious problem.' He shut up.

Now I've got to carry these two jugs of hot piss down to the doctor's room, so I've asked the screw to take the cuffs off. 'Can't be done, can't be done. Rules.'

'OK,' I reasoned, 'I can't manage both of them so you'll have to carry one for me.' He made a face, but he did it. As we're walking along I really don't know how I stopped myself screaming out laughing because I'm thinking, Go on, you arsehole, you wanted to take the piss, well, now you are. Even the doctor was a comedian. He looked at me without a smile on his face and said, 'Congratulations, Mr Knight, you've shown a profit.'

On the way back I could tell the screw had got the dead needle about what he'd had to do. He made it clear that no way did he want to hear that the story had been told to every inmate in Send. I assured him that I appreciated the gesture he had made on my behalf, but everybody knew about it ten minutes after we got back. I'll bet he'll be known as 'The Piss-taker' for years to come. Strange to say I haven't had to get up once in the night since that visit to the hospital.

Forget what you might have read in the papers. Not once had I stepped a foot back in this country in 13 years. Now over the last three or so I've been all over, but seen nothing of it, apart from glimpses through prison van windows. I wish I had a pound for every time somebody has asked me: 'Why did you come back, Ronnie? Why did you put yourself up for it?' I always answer, 'I got a bit homesick' and leave it at that. The real reasons are too compli-cated for prison chat, like many unanswered ques-tions in my life.

To explain why I am the person I am today and

what led me to the just described tour of Britain's finest institutions, I have to go back well over 60 years to a crumbling two-up two-down terrace in the East End of London.

2.
Early Days

ON TUESDAY, 20 JANUARY 1934, 10 Downham Way was turned upside down when I made up my mind to pop out into the world a bit earlier than expected. It was six o'clock in the morning. Pitch dark outside and freezing cold inside and out. With labour pains coming quicker and quicker Nellie Knight, calm as you like, organised her family. Jimmy, nine, and Billy four years younger, were got out of bed, washed, dressed and fed, then packed off next door until it was time for school.

Husband Jim, who'd got a fire going and was flapping all over the place, was given a big bag of sandwiches along with instructions to call the midwife on his way to work. I can imagine the old man couldn't make himself scarce quick enough at a time like that. No different from most blokes – in those days all that baby lark was for the women and certainly not his place to be involved.

With the house empty and the kettles boiling all Mum had to do was to relax and hope her little girl didn't arrive before the midwife. Half an hour later at about 7.30 am Ronald James Knight weighed in at 6lb 7oz. Small, beautiful and with a lovely head of hair. Bit like I am now. If Mum was disappointed that she didn't get the daughter she wanted I was never aware of it.

What can I say about my early years in that little house? Most of my memories are ones I can't really put my finger on. More feelings really. Of being warm, comfortable and secure. Two hazy memories of those years, before I was old enough or adventurous enough to go far from the front door, were of either playing in blazing sunshine all day long, or running little cars along the rug in front of a blazing coal fire and never being too far from Mum that I couldn't hear her singing.

From as far back as I was conscious of what was going on around me, I was aware of a sort of screeching sound that came from outside. No doubt it slipped into my mind even when I was months old, but it was always there. Well, not always, because I'd be lying in bed in the morning then this sound would start, and I'd know it was nearly time to get up.

As I got a bit older I found out that behind the fence just across the road was Jinkinsons sawmill, and the noises I had grown so used to were the massive circular saws they used for cutting up the timber. A by-product, and a very saleable one, of this constant milling was sawdust. And from this I gained two benefits. One was that Dad worked there. Driving a delivery lorry and dropping the stuff off to pubs, fishmongers and butchers so they could spread it on the floors. This was at a time when most blokes were struggling to find a job, so of course it put food on our table.

But second, and more important to me, was that sawdust was about as close to sand as you could get. Not that I'd ever played in sand, but I'd seen it in picture books about the seaside, so I had an idea they were much the same. How I got across the road and through the fence in the first place I can't remember. Probably Billy, who'd have been about nine then, dragged me over there after tea when it was closed, whispering, 'Don't tell, Mum.'

What a place! Everywhere I looked there were great heaps of the stuff. Some of it was white, some golden brown and in smaller piles some that was deep red. I learnt to leave that alone because it made you sneeze and itch from head to toe. But the other stuff, now that was magic. We rolled in it, buried ourselves in it, and we poured it out to make the walls of forts or mountains. And all the time I was in a cloud of this wonderful spicy smell. I remember not long before I moved back to England I was having some work done in the villa. The Spanish chippy was sawing up this big beam, and as I stood and watched him the smell of that wood took me straight back to

Jinkinsons' yard. All that's happened over years and years, and suddenly in a few strokes of a saw I'm four years old again.

Now Mum soon twigged where I was disappearing to because she'd had it all before with Jimmy and Billy. So I was told: 'Keep out of that yard, Ronnie – it's a dangerous place for kids.' I soon forgot the warning, and days later I've had a great time with two equally young pals, and it's time to go in. As soon as I stepped in the kitchen Mum looks up from her knitting and says, 'Have you been in that sawmill again?' I'm standing there like one of the characters out of the flour advert – white as a ghost, just two little eyes looking at her – and I've got the nerve to say 'No, Mum.' I get my second and final warning. Even at that age I must have had the makings of being a bit slippery because next time, before I climbed back through the fence, I dusted myself down, ruffled all the bits out of my hair and gave my face a hand wash.

Sunday night – bath night. Mum's got the tin bath off its nail on the outside toilet wall, put it in front of the fire and topped it up with kettles of water. She's standing there with flannel and soap, and I peel off. The last thing off are my little pants, and as I've pulled them down they're followed by a shower of sawdust. The heart-sinking thought that I'd dropped myself in it came at the same time as two neatly aimed smacks on the exposed cheeks of my bare bum. 'That's for telling lies. Now get in that bath.'

To me that little house in Hoxton, or 'Oxen in our cockney dialect, was the best place in the world. The truth was one bloody good shove would have sent ours and all the others in the street flying in a pile of bricks. Years later Dad told me that we took our lives in our hands every time we walked up the stairs or across the floor. And from what he said the patterns on my bedroom ceiling that to me conjured up castles and landscapes were to him more of a sign that one day we would be flattened by slabs of plaster.

So with demolition on the cards and the offer of the keys to a brand-new flat the Knight family prepared to move. One Saturday morning Dad borrowed the firm's lorry, swept out the layer of sawdust and with the help of his boys loaded up our bits and pieces. Jimmy and Billy fought over who was going to lie on the settee in the back, and I got in the front beside Mum and off we went.

As we pulled out into Kingsland Road I looked at Mum, and there were tears rolling down her face. At the time I couldn't understand why she was crying, and it was years later before I realised that just because a place isn't up to much doesn't mean it's any easier to leave behind years of memories. Again, it was a long time before I realised I'd left a little piece of myself in that old house.

By the time we were driving along Kingsland High Street Mum had cheered up, and as we turned right into Arcola Street her and Dad were laughing fit to bust over something or other. To me it was like we'd travelled to another country, though it would be stretching it to say we went more than a couple of miles.

Hindle House was one block of flats among many on a council development. When we moved in the site wasn't even finished, and there were piles of sand, bricks and scaffolding all over the place. To get into our block we had to balance our way up a ramp of springy boards because they hadn't put the steps in. Flats have had a lot of stick over the years, especially the sort Hindle House was – concrete jungles, high-rise ghettos and all that. But in those days, when life was so hard, it was different.

To get one of these places was the ultimate dream for most young families. Three bedrooms, lounge, kitchen and the best room of all – the bathroom. It didn't just have an inside toilet, but along one wall, sparkling white and surrounded by shining tiles, was a bath you could fill by turning a tap. Since then I've had a bathroom kitted out in marble, cut-glass mirrors and gold-plate taps, but none of them has filled me with such a feeling as I had that day.

This move turned out to be a milestone in my young life as I found the world was a much bigger place than I could have imagined, what with only being used to our little back yard, the front pavement or the sawdust yard. Being still young I wasn't allowed to wander so far that I wouldn't be able to hear Mum's 'Ronnieee' floating down from four floors above, but still a lot further than kids of five or six are allowed today. I suppose there were weirdos about in those days but nowhere like on the scale of today, where it seems a mother's only got to turn her head and the kid's nicked from under her nose.

On this unfinished site there were holes to jump down, pipes to climb up on and so many bits and pieces for throwing you didn't know what to pick up next. Being mainly young families in the flats there were loads of kids about so I was soon palled up in a little gang. Then came the day I'd been looking forward to – starting school.

Billy must have painted a pretty good picture of it to me because my head was filled with the prospect of picture books, toys and bottles of milk you didn't have to pay for. Shacklewell School was about two minutes' walk from home, so with one hand in Billy's and one in Mum's I skipped all the way there on that Monday morning. With a quick kiss she left me there and went off to do a bit of shopping. By the time she got back to the flat I'm sitting on the landing outside our front door. As far as I was concerned I'd given it a try, found it wasn't for me and made up my mind I wasn't going back.

Mum had a different idea. And if you were to talk a walk around those streets today I reckon you'd still see the marks in the pavement where I dug my heels in and she dragged me back. After that, encouraged by an occasional tanned backside, I went every day, but never without making a fuss because I hated every single minute.

Hoxton, where we'd just moved from, must have been as far down the slum-housing scale of poverty as it was possible to get. Yet as far as I could remember the few kids I mixed with were reasonably dressed.

Their clothes might have been handed down three or four times, but they were presentable. In hindsight perhaps the families around us were lucky enough to be in work like Dad. But as soon as I started school in Stoke Newington, as young as I was I couldn't help thinking how strange it was that mums would let their kids out dressed the way they were. Our Mum would have rather starved herself than let us step outside the door looking scruffy. All right, we might have been well patched, but always clean and tidy.

Now all of a sudden I'm mixing with kids who not only are black as Newgate's Knocker with dirt, but they've got holes in the arse of their shorts, no jerseys even on the coldest day and on their feet worn out rubber plimsolls and no socks. It was years later before I realised what a desperate hand-to-mouth existence so many families had to suffer in the East End during those years.

I didn't like the sums and spelling we had to do, but I did enjoy the playtime when we could run off a bit of pent-up-steam. The girls seemed to spend all their time skipping or singing games in circles, but the boys, well, we must have been like wild animals. Every word had to be at the top of our lungs and every move at high speed. Round and round the playground whooping and screaming like Indians. A quick stop for a drink out of the tap in the toilets, then off again.

Any one of us who was lucky enough to have been given or had managed to nick an apple on the way to school was followed around by loads of kids, every one of them begging for the core. If you were man of the moment you'd scrape away at the fruit as far down to the pips and pith as was possible, then hand it over to whoever you wanted as a friend. Though it was more likely given to the one you didn't want as an enemy.

Hygiene? We didn't even know what it meant. So it wasn't out of the way to spot one of the kids with a bulge in his cheek and ask if you could have a few sucks on the sweet. For the same reasons as with the apple nine times out of ten it would be handed over. It went without saying you didn't take liberties and crunch it. Half a dozen good sucks and back it went into the owner's mouth. Never did any of us any harm.

Funny how kids are. One minute Roy Rogers or Gene Autry are getting stuck into Ringo the bad cowboy, who always wore a black shirt. Most of this was a lot of pushing and shoving, and shouts of 'Get outta town, ya varmint.' Until one or other of them gets a punch on the nose a bit too hard for this sort of game.

Apart from my misery over going to school, at home life was very nice for all of us. Eldest brother Jimmy was working and helping out with a few bob. Mum had her beautiful home to look after. Us other kids were getting up to all sorts and having a good time, and Dad was still driving for Jinkinsons. Whenever I wasn't at school Dad would say, 'Want to help with the deliveries, Ronnie?' and I'd jump at the chance of driving round the East End with him in the lorry. I loved sitting up high in the big, old rattling motor. I doubt I was any help at all and probably drove him mad with questions, but at the end of the day I'd go home with a pocket full of coppers.

Dad was well respected, and everywhere we went the shop or pub people would be saying, 'Cor, Jim, is this your boy? Ain't he a chip off the old block!' and all that, then slip me a penny or threepence. Sometimes I'd be given a bit of fish. 'Go on, son, give that to yer ma,' they'd say, and when we got home I'd hand it over as proud as if I'd caught it myself.

What I didn't know at the time, but Mum and Dad must have, was that our comfortable life was going to get a knock back very soon. War had been declared between Britain and Germany, and round the table I'd often hear Dad talking to Mum about Mr Bleeding Hitler, which I always thought was a bit of an odd name for anybody. Kids at school who were better informed than me said that this bloke was going to come and drop bombs on us, but you could never believe half the things said in the playground.

Nothing happened. So as the months slipped past I knew those toerags had been lying. Then we started practising air-raid drill at school. At different times a bell would ring, and we'd all have to march out to the shelters that had been built in the yard. Sometimes we'd have to lie down, curl up and put our arms over our heads. Without a thought about how serious this was I loved every minute of it because it broke up the monotony of lessons. I nearly jumped out of my skin though when I first heard anti-aircraft guns practising on Hackney Downs. And we could even hear them when they were fired in Victoria Park. Then just as I got used to the boom of these guns the real bombing started.

Just opposite us in Shacklewell Lane there was a little market that had stables down one side. The bomb that flattened the market made a right mess of the place by blowing a deep crater right in the middle. Luckily it was at night so there were no people about, but every horse in the place was blown to bits.

A few days later the council came along, demolished what was left of the buildings, pushed the dead horses down the crater and levelled the site off. What I could never have imagined as I looked down at this bare piece of ground was that ticking away under the soil was a microscopic time bomb with Ronnie Knight's name on it. It would be a while yet but when it eventually went off it would damage me as surely as the German bomb would have done if I'd been there when it first went off.

That was to come. Right now Mum was in a right two and eight, and though she didn't want to see us go she made the decision it was time her boys joined the thousands of young children being evacuated to the safety of the countryside. By now all the inner London schools had been closed and taken over by Auxiliary Forces so at that time I was one very happy boy.

As if that wasn't enough, am I hearing right when Mum tells us we're going away for a bit of a holiday?

Imagine my excitement. I'd had a few day trips to places like Margate, Southend and Clacton-on-Sea, but actually to live somewhere else for two weeks was more than I could take in. Though when I found out I wasn't going to the seaside, and, worse, Mum wasn't coming with us I wasn't so keen. And though I don't really remember my feelings, I could bet that my face was no different from that of the other hundred or so kids gathered at King's Cross Station early one morning. Destination Cambridge.

I was luckier than most of those kids because I had my brother Billy to look after me. He was 13 now and to me almost grown up. Then of course there was the both of us to keep an eye on five-year-old Johnny. Losing her boys must have been heartbreaking for our Mum but she never let it show until the train was pulling out. We were away for what seemed like a long time to us kids. I lived during some of it on a farm and learnt a lot about growing things. I had to work for my keep but I didn't mind that because it made me feel independent, and I loved every minute. The farmer's wife got me looking after the vegetable garden, weeding and watering and even letting me plant a few runner beans of my own. Later, in the prison gardens, I got a kick out of planting things and watching them grow.

Although I did enjoy my time on that farm I think a lot of it was down to making the best of a situation I didn't have any control over. Inside I missed Mum and Dad terribly. The three of us would get a short combined letter from home quite regularly so we weren't out of touch. Then Billy would write back, and I would add a few words on the bottom of what he'd said. Not much as I'd be the first to admit I wasn't too clever in that department. To make up for my lack of words I'd draw a picture of different things I'd seen and I think that pleased Mum.

Then one Saturday, out of the blue, I looked up from watering the vegetables, and there was Mum. I'd grown up a lot while I was away so when we looked at each other I felt as though I should act the man. But tough guy or not, I couldn't stop the prickle behind my eyes as I walked towards her. 'Ronnie, love, I've come to take you all home.' That's all she said before giving me a great big hug.

Why she took us back home at that time I never even questioned. Though the war was still on perhaps the worst of the bombing was over. More likely she'd had enough of being parted from her boys. She wasn't alone, for by now thousands of kids were streaming back into London even against government warnings.

Back home we picked up the threads of our lives as though they'd never been interrupted. I couldn't believe what an interesting place our little bit of Stoke Newington had been turned into. I'd seen a lot of damage before I went away, but now everywhere I looked was broken houses, broken flats and big gaps where other buildings used to be – now just brick and rubble covered bomb sites.

What a playground for me and my best mate, Albert Lennard, who lived on the next floor down. I'd always wished he'd gone to Cambridge with me, but he'd been sent away two weeks before me to a place in Surrey. Still we were back together again and getting up to all sorts because he was a little rascal, same as me.

After a while Shacklewell School reopened, and I found myself back doing hated lessons again. By now Jimmy was working, and so was Billy, and they both had money in their pockets and loads of freedom, and I wanted the same. So all the time my mind was outside the school walls.

Up the road from us we had the Spurs Football Team in Tottenham. A bit further down was the Arsenal ground, so all us boys were football mad. Us kids used to organise our own football matches, leading eventually up to a world-cup game, except it was a very small world and no cup. I told you about the bomb knocking down the stables. Well, where the council had levelled out the site, grass had grown all over it, and it was a natural football pitch. This particular day I went for the ball, tripped over and cut my leg on a sharp stone sticking out of the ground. A bit of spit and a quick rub with my jersey sleeve, and I was as right as rain.

When I went indoors for my tea Mum saw the dried blood on my leg. She dug out a wet flannel, washed the tiny wound, then stuck a great lump of sticking plaster over it. Trouble was my shorts didn't cover it, so as soon as I stepped out of the door, off it came. I wasn't having my mates think I was soft or whatever.

A month later I'm in bed between Billy and Johnny, and I woke up soaked in sweat with my leg on fire. When I tried to move it I couldn't. I was terrified and screamed out for my Mum. With that my brothers have jumped out of bed like they were scalded, and both stood by the wall with their mouths open. Dad, who got in first, wasn't much better. But Mum – bless her – frightened as she must have been, kept calm. She only had to look at my bright red leg and feel my forehead to know it was serious.

Mum told the two boys to get into her bed, then sent Dad racing down to get the block superintendent to phone for an ambulance. The pain was terrible, and I felt like I was drifting away. The last thing I remembered was Mum crying and saying, 'Oh, Jim, I think he's got polio.' That disease struck fear into the heart of every mother in those days and would do for years after.

It turned out she was wrong in what she first thought. Though what was really wrong with me was even worse. Osteomyelitis, like polio, was a crippling infection, both caused by a virus, but mine had the potential of killing me as well. I don't remember anything about the following week except it didn't matter because when I opened my eyes Mum was always there watching over me.

Towards the end of the week the doctors managed to get rid of the poisons that had gone right through me, and slowly I came back into the land of the living. What me or none of the family realised at that moment of happiness, knowing I was going to live, was that this was just the beginning. Now I was going to have to suffer a three-year separation from everybody I loved and five serious operations.

After the dust had settled we found out that I'd picked up a virus that had come up through the ground from those dead horses the council had buried. It had got into my blood, then into my leg bone marrow and was slowly rotting it away. After a few weeks in Kingsland Road Hospital I was taken to a specialist hospital in Carshalton, Surrey. Nowadays you could jump into a motor and be there in less than an hour. But then it was a bit different and a trip over the water was like a day's outing. On top of that Dad didn't have a car anyway, and offhand I can't think of any of our neighbours who did.

Another thing was visiting kids in hospital was discouraged anyway. They had the idea that if you saw your Mum too often it would upset you and set back whatever treatment you were having. So visits were once a month, and that wasn't upsetting, was it?

I've blanked out the pain I must have gone through, and all I can remember is the never-ending pattern of my life. An operation, months of lying on my back, plaster cast on my leg, a few weeks of hobbling up and down the ward on crutches, then back for another operation. I'd like to be able to say that those three years prepared me for what I've gone through over these last years in prison, but I can't. The pain and frustration of separation from people you love is the same no matter how old you are.

I did make friends in there, but they came and

went so I could never find a special mate. One kid sticks in my mind because he was a bit different from me. He must have turned up overnight because I can remember waking up one morning, looking over to the bed next to me, and there's this kid, and he's as black as a coalman. I stared at him, and he stared back. Then I asked, 'Where you from then? Africa?'. And he's just looked at me a bit puzzled like and replied, 'Nah, Stepney.' I couldn't believe it, you just never saw black people round our way in those days. Well, there were a couple of blokes, but they were so what you might call exotic that they weren't like real people.

Apart from them I can't think of any others I'd seen so this kid was a bit of a novelty. Funny thing is after a while I never even noticed that he was a different colour from me. I don't know if he turned out to be a boxer or something like it, but he had the fastest reflexes I'd ever seen.

We were both up near a window that overlooked the gardens so there were always butterflies or moths flying in. As one's flown by the bed, Bang! he's caught it in his hand. Then he'd unfold his fingers, and it would fly off. He was doing it all the time. I only managed this trick once, and when I looked at this pretty little broken thing in my hand I wished I hadn't.

I suppose that sort of thing showed how little we had to do. There were no ear-phones or radio, and television was something only posh people had. There was no attempt at all to give us any schooling.

That suited me, but looking back it was a crime that I never looked at much more than colouring books for three years.

Though I had a livid scar on my thigh, I'd been out of pain for a while. So when I got a couple of fittings for a surgical boot – ugly great thing – I knew my days in the hospital were nearly over. It was one Saturday in 1946 when I was at last allowed home. One of my uncles had got a car while I was away so he brought Mum down to fetch me. I felt like royalty on the way back to the East End, and even more like it when the car stopped outside Hindle House. Talk about a reception committee. Here's me thinking that everybody must have forgotten about me, and everywhere I looked there's old girls hanging over balconies and waving. There was Poochie, dead chuffed because he was the best mate of the celebrity, and behind him every kid from the surrounding blocks all come to see what I looked like. Pretty pathetic, I should think. I was underweight, pure white, wearing a great built-up boot and leaning on crutches. Must have looked like Tiny Tim.

Back in my own bed after so long I lay and listened to the lovely sounds of home. When Mum started singing 'You Are My Sunshine' from the kitchen it swept over me just how much I'd missed her and the rest of my family while I'd been away. I might not have looked up to much but I was back to stay, and I had a lot of catching up to do.

3.
The Making of a Rascal

FOR A WHILE I was the local hero. Brave little
Ronnie who had suffered so much and now look
at him – a cripple, poor little bleeder. Well, that
was the mums. The girls wanted to mother me and
help me up the stairs and all that, like I was one of
their dolls. But the boys were less sympathetic, and
some of them were right bastards. They must have
lain awake at night thinking up some new name to call
me the next day. Booty, Hopalong, Peg leg, Long John
Silver, all of them trying for originality and maximum
hurting power. Original they were not. But painful?
They might as well have stuck a knife in me.

Though I was a cripple in their eyes I was not
what you might call a proper one. There was no pain,
and my leg wasn't paralysed. My problem was that

the disease had stopped the bone growing so one leg was shorter than the other, hence the boot. At the same time my muscles were weak so I needed crutches for a good while. Still by the time I got plenty of Mum's dinners inside me I reached a point where I could chuck away those horrible wooden crutches. Though not before I'd realised that they were offensive weapons that I could carry with impunity from the law.

Don't get me wrong, I didn't turn into Superman overnight. Caught on my own I wasn't brave enough to lash out so I took a lot of being pushed around. But with Siddy, Albert and Poochie behind me I managed to settle a lot of scores. Surprising how the threat or reality of a smack round the head with 30 inches or so of hardwood lessens the fun of piss-taking.

I don't think Mum ever knew what I went through during that time. I might have been a bit of a weakling, but I still had my pride. Indoors she spoiled me rotten, and I loved it, but the thought of telling her I was being bullied and have her fight my battles for me was something I could never contemplate. And believe me she would have done.

One summer evening me and the boys had a great time driving the neighbours crazy by knocking on their doors then legging it before they answered. What I didn't know was Mum was watching every move I made from four floors up. When the game broke up as we all rushed home to listen to our favourite wireless programme – Dick Barton, special agent, or Paul Temple – I walked straight into a clipped ear. But worse than that Mum said, 'If you can run about like a mad thing you're well enough to go back to school.' I couldn't believe what she was saying. School was a distant memory, something I'd put as far back in mind as possible.

Later that week a letter arrived like the 5th Cavalry coming over the hill. 'Unfortunately there is not an available place at Shacklewell School for Ronald.' Then I saw the coat going on and Mum marching out of the door. Next morning I'm sitting at my little slope-top desk wondering what the hell had happened. I'm like an alien. Remember I hadn't picked up a school book for years so everything was going right over my head.

If there had been such a thing all those years ago I could have been on *Mastermind* answering questions about my comic-book heroes, Roy of the Rovers, Desperate Dan or Korky the Cat. I knew there were 12 pennies in a shilling and 240 in a pound, but that was it. At first the teachers were easy-going, letting me catch up slowly, but I never even tried. After a bit they realised that stronger methods were needed and started to knock algebra (whatever that was) into my head and knuckles with a ruler.

Dipping into my extensive vocabulary I thought, Fuck this and started hopping the wag or playing truant. Of course this isn't any fun on your own so I roped in Albert and Poochie. These two were as good as gold. None of that about 'I'm not sure,' or 'We might get into trouble.' If it was a nice day and we were skint we'd take off down to the New River for a spot of fishing. This was strictly lying on the bank with string and bent-pin stuff, and I don't remember ever catching anything.

A lot of our time was spent in Harry's Cafe, owned by an ex-boxer by the name of Harry Chamberlain. He was a typical past-it pugilist. Cropped head, flat nose, misshapen ears – but a lovely bloke. He'd let us sit for hours over a mug of tea and if he was busy allow us to help out by clearing the tables and washing up for a couple of bob each. So how did we repay his kindness? We robbed him.

It pricks my conscience now, looking back, but then it was just the way of things. What we had noticed was that last thing when he locked up he always left his float money in the till. This wouldn't have been a lot, mainly change, but it saved him buggering about when he opened in the morning. It didn't take the three of us long to work out that this oversight could be turned into a nice little earner. So I waited until Harry's gone out the back, jumped up on a chair and flicked off the catch that locks the fanlight over the door. The place was empty as we were always last out, so there was no one to clock what I had done. All we had to do then was wait for dark, then in and out quick.

We made our plans like a military operation. Crept up to the cafe like commandos – and couldn't squeeze through the tiny fanlight. So much for master criminals. Next time we tried I made some excuse to Mum and dragged little eight-year-old Johnny along with us. All we had to do then was boost him up and shove him through the small fanlight. He managed to lift just under nine shillings. Two bob for each of them, and half a crown and a few coppers for the mastermind. Four times we pulled that stunt. On the fifth the till was empty. Harry had got wise that his float was floating off on its own. He never mentioned it to us, but we never tried it again.

Years later when Johnny went down for 22 years for being involved in the Easter 1983 Security Express job, the biggest robbery ever, I couldn't help thinking that I had some hand in setting him on that path.

School improved for a little while when I was put in a class under a teacher who knew nothing about me or my near psychotic hatred of all things educational. So when I volunteered myself for every odd job that needed doing in the classroom he must have thought, What a pleasant unselfish angel he is. I cleaned the blackboard, filled inkwells, emptied the bin and ran myself ragged with this message to Mr Reason, that note to Mr Dodge. My little bum didn't polish the desk seat for weeks and weeks. Until some grass blew down the earhole of Mr Carr the Headmaster. So it was goodbye Mr Nice Teacher, hello Mr Absolute Bastard.

From day one he set out to beat me into submission. He made up his mind that he would succeed where all the others failed. In his book there could never be a pupil allowed to think he was bigger than the system. Why didn't I just give in and accept defeat gracefully? I couldn't. It wasn't in me.

At the end of the day I'd be black and blue. But like the bullying, this was something else you didn't take home. 'How was school today, Ronnie luv?' – 'Lovely, Mum, lovely.' I got him one night though. Me and about a dozen other lads got on top of the toilet block roof with pockets full of stones, then waited for the teachers to show themselves. When they did we stoned the lot of them so they couldn't get out of the door. Thankfully for our futures none of them was hurt. Though unintentionally a school lamp and a couple of windows were broken. Once we had held them at bay for as long as we dared, we slipped down the back, over the fence and legged it as fast as we could.

There was bloody murder next morning. Old Carr said he was going to call the police in, but he never did in case his school got a bad reputation. And as we had not been seen they couldn't point the finger, even though they knew who the culprits were.

Another time, that teacher banged me three or four times on the head for messing about. I still didn't take any notice of him so, with a final stinging crack, he said, 'Right you'll stay behind tonight and do 500 lines.' I didn't say a word to him, but I told the other boys there was no way he could keep me in. Four o'clock the bell rang, and all the kids troop out with me behind them a bit smartish. Before I can make it to the door he's grabbed me and locked it. I can't believe it. He says, 'I told you, you're staying to do lines.'

'I fucking ain't,' I shouted. I thought he was going to have a heart attack. He went bright red, and I made a dive for the window before he could get hold of me. In half a minute I've got the sash slid up, and I'm out on the sill. Where's the drainpipe? When you are at school you know all the ins and outs of the place, but I have made a serious misjudgement – I've only got out the wrong window.

I'm 20 foot up. All my mates are down in the playground cheering, 'Good old Ronnie. You show him, Ron,' and there's this lunatic teacher behind me. I looked back in, and is he shitting himself. He must have thought I was going to commit suicide. 'Come inside, boy, and we'll discuss this.' 'Just open the door and stand back and I'll come in.' I offered, and, blimey, he did. I jumped in and went past him like a rocket. Outside they're all slapping me on the back, and I'm as cocky as hell, but inside I'm thinking, am I in trouble now.

Next morning I'm ready for the death sentence. He got me to one side and just looked at me. After a bit of this he said, 'Knight, forget the lines, forget any punishment. All I will say is this. One day when your schooling is far behind you, you will regret your lack of education and, though I seem to have failed, perhaps realise that I drove you hard for your own good.' I stood in front of him with a contrite look on my face, but inside I was bubbling. I'd got away with it. I'd beaten him.

His little speech didn't catch up with me for many years. But as he knew then it eventually did, and I regretted those wasted years a hundred times over. I've caught up now and think I can hold my own anywhere, but educating myself as an adult has been an uphill struggle and bloody hard work.

By now my bad leg was catching up with my good one. I had a horrible looking scar and a slight limp but other than that I was 100 per cent. While I was stuck inside the classroom I just ticked over. Once outside my life burst into action. I lived for playing football. I turned out for the school team with an enthusiasm I never applied to anything else. I was the star of the Shacklewell Youth Centre team, and when I wasn't playing for them enjoyed the less-organised games of endlessly kicking a ball around the streets or wasteground. But overriding everything else in my life was a daily need to scratch a few bob from anywhere I could.

In those days the question of pocket money from your parents was something that never came up. Dad always made a living and Mum never went short, but the thought of handing over a regular sum for a kid to waste never entered his head. So it was down to me to duck and dive to raise the necessary. Priority was pie-shop money. Once I'd got hold of a shilling or one and six I could get a meal in Cooksie's pie and eel shop up Kingsland High Street.

Most of the scams we tried were short-lived, for one reason or another, but we never ran out of ideas. Every house you went to in those days had a coal fire so that was always an earner, what with selling the people sticks and coal. The sticks came from the back yard of the Green Man pub. I'd nip over the wall and chuck out a load of wooden beer crates to Poochie, then with a little axe we'd nicked from somewhere else chop it into little bundles at tuppence a time.

Round the back of our school next to the boiler house was a mountain of coke. Nobody was allowed to go near it on pain of a good caning. Yet though every kid in the place knew it was there they never gave it another thought. But young Mr Knight saw the potential for a nice bit of wages.

Albert wasn't in on this one because me and Poochie had fallen out with him like kids do. Anyway, us two went back night after night with a load of sacks, filled them up enough so we could still carry them, then delivered all over the place. We were even taking orders during the day.

We thought we were made for life until over one weekend a big mesh fence turned up round the pile. Like I said scams came and went. In the cold light of day we were thieves, but it never seemed like that. It was more of a game seeing how much you could get away with. They could have put the crown jewels in one of the flats and left the door open. But we would never have dreamed of going in. That would have been dishonest.

Me and Poochie got a bit of a Saturday job on a fruit and veg stall in Garnham Street working for Yiddisher Solly. He'd give us five bob and a bag of fruit to take home, but as far as we were concerned that was just to get us there. The perks came at the end of the day. It was the same every week. Pack up about three o'clock, tidy all the old paper and boxes away, then into the cafe for a dinner and a count-up.

Solly would tip the cash out on to the table, and me and Poochie would sort it into piles. Every time the bell on the door jangled as somebody came in he'd look up, and I'd screw up a ten-bob note and drop it on the floor.

Once we were finished and the money was tucked in Solly's bag, I'd drop a spoon, cap or my hankie under the table, then with a 'Clumsy me' I'd bend down and wipe up the cash. Week after week we were getting 30 bob on top of the five shillings – fortunes. Then one of the barrow boys said, 'Here, Solly, you getting soft or what? Look you're dropping money everywhere.' Solly looked down, and there's half a dozen balled-up notes. Like Harry Chamberlain no accusations were made, but the job ended very suddenly.

Another liberty we took was with a guy called Bebe Moseley. He lived in Duke Street just round the corner from us. Me and Poochie were walking past his place one day and we saw his barrow out the front all loaded up with bananas. It wasn't like we were strangers or anything, we knew old Bebe and had done a few little jobs for him, so we looked in the yard and he's nowhere to be seen.

Good lads that we are we decided to do him a favour – and ourselves – by flogging the fruit. So we wheel the barrow up to the corner of our flats and start giving the old girls a bit of spiel. We knew what they were worth, something like six for a shilling, so that was no problem. I'm giving it all the old patter, 'Come on, ladies, this'll put lead in the old man's pencil,' and they're going like hot cakes. Poochie even had to go back to the yard and get more boxes. On the money side it was one for Bebe and one for us.

We're just congratulating each other on our shrewd move when Bebe turned up, and he's going fucking mad. 'You've robbed me – you've stolen my living,' and he's jumping up and down with temper pulling his hair out. 'Hang about!' I say. 'Is that all the thanks we get for helping you out?' Then trying not to rattle my pocket full of change, I showed him what we'd taken. He's all the other way then, 'Good boys – good boys' and he slipped us half a crown apiece. You had to get up early to get one over on a Jew boy like Bebe, but when we totalled up we had pie-shop and pictures money for a week.

So what with one thing and another my life drifted along, and time slipped by. Leading me slowly but surely towards that big moment when I'd teeter on the edge of adulthood. I don't know what I expected, but the day I left that hated school in 1949 was much like any other. No goodbyes, no fanfare of trumpets – nothing. I just walked out leaving nothing behind and taking very little with me.

My mind was full of nothing but what I would do with six or seven weeks' sun-filled holiday. It soon emptied though when that same night Mum said, 'Your Dad's put a word in for you at Baker and Sellsmans. You can start work on Monday.' I was horrified. 'Mum, I can't – I'm on holiday', I reminded her. She just smiled and said, 'No, son. That's when you're at school. You're a working man now.'

I lay in bed that night and felt I was on the brink of the good life. I knew about the firm I was starting with. They did upholstery. How much was there to know about stuffing a three-piece suite? Give it a little while and I'd move up to manager, then if I put a few quid to one side probably open my own shop up West, then a chain of them up and down the country.

Six o'clock in the morning, my career plan didn't seem so rosy. I don't think I'd ever been out of bed that early in my life. Dalston Lane was only five minutes from Arcola Street and I was at the factory door bang on seven am. By half past my dreams of a meteoric rise to fame and riches had smashed into smithereens. At least at school I was a somebody: bit of a tearaway, Jack the lad even. But at work I was suddenly a little boy who didn't know his arse from his elbow.

I was just wondering to myself which chaise longue they'd put me to work on when the foreman tells me I'm spring-boy – whatever that was. I soon found out. When one of the craftsmen wanted a few springs, he'd just shout out, 'Dozen number fives,' and I'd have to run to the racks and sort them out. 'Tacks' – 'Stretcher' – 'Blue Bolt, pattern four' – 'Cup of tea'. 'Fucking hell,' I said to the gaffer, 'stick a broom up my arse and I'll sweep the floor at the same time.' That got me a clip round the ear so nothing much had changed from school.

At home I noticed there was a subtle change in everybody's attitude. That night Mum fussed around me like an old hen, and my tea was on the table as soon as I stepped through the door. Dad and my elder brothers brought me into their working men's conversation like suddenly in one day I had formed opinions about life. While Johnny and baby Patsy looked at me as though I'd grown two heads.

Come the Friday night I forgot the frustrations of the week when I was handed what it was all about. A little brown packet with two notes sticking out of one cut-off corner and eight shillings and sixpence glinting through the perforations. This was so you could count your money without opening the packet. Typical of my dodgy character, it wasn't long before I learnt the trick of curling a note out of the corner with a lady's hairpin. All that had to be done then was to take the sealed packet to the office and kick up hell that they were trying to rob me. This could only be done a couple of times or they would cotton on to what the game was.

I practically flew home that night in my eagerness to hand over my wages. But Mum, bless her, said, 'A man's got to have money in his pocket – you keep the £2.00.' All right I know I'd nicked more than that in half an hour in the past but this was different, and I couldn't wait to get out and meet the boys for some manly pursuits.

Poochie was working at a place behind the garage opposite – Fentons, I think it was called, something to do with antiques. Albert had got himself fixed up where my Dad worked, and Siddy Smith had joined his dad's haulage firm. We were all roughly on the same wages and raring to go – for a night on the town.

Dance halls were where the action was, and we had plenty of choices. Barry's in Mare Street, Grey's in Seven Sisters Road or the town halls of Hackney or Stoke Newington. Top of the list though was the Royal Ballroom in Tottenham. The whole point of the exercise was to show off and impress the ladies and with a bit of luck pull one who knew what it was all about, which, God help me! would be more than I did.

I'd put two and two together over the years, and I'd studied the corset adverts in the *News of the World* until my eyes nearly popped out. I knew what I wanted but getting some practice in was proving more difficult than I imagined it would be. I remember walking a girl home one night and never even so much as shook her hand. But next day I told the boys all about my good luck in graphic detail; had I given her some. They had about as much success in that area as I had, so their eyes were popping when I explained, 'She was still begging for more when I left her.' Good job they never had the imagination to ask me more 'what' because I would have been stumped for an answer.

Trouble with these gatherings of females and young stags, it didn't take much for a scuffle to kick off into a fight. My years as a scrawny cripple were way behind me, and I'd filled out nicely. Didn't go upwards very much, but I could handle myself even if I was a bit slow in technique.

One night we all got a good hiding – must have bumped into the wrong guys, so I've said to the others,

'Why don't we go down the Odeon and join the boxing club? Can't do any harm.' The next day we strolled off to the cinema in Kingsland Road. For a while we just sparred around getting the hang of a few moves. Then we had to get in the ring with the trainer, and his idea was he'd show us how to fight proper.

I saw this young kid get in one night and instead of being shown what to do he was getting knocked about terrible. The trainer was steaming into him, punching the kid all over the place, showing off in front of all us lot. Course, all my mates are saying, 'Go on, Ron, get in there – show him what it's about.' I can hardly say no to this vote of confidence, so I'm giving them all the 'Yeah, I'll have some of that. I'll knock his fucking head off.'

I've gloved up and jumped in the ring. Hadn't got a clue really. I'm ducking and weaving, and he hasn't even moved yet. Bang! I've taken one right in the solar plexus. Soon I've gone down like a sack of shit. I'm laying there thinking, Sod this, and my mates are laughing and shouting, 'Give him some more, Ronnie.' I told them all afterwards that he'd taken a liberty, and if I caught him in the street any time I'd give him a seeing to with something heavy in my hand. They were still laughing when we said ta-ra at the flats.

When I got indoors my brother Billy took one look at me and said, 'About time I showed you how to look after yourself.' I'm aching from head to toe and just want to fall into bed. 'One minute,' he said, 'Give me one minute, and you'll never lose another fight.' How could I turn down an offer like that! 'As soon as some geezer says, "Do you want to fight?"' he advised, 'don't even answer – whack him straight in the mouth. Never mind walking round in circles like they all do – straight in, no messing. If you have to say something say it to his mate, they've always got one. Your oppo's bound to look round as well, then punch him on the jaw by his ear, and it'll break like an eggshell – all over.'

That was some of the best advice I ever took, and it never let me down. Thinking about what he'd said I couldn't wait to put it into practice, but what I didn't know then was that my next good hiding was going to come from my eldest brother, Jimmy, and I respected him too much to fight back.

I was knocking about with some lads from Stoke Newington one night. I don't know where my own little mob was, but these fellas were a good laugh, and we were just wandering about kicking a few cans and eyeing up the girls. We turned a corner, and there was this beautiful Jaguar. We've crowded round like boys do, imagining if we had a motor like this. Next minute one of them's got the door open. What he did next I haven't a clue because it was out of my league, but the engine burst into life, and I'm shoved in by the other lads piling in behind me.

We must have driven around for about an hour, when suddenly the driver pulled up and got out. He stuck his head back in the window and announced, 'I've gotta go. If I'm not in by ten my Dad'll have the skin off my arse.' He started to walk off, then came

back. 'Get rid of the car sharpish, there's good mates.'
No wonder he had to be in early – turned out he was
only 13.

Now what? All the others look at me until one
of them says, 'Go on, Ron, get a move on. None of
us knows how to drive,' and they're all hoping I'm
a younger version of Donald Campbell. Never one
to lose face I climbed over from the back and tried
to remember what I'd seen Dad doing in the lorry.
Before long we've taken off down Seven Sisters
Road like a greyhound out of the trap, and all I could
do was hang on to the wheel for dear life and steer.

Only problem was I couldn't stop the bloody thing,
and we're heading straight for the junction with
Stamford Hill! In the back they're screaming, 'Under
the wheel – pull the fucking wires off.' I was
frightened to let go of the steering wheel so I held it
steady with my chest, leaned under and with both
hands grabbed anything I could feel. I must have
broken the connection where it had been hot-wired
because the engine cut out, and we kangarooed to a
stop with the wheels up on the pavement.

I sat there with my eyes closed, and all I could
hear was four hearts thumping like the clappers. I
opened my eyes, wiped the sweat off my face, and I'm
looking straight into the distinctive chromium-plate
grille of a big black Wolseley police car. We're lifted.

Two minutes later we're in Old Street nick getting
the bollocking of our lives. I couldn't grass on the
other fella so I was treated like Britain's Number 1
wanted. Then they bring Mum in, and the look on her

face guts me. This wasn't the first time she'd had to suffer the shame of digging one of her sons out of custody and wouldn't be the last.

In a way I think I would have felt better if she'd belted me, but she just looked sad, tired, and, what hurt, suddenly a lot older. Once we got home I thought the best thing I could do was slip into bed before the old man got in from the pub. Instead I walked straight into a right-hander from Jimmy. One of the biggest rascals in the district, and he's doing his nut. 'How could you do this to your Mum? How can you let the family down?' and between every word he's given me another slap. I wanted to say, 'You were up for one yourself last week,' but thought better of it. I was black and blue before Mum told him that was enough.

For three weeks I suffered nightmares about Stamford House remand centre and Hollesley Bay borstal, places I'd heard about from local young tearaways. But after worrying myself sick, my day in court ended with 12 months' probation, a record that would follow me like a tail, and, worse, a write-up in the *Hackney Gazette*. Local parents marked me down for ending up on the rope, which a few boys from the area did years later. Though as far as my mates were concerned I'd turned into Jimmy Cagney overnight. Naturally this gave me even more of a swagger when we all met up at the salt beef bar in Stamford Hill.

Trouble was, getting dressed up for a night out and preening myself in the wardrobe mirror, the image that stared back at me wasn't quite my idea of how a local 'face' should be dressed. White open-neck shirt, grey flannels and a tidy jacket. Smart, same as the other lads, but what did it say? Kid that's just started work and skint. Bang on. I was finding my two quid a week hard enough to stretch to my next bottle of Old Spice aftershave, let alone five bob a week for a suit from Burton's. So I did the next best thing and helped myself to one of Jimmy's. He was doing well and had half a dozen suits hanging up, and let's face it he couldn't wear them all at once.

Did I look the dog's or what? All right, it might be laughable now, but then that's what it was all about. Standing out, being noticed, looking like you were well heeled. I suppose that was one of the reasons why two very likely lads on the up by the name of Ronnie and Reggie Kray introduced themselves to me down the Royal one night. We had a few words, shook hands and had respect for each other thereafter.

One of the drawbacks of wearing Jimmy's suits was that I lived in fear of getting a mark on them. In case I dribbled beer down the front I got in the habit of holding the glass out and dipping my head down to it. I must have looked like a sparrow on a bird bath. On top of that I stuck my elbows out to keep people away from the whistle. My other fear was Jimmy getting home before I did, which played hell with me trying to do what comes naturally with some right little smasher, or to hear me next day – a raving sex maniac.

Courtship took a long time in those days. I don't mean up to marriage but to the point where I could build up enough courage to ruffle the bottom of a petticoat. No sooner had the object of my rampant desires started the old cry of 'I'm not that sort of girl,' than there was no chance she was going to be that night anyway, because I had to leg it home like some bloody Cinderella.

Dad had packed up working at Jinkinsons, and though he was still lorry driving he had started with a firm called Scaffold Erection. My career prospects had blossomed when, instead of fetching springs, I had been promoted to nailing them into place. For this soul-destroying enterprise I was taking home the princely sum of a fiver or so a week, and to put it mildly I was totally pissed off. So when the old man said there was an opening down his firm I couldn't wait to get started. My wages trebled overnight, and at last I could stop nicking Jimmy's gear and get suited and booted out of my own back pocket.

The work was hard and a bit dangerous, what with being up high, but that's why the money was so good. I loved it. It got even better when the fiddles started to show. These didn't happen straight away because I had to learn the business first before I could suss out the angles. But after a while I worked out that if I could put a scaffold up I could take it down in half the time. All I needed was a couple of mates and I'd be on a nice earner. I didn't ask Siddy, Albert or Poochie because though they pulled a few strokes when we were kids they were all straight guys. I was the only rascal, so I pulled in two fellas from the Angel, and we got to work.

If the firm had put a scaffold around an empty house in the week, on Saturday afternoon when the painters or whoever had gone home we took it down. A quick phone call to brother Billy who was doing nicely in the scrap game and Bob's your Uncle. He'd pick it up in his lorry, part with a bit of greenstuff, and everybody's happy – except the firm. Dad never had a clue that it was us doing it and he'd sit at the tea table talking about these bastards who want their hands chopping off. This wasn't every week. I'd do one, wait for the fuss to die down, then dive in again.

The long terraces of those five-storey London houses were a goldmine. When we were backwards and forwards up and down the street I'd look out for any that were unoccupied. Then once we'd scaffolded the house we were working on, I'd go back at night with the boys, walk along all the roofs to the empty one, then strip all the lead off. Anybody watching probably thought we were on overtime and once we were on top we couldn't be seen. Another call to Billy!

So what with the wages and the thieving, I must have been picking up £30 a week easy. In my spare time I still loved a game of football. Not kid's stuff, just kicking a ball about, but to almost professional standard turning out for Tottenham Juniors. I really did think the big time was just round the corner for me. Not bad for a kid who'd spent years as a cripple. I never missed an evening training session or a Saturday game, and that's what put the kibosh on my career.

One Monday the governor of the firm gave me a pull. 'Knight,' he said, 'I see by your time sheets that you never work Saturdays, and you know we do six days here.' I've explained that it was important that I played football every week and hinted it might not be long before one of his workers would be wearing an England shirt. Must have been a cricket fan because he wasn't impressed. 'The choice is yours. If you don't work next Saturday your cards will be ready for your collection.' Pompous arsehole.

I could have wept, and probably did when I was on my own, but the old shekels won in the end. Back then my hero and top player, Tommy Harman, was taking home about twelve quid a week for blinding the crowds with his talent. Me, scaffolder-cum-rascal, three times that on a good week. No argument.

4.
Some Work with the Krays

I T WAS THE QUEEN'S Coronation in the summer of
1953 that finished me in the scaffolding game. The
firm I was working for got part of the contract to
put up stands down the side of miles and bloody miles
of road. The money was blinding, but I was so
knackered by the end of the day all I wanted to do
was fall into bed. Even then I'd spend half the night
dreaming about poles, put-locks and boards. I was
doing well, but my brother Billy was doing even
better in the scrap business and had taken over a big
yard on Hackney Downs. Give him his due he could

graft when he had to, but half the time when I popped in to see him he was on the phone setting up deals. How hard was that?

So I made myself busy – slung a load of iffy deals at him to butter him up, then put it to him that if he didn't take me on the firm he was missing the chance of a lifetime. Now Billy was no mug, and he didn't get where he was by giving out free rides, but weighing up the moves I'd made up until then he asked, 'Could you handle making your own contacts, then bringing in the gear to the yard?' I babbled something about 'Just give me the chance,' and he remarked, 'Shame you can't drive yet, but start work Monday, and I'll sort something out over the weekend.'

Next few days I practised my telephone manner. 'Knight Brothers – Ronald Knight speaking. Cut up and remove Tower Bridge? No problem, sir. I'll call you back.'

I was in the yard bright and early to make a good impression. Billy's not about, but one of his blokes told me I should be down the end where the old buildings are. An old fella's down there already, and he says, 'She's all ready for you, son.' She? What the fuck's going on. I soon found out when he led a horse and cart from behind the shed. No wonder Billy's made himself scarce, it was so he didn't piss himself laughing at the look on my face.

I didn't show what a shock all this was, I just said, 'Right then, what's the game?' 'Yer balloons are in this bag, goldfish haven't turned up yet. Sit up behind Rosie here, shout "Gid-up" to go, "Whoa" to stop, and she'll do the rest. Oh, yeah, and as long as you keep calling out "Ragsabonalumba", business'll fly in. Away you go then.' And away I went.

Now Hackney Downs is only about five minutes from Arcola Street, but no way was I going anywhere near where I might be seen, so I took a left and headed towards Clapton Park. It must have been half way through the morning before I plucked up enough courage to start advertising at the top of my lungs. The art of it, like I'd heard many times round the streets, was to roll all the words together like a little song. Didn't make sense really but it was expected.

End of a long day staring at Rosie's enormous arse, and I was glad to get back to the yard for a weigh-in. Rags I understood, especially woollen ones. If I was offered a bag of bones for a balloon I'd have told them where to stick them, and as for lumber – what the hell was that? It turned out to be a good one though what with it being the school holidays, and I began to see that the totting lark had a fair potential. I think Billy expected me to kick up when I saw him but I never said a word.

As I learnt more about the tricks and dodges it got more interesting and more profitable. Sometimes it was a bit like thieving by proxy. Some kids would come running up with a little armful of clothes and stare wistfully at the goldfish swimming about in a glass tank. I'd look through whatever there was, and I'm shaking my head. I could see their hearts sinking slowly into their boots. What a shame! If there was just a few more bits I could part with one of these lovely fish. One minute later they're back with a jam jar, three of Mum's best jumpers and Dad's sunday suit. Terrible really, but at the end of the day a tanned arse was a small price to pay for a pet. Me, I'd give each area a miss for a long time after I'd pulled a few stunts like that.

I didn't always get away with it, and more than once I'd have some irate mum pounding after me, pinny flapping and stockings rolling down, shouting 'Oi, you bastard. I'm calling the law.' I'm caught bang to rights, so I just turn on the charm and swear my innocence. Good practice for later on in life.

Always looking for ways to catch the eye I laid out a few quid on a great big soft toy panda. This was when the first one ever had arrived in London Zoo from China, and they were all the rage. I stuck it on the front as though it was up for offer, and it brought the kids from every house in the street. What they didn't know was that they'd have to dolly up about two ton of best woollens to get their hands on it, but, bless them, they all lived in hope.

I got in from work one night, and there was a letter on the sideboard for me. Bit of a novelty really, because apart from the occasional summons it was very rare for anybody to write to me. Brown envelope. HMS on the back. Very dodgy. Without even opening it my stomach gave a little somersault and then a double one when I finally read it. It was my call to arms that every kid grew up facing, and, though inevitable and expected – dreaded. National Service. Well, it wasn't exactly my call-up papers, but as close as you could get. I had to report for my entrance medical examination.

I hadn't finished my dinner before Poochie was banging on the door clutching a similar letter – they'd got him as well and a load of our other mates. By the time we took a bus ride down to the recruitment place behind the British Museum, we were mob handed. I didn't fancy it at all. I was having a good time and earning good money. I didn't want to drop down to two bob a week and suffer having my best feature, the barnet, shaved down to my skull.

I thought you had to do your time no matter what, but I think it was Jimmy who marked my card with a bit of advice, so by the time I've been called into the cubicle my limp has come back. No young fella fancied losing two years out of his life, and every second one of them is trying it on with a gammy leg, dodgy chest or a bad back. The doctors have seen it all before so don't take a lot of notice. But when I got my kit off and they saw this nasty-looking scar, one of the geezers told me, 'You'll be no good in here with that.' So I played on it even more. I thought the game was up when he banged my right knee with a rubber hammer, and it shot up. I'm praying, Please, Jesus, don't make the other one move. And it didn't. He even gave it one for luck, and it just sat there.

When the third doctor, the one who makes the decisions, looked at my leg he said, 'Now what's the problem here, young man?' I looked a bit upset and answered, 'I had osteo-what's name as a child, sir.' He's sat there shaking his head making his mind up.

Now I know when a bit of brown-nosing comes in handy, so I said, 'Does this mean I can't serve my country, sir?' I might have been wrong, but I'm sure his eyes filled up. 'I'm afraid not, son,' he replied. 'I'm marking you down as unfit for duty.' I could have danced the hornpipe, but instead I managed to walk out with my useless leg dragging on the floor.

Outside the other boys, including Poochie, have all got long faces. Then we saw our bus turning the corner, and they all started to run. I've overtaken the lot of them and got to the stop first, so when they've caught up they're all shouting, 'Bastard – you're fitter than all of us,' and I'm laughing my head off.

As it turned out there was a lot of people lived to regret the day I wasn't taken out of circulation for two years – it might have saved a lot of aggravation.

I'm an old hand at the rag-and-bone trade by now, and I don't care who knows it. I go anywhere I can get a living. I'm rattling up Kingsland Road on the cart, and I spotted June Billingham, an ex-girlfriend, waiting at a bus stop, and she's more beautiful than ever. She'd left me for a schoolmate, Donnie Leach, who was everything I wasn't: quiet, polite and always had his head in a book. When she took up with him, being young and full of myself and too proud to admit defeat I consoled myself with the thought that it wouldn't be long before she came running back. So I've slammed the brakes on with a quick 'Whoa, girl' and offered her a ride home. She never turned a hair, what with all the bus queue watching, just stood on the wheel and climbed up. The conversation was a bit of the nice-weather variety for a while, then she said, 'When I was little I used to dream that a knight on a horse would sweep me off my feet, like in the books. This could be my dream come true.'

After that I saw her every night and a month later suggested we got engaged with one of H. Samuel's finest. We had to speed things up, though, when June got in the family way when I was not quite 18. In 1952 Lorraine was born – just four and a half months after the wedding.

For a while we lived with June's mum, until eventually I got busy and found us a small flat on the top floor of a house in Highbury. Couple of tiny rooms, a shared bathroom, but it was all ours. Now things could be a bit different, and we could start being a proper married couple. Some hope. Only change was that June took over looking after me, and I sailed on like the single bloke I thought I was. I loved June and little Lorraine but looking back it was a terrible way to carry on. Though to be fair I was only a kid, and I was only acting the way I'd always seen it.

In my young man's ignorance, as far as I was concerned I had done everything to make June happy. I'd given her a baby, a nice place to live and put money on the table every Friday. So it was only natural that I should get something out of life myself.

About this time, around the mid-fifties, I got into something that could have turned a bit heavy. I was having a drink in one of the locals when in walked Reggie and Ronnie Kray. By now they're starting to make a name for themselves even though still in their early twenties. We shook hands and stepped away from the fellas I was with, and Reggie, in that quiet, polite voice of his, asked me, if it's not too much trouble would I do them a favour on the coming Saturday? Of course I've agreed, and he's suggested I call in at their house about eight o'clock. Ronnie never said a word.

On the arranged night I turned up at Vallance Road. I'd never met Violet Kray before, but she opened the door, all smiles and friendly, and told me to go upstairs. She seemed a lovely woman, and obviously treated their mates like my own Mum treated mine. There were three other young blokes already up there with the Twins, and though they didn't know it each of them would end up a household name in years to come. Anyway Reggie explained to me that the idea was to slip out later, drive up to the Royal in Tottenham and put the frighteners on a North London mob who were getting a bit stroppy. Was I up for it? Of course I was – mates in trouble and all that.

Next thing Ronnie's pulling a big box from under the bed and sharing out enough weapons to start a war. The other fellas are getting swords and knives. When it came to me, he handed over a sawn-off shotgun like I was the luckiest man in the room. 'Tuck it in your coat for now, Ron, and leave the safety on until we get there. I've already loaded it.' I was so shit-less I couldn't speak. Then we're all trooping out the door – 'Goodnight, Mrs Kray, Goodnight, Mrs Kray' – like a bunch of kids going to the pictures.

The appeal for the Twins to rope me in on this caper was less to do with my abilities as a hard man, than the fact that I was the proud owner of an impressive black taxicab. A car that in private hands could look every bit as sinister as the film gangsters' favourite, an American Buick. This didn't mean I'd gone up in the world – the motor only cost me thirty quid, but it did look the bollocks. We all piled into my motor, and ten minutes later I pulled up outside the Royal. Five minutes after that the ten-handed firm are dug out of the dance hall and confronted up a side alley.

Suddenly their threats and offers of aggravation towards the Twins turned out to be some sort of misunderstanding – perhaps someone with a grievance has been spreading malicious rumours. Honour satisfied, it was handshakes all round. But I'll never forget how those ten pairs of eyes stayed glued on the shooter I was carrying the whole time. I was dropped off at my flat after a bit of a drink, and I never heard any more about it. But I've often wondered if I would have pulled the trigger in the heat of the moment if something had gone off. Just shows you how you can get pulled in.

Every now and then some journalist throws in that Ronnie Knight was a former Kray henchman. What the fuck is that supposed to mean? OK, I did a few favours for them, and they did the same for me, but I was never a paid-up, cards-in member of the firm. Newspapers again, always got to blow everything up where I'm concerned.

Billy gave me a bit of promotion at work, and Rosie the horse, who I became very fond of, was retired to a farm in Essex. So instead of the cart I was driving round the streets doing the same old game but in a clapped-out old lorry. I was two different people really. During the day I lived the part that was expected from a rag-and-bone man. Scruffy as arseholes and full of cockney banter and old bollocks. But once I put on the suit and fancy shirts that June had laid out for me, I was something else altogether, and I could hold my own anywhere. Inside I was still pretty shy, but, with more front than Brighton Pier, nobody had a clue.

I was getting around quite a bit and meeting people in the clubs and pubs who, to put it mildly, were a bit on the dodgy side – just like me. I was getting a bit of a name amongst the up and comers as a fella who could be trusted and had plenty of bottle. Nothing's a secret in that society, and after the shotgun business and a few other bits and pieces, stories about what I had done, or would do if pushed, got blown up out of proportion. Still a bit of a rep didn't do any harm – true or not – so I let everybody think what they wanted.

Perhaps I was getting a bit flash, or it might have been, what with the lifestyle I was leading, I was changing from the kid I used to be. But whatever the reason me and June were growing further and further apart. I've got to hold my hands up, it was all down to me. All she ever wanted was to have a few more kids, put a nice home together and have a husband who would spend a bit of time with her. I was too young and very selfish – though I wouldn't have believed it at the time – and I had ambitions to be somebody.

When I wasn't doing deals and playing the rascal I still had time for my old mates like Siddy, Poochie and Albert, and we often went out for evenings together. One of the places we used was The Pegasus in Green Lane, Stoke Newington. It was a lively place, and as usual I'd get up and belt out a few Al Martino numbers. I loved singing, always had. Something I'd picked up from my Mum because she was at it all day long. I couldn't have been that bad either because I used to earn tens and twenties all over the place – in the dance hall or pub concerts.

We got friendly with Ronnie Ellis who worked there, and because he did the tables and glasses and also got up and did a turn on the stage he was known as the singing waiter. I was chatting to him when he said, 'Hang on, Ron, my niece has just walked in. I'd better go and have a quick word.'

She was about 20 years old, lovely face, bubbly blonde hair and a giggle you could hear all round the bar. Oh, yeah, and RK being the randy little sod he was couldn't help noticing she had a pair of lungs that could have knocked your eyes out. Barbara Windsor, rising star of musicals, was related to my mate Ronnie, and he'd never said a word about it.

I had a fleeting mental picture of mumsy June sitting at home looking after our little girl, but knocked that on the head, remembered I had something urgent I had to talk to Ronnie about and shot over to him. Being the polite fella he was he just had to introduce me to his niece. I turned on the famous charm and was rewarded with a 'Hello, darling, nice to meet you,' a light handshake, and what I took to be an unmistakeable hint of promise.

If I'd had a crystal ball and taken a quick peek that night in the late fifties I'd have run home to Junie, locked the door and never come out again. But I couldn't see into the future and was too weak to fight my feelings and do the right thing by my wife who loved me. I couldn't get the vision of that lovely girl out of my mind and dreamed of what she was trying to tell me with that touch of her hand.

Weeks went by, and things got worse indoors, mainly because I was touchy and moody. Every paper I picked up seemed to have a picture of Barbara staring out at me. This wasn't so much about her being a big star or anything, because then she still had a long way to go, but more to do with her looks and cheeky personality being great newspaper copy.

Though she was a local celebrity, the biggest thing she had done at that time was knock them out in a show called *Love From Judy*. Still the papers knew they were on to a winner and gave the punters every detail about her, which didn't do my lovesick little heart any good as I read about this bloke and that bloke doing what I desperately wanted to do. The latest following her about like a puppy was Gary Crosby, son of the famous Bing. There might have been nothing in it, but it didn't stop a feeling of jealousy creeping into my stomach and thinking, what's this flash Yank doing sniffing round one of our local girls?

The next time we were destined to meet was at my favourite start of the night place, the salt-beef bar at Stamford Hill. I'd changed my image, got rid of the cab and was driving a tidy-looking Zephyr Zodiac. I parked it up, walked over to the beef bar, and there she is standing with a bloke I recognised from my schooldays. I gave them both a nod, and she returned it with a look that tightened my throat up. Now I never had two minutes for Neil when we were at school, but suddenly he's my best mate. When I clocked that the two of them were just friends having a sandwich, I got him to one side and asked him for Barbara's phone number. He obliged, and I felt ready to go to work.

Next morning I phoned her about eight o'clock. I think I got her out of bed and certainly got a blank at the other end when I gave her my name. I was desperately trying to paint a word picture of myself to jog her memory, and things were getting embarrassing. So to make a little joke I threw in that I was the fella with a big hooter. 'Oh, yeah,' she says. 'I met you at Uncle Ronnie's pub.' Some impression I'd made. Couldn't wait to meet me? No, too busy.

She didn't tell me to sod off, so I rang her on and off for the next couple of weeks. Same excuse every time. Then I started to get her answering machine – her mum – and she sounded frostier every time she recognised my voice. Not available. I wasn't only kidding myself that I stood any chance against the big names she was rubbing shoulders with, but I was beginning to suspect that I was making a fool of myself as well.

It's funny how two people can share the same experience and yet remember it so differently. To me our first meeting was mystical, and I definitely felt something electric between us. Yet in Barbara's autobiography she writes that far from our meeting being a magical moment, she hardly remembered that first hello, and when I started telephoning she thought, Who the fuck's this bloke pestering me? Perhaps old age was fading her memory when she wrote the book.

So I gave up the chase. Until one day I saw a picture in the paper of her sitting in a restaurant on her own, and the caption underneath said something like LITTLE MISS LONELY. She might have been let down by her boyfriend or it was more likely to fill a gap in the newspaper. Either way I'm straight on the blower, got through to her and asked her out. 'OK, Why not?' she said. And that was the beginning of a love-hate relationship that would turn me into Mr Barbara Windsor.

That night I took her to one of the West End's plushest clubs and really rolled out the wagon – champagne, flowers and expensive food. The whole nine yards, plus the smoothest line of old chat you've ever heard, most of it about me being free, rich and single. Worked though, and we finished the evening with a nice kiss and cuddle in the back of my car. If I'd known that night what I learnt a long time later I'd have gone all the way. But I was completely naïve and didn't dare force myself on this beautiful and innocent young lady.

I had fallen in love the moment I clapped eyes on her. She took a good bit longer to return the feeling, but with woman's intuition or whatever you call it, she must have seen right past the Jack the Lad front I put up, and after a few weeks she was calling me her Prince Charming. Barbara was everything I could have wished for. Passionate, loving, funny and often crudely down to earth, which suited me because I didn't have to pretend I was clever with words or that I was anything else but a successful scrap dealer.

Our lovemaking was acrobatic and exhausting. The problem came afterwards when, like most women, she wanted to talk, while all I wanted was a quick kip before going home to my own bed. It wasn't the talking that bothered me so much as the fact that she was chipping away at the fictional life story I'd spun her.

The truth was the thought of her finding out that I was a bit of a Cinderella man then dumping me in disgust frightened the life out of me. I don't think she disbelieved what I'd told her about myself, she was just interested to learn more than the very sketchy details that were all I wanted to give out. When she asked me where I lived or where I had my business, a mental picture would light up in my mind, and a lie would roll off my tongue as plausible as you like. I'd tell her that I'd just taken over this run-down flat, and I didn't want to take her there because it was filthy, and the decorators were working on it. That wasn't enough. I'd then rabbit on about colour schemes, wallpaper and what furniture I'd probably get, and the more I spoke the more I got to like the way this non-existent flat was turning out.

As for work, I drove past Billy's yard with her early one evening, pointed it out as mine and then went into detail about my plans for expansion. Past girlfriends? I'd had one or two, but right now there was only one girl in the world for me – then we'd laugh and cuddle and start another romantic session.

I must have been stark-raving mad. How long did I think I could keep up the pretence? Talk about burning the candle at both ends – I'd set fire to the middle as well. I'd graft all day long, rush home to change, tear round to Barbara's and act the stallion until the small hours, then fly home for a few hours in bed beside June and be up at six to start all over again. Most of the time I walked round in a daze absolutely knackered.

Before things got so bad that June didn't want to know me, I dreaded crawling in beside her to find she was awake with needs of her own. After all she never set out to be a nun. So as always thinking of number one and making sure I didn't blow the whistle on my double life, I had to call on reserves that even Casanova couldn't have matched. Eventually June twigged that Chanel No. 5 wasn't amongst the dozens of bottles on my aftershave smellies shelf, put two and two together and decided to spend a lot of time with her mother. Naturally the block was put on my marital conjugals but not before she told me – 'If you're interested!' – that she was pregnant again.

What is it with me and mothers? I mentioned that Barbara's was a bit frosty on the telephone, well, when she clapped eyes on me for the first time her manner was sub-zero and never got above freezing point. While Barbara saw past the flash exterior Rosie Geel (no wonder Barbara changed her name) never did. She must have thought, what you see is all you get, and never missed a chance to dig me out whenever Barbara turned her back.

She didn't know what subtle meant, and I must admit I didn't myself at the time. So she'd get straight to the point, buttering me up with things like, 'You're nothing and never will be – a chancer – a no-hoper, and the quicker my daughter sees through you the better.' That was telling me. Still, I kept smiling and kept coming back, forcing her to pull out an ace from her sleeve or, as it turned out, her handbag.

I arrived a bit early at the flat one night, and Barbara was in the bath. So I had to sit in that cold atmosphere, me on one side of the table and Rosie on the other. After ten minutes of the silent treatment, she leant backwards, picked up her handbag, pulled out a bundle of notes and spread them in front of me. 'That's £100.00,' she said, cool as you like. 'Is that enough for you to clear out of our lives?'

I looked at it and very politely said, 'Rosie, a million wouldn't make me walk away.' Then she started crying. Barbara's walked in, and I had to explain what's gone down. She went crazy, shouting at her mother that she was an evil old cow, and no wonder Daddy had left her. In the end they're both howling the place down. That was one night I was glad to slip into my own bed before midnight.

What I didn't know at the time was that Rosie had a secret, which if she'd cared to share it with her little girl, would have brought our love affair down in flames quicker than the Hindenburg. For some time I'd noticed that she'd been giving me strange looks that were a bit different from the normal 'Why don't you drop dead?' I can't explain what they were really – it was as though she was trying to solve some sort of puzzle written on my forehead. What she was really trying to work out was how to protect Barbara from the knowledge that 'Mr Eligible for a walk up the aisle' had not only got a wife and daughter hidden away but was also expecting another delivery from the fruit of his rampant loins.

Can you believe it? The very man who'd been instrumental in bringing us together, good old Uncle Ronnie from the Pegasus, had heard a bit of bar-room gossip and done his duty by passing it on to his sister Rosie. A few weeks after the pay-off stunt Rosie spilled the beans to stop Barbara defending me once and for all. When I turned up that evening I walked into one of the most frightening experiences of my life. Being on the receiving end of little Miss Windsor's uncontrollable rage.

She screamed, she swore, she went for me with her fingernails, and all the time she's ripping every one of my lies to shreds. I was an effin' rat, a dirty lousy scheming bastard and even a filthy ——, a word I'd never heard a woman utter before. It was like being in the path of a howling storm. I couldn't defend myself. I just stood there as she pummelled into me with her tiny fists, because it wasn't my nature to raise my hands to the opposite sex. As for the verbal attack, all I could do was hang my head and do my best impression of Little Boy Lost that never failed to soften the hardest heart. Eventually the steam went out of her, and she just slumped on the settee and burst into tears. I was still looking contrite enough to make a block of stone weep, but inside I'm thinking thank God it's all over.

It was, but not in the way I wanted. Barbara looked up very quietly, which made it worse, and said, 'It's finished, Ronnie – I can't love you after what you've done.' I wanted to argue that she was being unfair and overreacting to my little bit of economy with the truth, but I couldn't speak. As I walked away my bubbly, confident, always giggling Barbara was rocking backwards and forwards with her head on her knees like a little girl.

So what did I do? Get myself a bed sit and keep my head down? No, I went running straight back to June. Not because I wanted to make a fresh start, but because I couldn't bear to be on my own. Poor June, bless her. I think she blamed herself for the way I was. Like now she was a mum she was no longer attractive. To try and get me out of my black moods she'd sit and talk as though we could resolve our differences, and things would get back to how they were. I was so wrapped up in my misery that sometimes it was on the tip of my tongue to tell her about Barbara, hoping in a stupid male sort of way that she'd understand, sympathise and advise me what to do. She'd have probably knifed me so it was just as well I didn't, but I was so gutted by what had happened that's how I was thinking.

For two weeks I wallowed in self-pity, then snapped out of it with the idea I'd go back to square one and pick up the phone. No answer. I knew Rosie wouldn't be there because she was working, but Barbara was what she called 'resting' and I called unemployed, so she had to be in the flat. I rang so often my finger was getting a corn on it, and I began to wish I'd stuck to my school lessons so I could write a touching letter begging forgiveness.

Then she picked the phone up. I took a deep breath and said, 'Give me two minutes to explain why I acted the way I did and if you still feel the same about me I'll never trouble you again.' That few seconds before she answered were like for ever. I was biting my knuckles and holding my breath, when she said, 'Come round then.'

If the truth was known Barbara had missed me as much as I had her, but she was a woman after all, and she wasn't going to admit it until I'd paid penance and got down on bended knee. That night I gave her the truth. Finishing up with, if I ever so much as told her a lie or was unfaithful I hoped something terrible would happen to me. I didn't leave her bed until the milkman came up the path.

With a promise of marriage tucked in her bra top, subject to my divorce, Barbara started to introduce me to her world of show business, which she hadn't been confident enough to do before. That caused problems for me. I was an old-fashioned East End guy, and I didn't take too kindly to all the kissing, cuddling and luvvieness that my girl was on the receiving end of. I told myself that most of the blokes were gay, but I couldn't always be sure, and it's a wonder I didn't show myself up by thumping a few heads.

Barbara shrugged it off with a 'Don't be daft – they're just being friendly,' but I still got the hump on too many occasions. Apart from that I loved the novelty of meeting famous celebrities. It was so different from what I knew, it took some getting used to. I'd drop Barbara off at wherever she was doing her turn, like in a cabaret or theatre, shoot off and have a few drinks with Poochie, Siddy and Jim Lumley and have a good laugh until it was time for me to pick up Barbara. One minute I'm with my down-to-earth mates, next I'm in Danny La Rue's house listening to Noel Coward banging out show tunes on the piano. I was so star struck I nearly showed a few of these names that I was Mr Nobody by asking for their autographs. Still, most of them were so full of themselves they never noticed who was around them unless there was a danger of being upstaged.

Though I'd been pretty vague about it I wasn't ashamed that I earned my living in a scrap yard from the back of a clapped-out old lorry. Now she knew the truth Barbara didn't give a monkey's either. So it wasn't to drag myself up in the world that I made up my mind to try something where I didn't get my hands dirty. My new venture was going to be in the rag trade – well, one end of it anyway.

The idea was planted by a mate of mine, Peter Gibson. This fella was a tailor with aspirations to do with needle and thread what millionaire John Bloom had done with washing machines. That he was a wide boy with a plausible line in old chat and was as reliable as the weather was an extra he threw in for free. Flash Harry or not he could knock up a silk blouse out of a pair of old drawers quicker than you could down a pint.

Pete came to me with what he reckoned was a sure-fire money-spinner. Women were going crazy over these items. They would be cheap, colourful and a fashion accessory for every home. With visions of a line in summer frocks I cut off the sales patter and asked him what the fuck he was talking about. 'Ironing-board covers and oven mitts, mate – can't go wrong,' he said.

Whatever Pete was he wasn't a con artist, so in the end I allowed myself to be worn down and agreed to invest a small bundle into the venture, plus my nimble fingers on a pair of scissors. I was voted to get the design sorted, which meant nipping down to Woolworths and buying one each of a cover and a pair of mitts. Then back to Peter's flat where his missus Betty took them to pieces so that we could draw round the sections on a piece of wallpaper and cut the patterns out. After all the clever technical stuff, it's left to me to cut out the material, while the other two get a couple of old treadle sewing machines going like the clappers.

I could not believe how quick the goods were piling up. Once we'd made enough to fill four suitcases the sewing was out of the way and it was over to the sales department for a quick trip to the West End. Offer these fine lines to Harrods? No chance. Peter's set up on a corner in Bond Street. And me, suitcases on the pavement, down the other end. After my years on the cart I'm not slow at geeing up the ladies, and the gear's gone like hot cakes. We're on a winner – in fact the line was so popular we were getting other street traders begging for the address of our supplier. Naturally we've offered to fix them up.

It got ridiculous. The money was rolling in, but we couldn't keep up with demand. It got so crazy most nights I couldn't get round to Barbara, let alone show my face at home. Me and Pete decided to expand, and in one week went from his kitchen to a large lock-up, kitted out with a dozen second-hand sewing machines and the same number of girls to keep the merchandise pouring on to the streets.

I was the first to admit that the success of our little operation took me by surprise. I know I'd sunk a bit of cash into the business, but all the same I couldn't help thinking the whole thing was a bit of a joke. Ironing-board cover and bloody oven mitts, I ask you! But what with renting a bit of real estate, grandly called 'The

Factory', and employing people, it had all turned very legitimate, and it felt good.

There's something in my character that insists that whenever my life is on the up I've got to take out a very large gun and shoot myself in the foot. I can't help it. I've always got to live on the edge. So here am I stuffing loads of cash into the old sock week after week, and I get a very dodgy offer. Do I look at what I've got and think, No, I'm quite comfortable as I am – I'll give it a miss, mustn't rock the boat? No, I don't – straight in with both feet. Five grand's worth of top-quality cloth going for a song. It's fallen off the back of a lorry, and there's not a mark on it.

With these deals you don't ask questions, and if you did you wouldn't get any answers. So I didn't waste my time enquiring why the delivery was all cloak and dagger. No, my dealer couldn't drop the cloth round to my lock-up, but he'd park the lorry in a certain street with the keys above the sun visor. I collect it, deliver it to wherever, then return the lorry. Half up front, the rest once I've got it tucked away. No skin off my nose, so I agree.

I got a phone call telling me the stuff was waiting where we'd arranged so I drove down and parked behind the lorry. As I was retrieving the keys from their hiding place, the cab door opened, and I was pulled out of my seat by the law and cuffed before I knew what was happening. A police car screeched to a halt beside us, they bundled me in and drove off at high speed to Islington nick – I was still clutching the keys to the lorry.

At the station the arresting officer went through the standard spiel to a bored desk sergeant while I stood there like a kid brought up in front of his headmaster. Then I'm processed. First I have to turn out my pockets and the contents have to be written on a form before all my bits and pieces are tucked into a large envelope. Next I'm whipped into a side room for a fingerprint job then stuck in front of a camera. Funny how it's automatic to put on a big cheesy grin when you're having a snap taken. But I'm soon told there's no need for that as the whole point of a mug shot is to make you look like a mass-murderer. Finally I'm told to hand over my belt, tie and shoelaces in case I try to hang myself when I realise what a naughty boy I've been, and I'm locked in a tiny cell.

It's like a public toilet. Tiled floor to ceiling and the only break in the monotony of these cracked white tiles is a notice telling me that anyone defacing these walls will be in serious lumber. Short of having a hammer and chisel handy I can't imagine any possibility of leaving the message 'Ronnie woz 'ere'.

One hour ago I was a key's turn away from a very healthy earner. So close. I'd made plans to treat myself with the proceeds. New car perhaps, or if I could have talked Barbara into taking a bit of time away from her cabaret, a nice week in the sun somewhere. Now it's all down the pan, plus my investment money.

The charge was all bollocks and not worth worrying about. Little bit of receiving – only slightly worse than shoplifting – would only get me a slap on the wrist and a stiff fine. What was making me break out in a cold sweat was how the family were going to react. After a few other brushes with the law I'd sworn to Mum that I would never give her any more grief. I was definitely on the straight and narrow. Same with June. What with being a responsible father my dabbling in crime was a thing of the past. And – Oh Christ! – what about Barbara? She didn't have a clue that her Ronnie was anything other than as straight as herself. What a mess!

When I told June she suggested I should clear off and take my criminal influence as far away from her child as possible. Mum didn't say much, but Jimmy and Johnny knocked me all around the room when they found out. Barbara was the only one who didn't give me a load of grief. But this was because with no one else to put her straight I bent the truth a little. Largely forgiven I decided to forget about it. So much so that by the time my court summons turned up I'd almost forgotten about it entirely.

Barbara had been pulling the punters into Winston's Club in Bond Street with her act and getting her name up where it counted, so she was happy, which meant I was happy. Come court day I dressed in my finest and made sure I had enough cash in my back pocket to square the fine. I wanted to pay my dues and get a shift on, because I had arranged to run my eye over another deal later on. It didn't take long at all, an hour tops, I suppose, while they went through all the legal stuff. Then about one minute for the judge to hit me with a 15-month prison sentence.

For the whole 61 minutes I'd stood in the dock and taken the piss. I never spoke out of order, but I let them all see that I thought they were all a bunch of tossers. I'd given June a little wave when I saw her sitting there in the bloom of imminent motherhood. And when she wasn't looking, a little wink to Barbara who had taken a seat at the back. I didn't know it then but she was in the same delicate condition as June. I bet that judge dined out on the story of how he'd knocked the arrogant smile off this cocky little bastard's face. Suddenly it wasn't a joke anymore.

5.

First Taste of Prison, Second of Marriage

A PART FROM THE DAILY ritual of slopping out and the absence of TV – they didn't have television in prisons in 1960 – the regime in Brixton could have been a lot worse. Being a remand prison, it was really like an oversize waiting room. A place where they held the guilty and the innocent while they chased up the evidence to prove the point either way. Or, as in my case having already been sentenced, waiting while they sorted out which prison I was going to, where the punishment could start with a vengeance. My first time inside – how could I know this was the lull before the storm?

I had just got round to thinking that if this was the price of crime, it was no wonder everyone was at it, when they moved me to Wandsworth. Nothing could have prepared me for that place. It was like a zoo packed wall to wall with a cross-section of the lowest forms of criminal life. Spotty granny muggers, raving lunatics and crazed body builders who wanted to smash everything that moved. I sat on my bunk and asked myself what a straight rascal like me was doing stuck in with people like that.

Anyone who normally lived on the right side of the law and had been unfortunate enough to get time for nonpayment of fines or maintenance would have no chance of surviving unscathed. They would be robbed, done over and probably beaten in two minutes, because without friends inside you are out on a limb and completely vulnerable. At that time I didn't have a name that carried much weight. Luckily for me though my brothers Jimmy and Johnny had been through the system quite a few times and gained a bit of respect, so because of them I was well looked after.

The few run-ins I did have were down to me and caused by the jealousy I felt about Barbara. Some poor bastard would open the daily rag, see a photograph of her and go, 'Cor, I wouldn't mind some of that'.

If I was around I'd say, 'Well, how about some of this instead?' and give him a whack. I suppose I was a bit out of order really because they didn't mean no harm by it, and we've all leered at young ladies in the papers. But this wasn't just any bird, it was my Barbara, and I was having none of it. Word got around, and after that they made sure any comments were made well outside my earshot.

I expected Barbara to give me the elbow as soon as I was sent down, but instead of that she was as good as gold and visited me all the time I was in Wandsworth. Nothing to do with me getting some time, but no sooner had the door slammed behind me than Barbara became a national star. She'd got herself one of the main parts in *Fings Ain't Wot They Used T'Be*, Lionel Bart's 1959 smash-hit musical comedy. And if that wasn't enough, at the same time she started appearing in the *Rag Trade* comedy series on television. If that little box couldn't make her famous nothing would.

While her almost overnight success was great for her, it did nothing to make my sentence any easier to bear. I worried endlessly that now she was a proper star she wouldn't want to know me. And on top of that I had something more tangible to worry about. Some kind soul took it upon themselves to whisper in my ear that Barbara had been seen out with Charlie Kray. Frustrated that if it was true I could do nothing about it, I suffered a lot of grief until I convinced myself that with a wife and young boy no way would Charlie be messing about. I was wrong, and in fact the two of them did have something going, but luckily for my peace of mind I didn't find out the truth until years later.

Same as I didn't know Barbara was pregnant when

I was sent down. Just as well, I suppose, otherwise it would have done my head in not being with her at a time like that. I was also unaware that before I would taste freedom again, she would have had the second but by no means last abortion. My ignorance was certainly bliss. Knowing nothing of what she was getting up to outside I eagerly looked forward to her every visit and was grateful for the couple of quid she slipped me every week.

My daily life was difficult enough without the added complication of worrying about my tangled love life. June had started writing to me suggesting that with a bit of honest commitment from both of us, we could sort things out. So, could she visit me and talk about our problems face to face? Bless her for trying, but the last thing I wanted was her bumping into Barbara in prison reception, so I put her off. Then I had to start putting Barbara off just in case June ignored my letter and came anyway. That problem was resolved when I was moved to Eastchurch open prison on the Isle of Sheppey, and neither of them would find it easy to pop in. They kept writing though.

In case the new prison had a policy of hard labour, like breaking rocks, I developed a limp from day one. A quick flash of my still livid scar and I was given light work detail and signed up for the kitchens. I played my cards right, made an impression of being keen and in no time took over as head kitchen boy. This was one of the most sought-after jobs in the place, because the perks and power were unlimited. Overnight I became the most popular con there.

I gained benefits from my bad leg. With pain written across my face, I would limp past the screw in charge and say to him, 'Got to take a little walk, guv, pain's terrible,' and I'd shuffle past with half a dozen frozen lamb chops down my trousers. Other odds and ends, like butter and cheese and fruit for fermenting hooch, were easier to get out of the kitchen. Everybody was desperate for these extras, and I didn't give away the stuff. It had to be paid for in prison currency – namely tobacco.

I'd never been a smoker so it was easy for me to build up a good supply of this valuable commodity, putting me in a strong trading position for the good things in life. So one way and another I was living like a king, never dreaming for a moment that I'd cut myself into a time-honoured prison tradition, which is that only the toughest, hardest and meanest lags get to run the tobacco racket.

Everyone else, except me, knew to keep their nose out or have it removed in the showers. Perhaps my favours in the kitchen held back some violent assault. Instead the big boys took the easier option and grassed me up to the Governor. I don't think he could believe his luck. Tobacco barons are a pain in the arse to the system. They might appear to be providing a service, the same as moneylenders on the outside. But as soon as there is a hiccup in repayments, violence and intimidation are used, causing aggravation for the screws and the Governor. So he was well pleased to have one of these troublemakers delivered to his office.

Until he accused me of being one of these barons I hadn't been aware that that's what I had been. I protested my innocence and swore it was a fit-up. No good. Next morning I was in the van on my way back to Wandsworth. With only a month to run on my sentence, the place didn't bother me so much as it had the first time. At least Barbara could drop in and see me more often. One thing I did promise myself – once I walked out of that gate I was going to lead an honest life. It would be the last time they would ever see me behind these walls again.

Unless you have experienced some time behind bars, there is no way you can understand what it's like to step out of a prison door with your porridge all done and behind you. There I was, a man who loved a new suit every month, standing outside the walls of Wandsworth still wearing the same clobber I was lifted in nearly a year and a half ago.

I was excited, nervous and bewildered, wondering whether to head for home and see my new-born son. Drop in and see Mum and Dad. Or give Barbara a ring. Then I heard that giggle, and there she was, my lovely Barbara, standing by a taxi with a great big smile on her face.

After a bone-crushing cuddle, instead of telling the taxi driver to head for Stamford Hill, Barbara directed him to take us to Green Lanes, Haringey. We pulled up outside Carson's the tailors, and I was thinking I love this girl, she's going to kit me out with some new gear before we go back to her Mum's place. But I was wrong.

She led me to a door beside the shop and up a flight of stairs to a beautiful flat that she had taken over for the two of us while I had been inside. I was knocked out by the luxury of it all. Not only had she got the lease, but she'd had it decorated from top to bottom, carpeted and filled with furniture. The lounge was bigger than the whole flat in Arcola Street, and all around were placed fancy bits and pieces that I had never been used to. The whole set-up was like a West End showroom or something out of a magazine.

Glass-top tables, expensive lamps and – straight out of a film – a bamboo drinks bar across one corner. The two bedrooms were massive, and the kitchen and bathroom were both bigger than four of my cells knocked together. Remember my home for ages had been a 12 x 8 tiled shit-house, now this. I couldn't take it in. And for a long time, after what I had gone through over the last year and a half, was only ever really comfortable in the confines of the smallest room. That night I gave her the biggest thank you I could raise.

After a magical first few weeks things started to slip downhill a bit. As usual due to me. As I said, this little lady had turned into a big star while I was away, and to be honest I wasn't sure I could handle it. I was very happy that at last she'd reached the goal she seemed so obsessed with, but it didn't please me that for the moment she was paying my way.

With being out of touch for such a long time, I hadn't got back into the swing of wheeling and dealing, so quite honestly I was skint. I felt like a ponce. Barbara never complained that I wasn't bringing in a few shillings. All she said was, 'Something will turn up soon, darling, and I've got plenty for both of us.' She had and was grafting for every penny of it.

The more popular she became the more she was called on to appear in television chat shows, stick her chest out for glam-shot sessions and go here and there for endless interviews. All that was just the spin-off from filming all day and doing cabaret or a show at night. It made me tired just thinking about her schedule, but she couldn't get enough of it. Out of bed in the small hours – full day – then back into bed in the small hours.

So where did that leave me? Bored, a bit lonely and getting more and more pissed off. I suppose my state of mind was mainly brought about by the delayed reaction to my prison sentence. You don't just shrug it off and walk away untouched. The early part of 1961 was not a very good time for me, but I knew I had to make the most of what I'd got and snap out of it. I did have a lot going for me. There was Barbara, who every red-blooded male in the country was lusting after, but she was more than content for me to be the only man in her life. I had a lovely place to get my head down. And what with night clubs, pubs and celebrity dos, had a lifestyle that many would have envied. The drawback was being a bit short on the readies, and the answer to that was to make myself busy and put my face about where it counted.

I put the word out that I was up for a bit of work

and within a few weeks had a few deals on the table –
at last I was earning. What a lovely feeling it was to
have a thick bundle in the pocket again. It boosted my
confidence no end. I might have imagined it before
but now instead of thinking of Barbara's friends all
muttering, 'Here comes that hanger-on', they would
cop the fancy jewellery round her neck and say to her,
'Lucky girl, you've got a lovely bloke there.' Funny,
really, the easier money came in the easier it was to
get rid of.

I'd go into some posh West End jewellers and tell
her, 'Go on, Windsor, get yourself something nice,'
and she'd be going 'I'll have this – I'll have that,' and I
would peel off a wad of paper to settle up. I happily
paid for everything – even her clothes, which I felt
gave me some say in what she dressed herself up in.

Strange how a man's mind works. When I first
clapped eyes on her she was everything I'd ever
wished for. Lovely hair, lovely face and those tiny
skirts and low-cut tops – Wow! Yet once our
relationship was well established, and I felt she was
100 per cent my property everything about her was
wrong. What attracted me to her in the first place,
suddenly turned into an indecent display of legs and
boobs. A flagrant show for anyone who wanted an
eyeful. I dug her out on the subject over and over
again. I went quiet, I sulked, then it would all blow up
in a row, and I'd ended up telling her she looked like a
ten-bob whore, adding, 'No wonder they gave you
that job as a tart in *Fings*. They saw you coming a
mile off.'

I'd been at the wrong end of her temper more than once so I couldn't believe I was putting myself up for it again. But instead of quite rightly telling me, 'I am what I am – if you don't like it piss off,' she said, 'OK, Ronnie, take me shopping tomorrow, and I'll get something to suit you'.

Not only that, I stuck my oar into her personal manners as well. At the table I'd tell her, 'Don't slouch when you're eating, shoulders back, chest out. Bring the fork up to your mouth, not the other way round.' Talk about *Pygmalion*. Bloody cheek on my part or not, she loved the new image. When directors and film people that she took notice of complimented her on the new look, she proudly told them that her Ronnie had turned her into a lady. That's one of the few things I did for her over the years that she hasn't turned on its head with the passing of time.

Most of my income was coming from very iffy sources. But with being so busy Barbara never stood still long enough to enquire what I did all day, or where all these bundles of cash were coming from. She got a very sharp hint very early one August morning.

Nothing like the summer sun streaming through the window at first light, plus a bit of birdsong to get the sap rising. Ten minutes earlier we'd have been caught *in flagrante*. As it was we were dozing in each other's arms when the front door was smashed off its hinges, and the law was all over place. My sarcastic 'Why didn't you knock like everybody else?' fell on deaf ears. Considering the terrible shock it must have been to experience something like that for the first time in her life, Barbara went at them like a terrier. Kicking off with 'Ere, what's going on,' she shouted and effed and blinded until I was escorted out of the door and into a police van.

Before we drove off an inspector plonked himself down opposite me clutching a blue vase and a copy of a previous day's newspaper that had been on the kitchen table. He never said a word, just unfolded the paper as though he was reading the inside pages. Leaving me to stare at the screaming headline on the front: ARMED ROBBERS NET £8000 IN POWER STATION ATTACK. After a while he put the paper down, gave me a smug look and said, 'You can have this back for your scrapbook in ten years' time.' I told him to fuck off.

Not long afterwards I was back in the usual situation of no tie, no belt, no shoes, a different cell but those same cracked and dirty tiles. Eventually they get round to charging me with taking part in the aforementioned armed robbery that had taken place in Lotts Road, Fulham. In case there was some chance of me wriggling my way out of that, they covered that eventuality by adding a charge of receiving cash from said robbery. Now where have I heard that recently?

I actually laughed at the charging officer. I told him, 'You've got no chance.' Then I asked, 'Did you get any prints off the job or find guns under my bed?' All I got from him was, 'It's not for me to discuss, but I'll tell you this. The officer in charge wasn't pinching your vase for his missus to put flowers in. It's here as evidence and full of bent money.'

After that little put-down I kept my mouth shut until I found out I was being bailed, which was a result in itself. If they had been taking it seriously they would have kept me locked up. Barbara turned up and dished up the money without argument. In the taxi home she was a bit quiet, then she asked 'Another little misunderstanding, Ronnie?'

I put my hand on my heart and said, 'God's honest, sweetheart, they just want to fit up all the Knight brothers. You know how it is, the law get a bit paranoid about families. A few brothers get a bit of form, and they've got them down as a firm of gangsters. It's a liberty.' She accepted that.

I couldn't see they had anything on me so, apart from weekly visits to the local police station as condition of my bail, we got on with our lives. Or at least pretended to, because with something like that hanging over your head it's a worry whatever front you put up. I didn't enjoy my turkey like I normally do that Christmas 1961. A summons had arrived, giving me my court appearance date, and by then I was well up on what they were putting against me.

It was no secret that the other men involved in the robbery were friends of mine. They had been dealt with earlier and had already been sentenced. Alfie Hutchinson went down for ten. Peter Davis seven, Terry Shaw a five and Yocker Robinson eighteen months for receiving. Heavy stuff, and if it all went pear shaped I'd be two steps behind them. As for the vase 'full of bent money', one single £5 note had been proved to have come from the raid. The rest were white as snow. As a little sweetener for themselves the police had thrown in as evidence that my telephone number was found in Alfie's phone book. They must have been really desperate to pin this job on me.

When I turned up in court I was smartly suited, just as I was when I got the 'Guilty' over the cloth. Unlike my last appearance though, this time I was sober-faced and respectful. I'd learnt a painful lesson that day: 'Don't take the piss out of the judge'. No evidence was offered as to me actually being on the raid, and the whole court had a good chuckle when the phone book was brought up. But when they got down to the business of receiving that measly fiver, my brief produced, like pulling a white rabbit from a top hat, my lovely neighbour Betty Cronk. God bless her for ever.

Betty lived in the flat below ours, and she thought the world of me. This was largely down to the fact I did loads of odd jobs for her. And, the icing on the cake, I used to take her poodle for walks, rain or shine. And she wanted everyone in court to know about it.

As a bonus to the glowing character reference she gave me, she happened to mentioned that one afternoon in August 1961 she was having a cup of tea and biscuits in my flat when a certain Alfred Hutchinson called in to repay a long forgotten loan. Not only, she told the court with an honest look on her face, did she witness him handing me a few banknotes but also, she couldn't help noticing, she saw me place them in a blue vase on the shelf. Her air of innocence and that vital evidence won the day for me. I could see the jury were impressed, and even the judge had a benign smile on his face. Verdict? I was acquitted and discharged. But I could bet my life that the law would have me marked down from then on.

I thought Barbara might have got the hump over being associated with a man on an armed robbery charge, what with her career to think about. But no, there she was hugging me to death outside the court, proudly telling reporters, 'Ronnie is a wonderful man. I never doubted his innocence for a minute.'

In the run up to the trial I'd had an idea for a nice little scam. Though not knowing which way things would go I had put the brakes on it. Now there was nothing to stop me so it was full steam into the 'long-firm' fraud business.

No marks for originality because this moneyspinner had been going on since time began, but it was a new move for me. The idea is to set up a front – shop, offices or a warehouse – all nice and legitimate. Letterheads, a few dodgy papers and a sticker on the side of the lorry. Then, depending on what line you intend to trade in, start ordering electrical goods, clothes, toys or what have you.

This takes a bit of up front money, because after a month when the invoices come in – Bang! Paid on the nail. The suppliers can't believe it. 'What, haven't got to chase our money? This firm's got to be looked after. Give them extended credit and anything else they want.' That's the game. Get them hooked and they can't deliver whatever's been ordered fast enough. Then we hit them. With the warehouse stacked to the rafters, the word is put out to our contacts, and the place is cleared at half price. By the time the suppliers realise that things have gone a bit quiet, we've already set up somewhere else under a different name.

I went into all this with two other fellas. One of them had a couple of big supermarkets, so obviously he was in a good position to know what was required and also to be able to move the stuff on without anybody getting suspicious. I'd better just call him Harry, because since then he's gone right up in the world, and I don't think his shareholders would like to hear he used to be a rascal. The other one was Jimmy McLean, and his job was to order whatever Harry or I told him to.

Half the time Jim was a fucking nuisance, and I used to wonder why I'd got webbed up with him. He'd be told what was wanted, then off his own back he'd order something else. Or the reps would tell him that this was a good line or that was new on the market, and mug that he was he'd let them load him up with a thousand cases of a line we couldn't shift. Harry would come to me pulling his hair out. He wouldn't say nothing to Jim because he was a bit intimidated by his size so it was left to me to straighten him out. I told him, 'You work for me, not the other way round, and next time you leave us with a ton of stuff we can only sell for pennies, you can piss off.' Big as he was, he swallowed it, and I left it at that.

If it hadn't been for a certain young lady, instead of coining the cash in I would have been earning 50 bob a week scrubbing out the bogs behind the wall. So when we needed a secretary for typing and answering the phone, I was straight downstairs to Betty Cronk. She had stood up in court and given them the story that got me acquitted, so the least I could do was to put some wages her way when I knew she was short of a few bob. She wasn't involved in the naughty side of things – just did her job and that was the end of it.

Betty was a nice-looking girl, and, unbeknown to me, whenever I wasn't around, Jim would slip up to the office and try his luck. She knew he was married and told him to leave it out. He wouldn't take no for an answer and kept at her, threatening he could sack her if she didn't come over with it. He even took a few personal liberties.

I noticed she was becoming a bit on the quiet side, which was unusual, because normally she was a live-wire. I asked her what was the matter, and she told me about Jim pestering her. The bastard. I shot straight downstairs and gave him a pull, and he was right cocky. He's about six foot three, and I wouldn't reach that if I stood on a couple of bricks, but I was steaming. As soon as he said, 'You don't fucking own me. What you going to do about it?' I took Billy's advice and punched him right in the mouth. Just in case he came back at me, I gave him another right-hander that knocked him arse over head. Harry came flying in and grabbed hold of me, but it was all over. This 20-stone bully was going to stay on the floor until he was sure I'd cooled down.

Funny how you can work with somebody every day and know nothing about them. If I had known then what I found out years later I would have broken his back. I always thought he was one of the McLeans out of Pickwell Street, Hoxton. I knew the sisters, and they were lovely girls. Turned out, though, his real name was Jim Irwin, and what he'd done was marry a widow, Rosie McLean, and taken on her young family. When it suited him he took on their name as an alias.

When he wasn't being a pain in the arse at work I found Jim was OK. We might have a drink and a few laughs, then like some bloody Jekyll he'd go back to his flat in Kent Street and beat the shit out of those little kids. Rosie McLean as well if she got in his way. He took a particular dislike to Lenny, one of the kids, and gave him the works. Not clips round the ear or a belt across the backside, but broken jaw, leg and arm.

I remember taking Barbara round to Jim's for something or other and seeing Lenny keeping quiet in the background. No bloody wonder. It's a small world. Years later I used to put money on a bare-knuckle fighter who was the best the East End had seen for years. Giant of a bloke, ferocious and unbeatable. Young Lenny McLean. Big man, big heart and I've got the greatest respect for him.

The last time we met was when I bumped into him in Spain. I had a lovely drink with him and his wife Val, and he told me that he was retiring at the top, putting the unlicensed fight game behind him and going in for a bit of acting. Me and the boys in Send sat and watched him on television, acting in *The Knock* with Dennis Waterman. He died a couple of years back, and the world is a worse place without him. God bless you, Len – you rose above what that scum did to you.

Me and Jim did settle our difference of opinion, and he behaved himself after that, but I got a whisper that Old Bill were making discreet enquiries about the business so thought it was time to pull the plug. Harry went legit when I walked away, but Jim carried on somewhere else until he got his collar felt, and he was stuck inside.

It had been a good run for me, and I'd stashed away a nice few quid, but Barbara was getting the fidgets and wanted me to get into something that didn't have the law breathing down our necks all the time. Now she says she didn't know what I was getting up to in those days. Come on! What did she think I was doing? Window cleaning? Does she expect people to believe all we did was screw? That we never had conversations, just bonked each other's brains out? That might have been true early on. But then I was frightened I'd lose her if she found out my wages weren't quite kosher.

Certainly she got fed up with having a new front door fitted after a visit from the law, but that didn't prevent her from dropping very heavy hints that she fancied being the second Mrs Knight. By then I had nothing personally to do with June or my kids, though

Top: From my base in HMP Send, I was allowed out to work unsupervised in a National Trust garden, a bit like Little John in Sherwood.

Below left: I never did grow into my brother Jimmy's suit. George Massey, my mate Poochie, is on the far right – too big for his brother's clothes!

Below right: Third from the right, I'm out and about with a few of the Dalston boys.

Right: My sister Pat was the ideal daughter to my Mum, Nellie, and Dad's favourite.

Below: Just a quick one at my local before I set out for the night.

Top: No smiles on my wedding day, but I got the cream of Dalston in my June.

Left: I left my son Gary, seen here with my daughter Lorraine, when he was a babe in arms. Later, (*above*) he has me in his arms.

Top: We were Mr and Mrs for 22 years, seen here in the 70s in a still from the TV programme of the same name.

Below left: My first nephew, Johnny's and Diane's son, seen here with Barbara.

Below right: Two of my favourite people, my brother John and wife Diane. John's just a bit greyer but the same man after serving 13 out of 22 for the Security Express robbery.

Barbara's second husband
Stephen was a qualified chef, and
they went into partnership to run
a hotel in Amersham.

Left: My third wife, Sue.

Below: In Spain, we generally dined out, but when we ate in we did it in style – on our own in the dining room of our Spanish home, the Villa Limonar.

Above: Just taking tea in Parkhurst before the bingo starts! Poochie (*left*) and Jim Lumley stand behind me, flanked by Joy Lumley (*left*) and Edie Massey, Poochie's wife.

regular as clockwork I got my solicitor to send an enquiry about a divorce. Just as regular came back the reply that I could forget it.

Then out of the blue the tables were turned. June had got herself romantically attached to the fella who had lived in the flat below, and she wanted a divorce. I had no problem with that because he was a decent sort, and I agreed by return. Months later when the decree absolute dropped through the letter box Barbara's eyes lit up like spotlights. This was around Christmas 1964, and two months later I was getting suited up, ready to tie the knot again.

As far as I was concerned marriage had always been on the cards, only held up by the complication of still having wife number one. Now that was squared away, all that was needed was a couple of phone calls and a quick ride up to the local registry. Women are funny creatures, and Barbara was no exception. She said to me ''Ere, haven't you forgotten something?' I've gone, 'No, like what?' She said, 'You haven't bought me an engagement ring and haven't even asked me to marry you yet.' 'Leave it out,' I've said, 'I wouln't be here if I didn't want to marry you, and I've shelled out for so many rings you haven't got enough fingers for any more.' So that was the proposal. For ever after she told anyone that would listen that she had to propose to me.

If ever any bloke got on his knees in some romantic film on the telly she'd be sniffing with disdain all through it just so I'd get the message. Same with weddings, I'd have to leave the room if one of those came on because she wouldn't let me forget ours was a bloody disaster. Our first attempt was hastily cancelled when we drove up to find the press all over the place. Not like her to turn down a bit of free publicity, but she made me drive straight past, take her home and phone up with some excuse. Second time, the studio wanted her on set all day filming an important scene in one of the *Carry Ons*. If the film director had pointed his camera at us two he'd have had a smash hit *Carry On Wedding Day* on his hands.

Even more so on the day. It pissed down. No, it didn't, it was a bloody monsoon for one hour before and one hour after. We had got off to a bad start that morning in February 1964. The studio had rung at seven and told her she was on stand-by. That did it. Ever the professional, she's ready to put the block on her big day on the off chance of five minutes filming. I had to get firm then. I took the phone off the hook and told her, 'Just once will you put me before your career!' and she swallowed it. Then the suit she'd bought a couple of months before didn't fit because she'd lost half a stone for the film part. She looked beautiful to me, yet she was crying that she looked like a bag of spuds.

She was still crying when we got into the car. When we got out at the Register Office in Tottenham no one would have noticed because we were both soaked to the skin as we dashed for the door. During the short ceremony my heart went out to her. Appearance was the most important thing in her life, and there she was on a woman's most special day, looking like a drowned rat. Her wig had lost its bounce, her make-up had run, and she was right – the suit hung on her like a small tent, but I loved her more than anything else in the world, and to me she was beautiful. Though if it's true that you start as you mean to go on we were in for some stormy weather during our marriage.

Not only did I get the unspoken blame for the weather but she always harped on about the fact that I hadn't whisked her off to some Caribbean island for a romantic honeymoon. Though the way I remember those following months was that Barbara had her feet firmly nailed to the studio floor on the *Carry On* set.

It was on the same set that we were discussing where to go once filming was completed. Kenneth Horne, who was filming with her, chipped in and asked me what I thought of Madeira. I told him a large slice of ginger cake was more up my street, but he said, in that voice familiar to fans of *Around the Horn*, 'No, no, dear boy, I mean the islands off the west coast of Africa. Wonderful unspoilt paradise – just come back from there myself.'

Barbara was jumping up and down with excitement as Ken went on and on about peace and tranquillity, exotic birds and beautiful orchids. I still had very fond memories of my last holiday in Skegness. Lovely place – plenty of people, loads of noise and a pub every five yards. Apart from that I didn't fancy getting in a plane bound for some God-forgotten desert island. But as Barbara was now very firmly 'Her Indoors' I kept my lips sealed and let her be talked into it. There was always the possibility that this holiday might make amends for her disastrous wedding day.

Kenny Williams was nonchalantly leaning up against one of the sets, nose in the air like he did, but earholing our conversation in case his name popped up. Eventually he came over and gave one of those nasal 'Ooers' that he was famous for and said to Barbara, 'I wouldn't half fancy a nice little holiday myself. Mind if I join the party?' Barbara gave me a quick look and said, 'That would be lovely, Ken.' I knew she thought the world of him, and I must admit I liked him myself. And one thing in his favour was that I didn't see him as posing any threat, unlike most of the other males that hung around Barbara.

On the other hand this overseas' jaunt was for us to spend some much needed time together, so afterwards I got him to one side and said, 'You know this is our honeymoon we're talking about?' He flared his nostrils, and it was like looking up the barrel of a shotgun as he said, ''Oneymoon – 'oneymoon? You've been shagging the arse off her for years. Whatcha want with a fucking 'oneymoon?' What could I say to that, so it was all booked up. It got worse.

When we arrived at the airport, there was Kenny waiting for us with his sister Pat and sitting on her suitcase with a beaming smile on her face his old mum, Lou. My face must have spoken volumes, but Ken just announced in a lofty voice, 'Couldn't leave them behind, could I?' and shepherded us towards the take-off lounge.

My first flight ever was everything I expected it to be. From London to Lisbon an absolute nightmare. Not a parachute in sight and I was being thrown around like a pea in a bag. Kenny and Barbara were laughing, singing and entertaining the rest of the passengers, while all I could do was hang on for dear life staring straight ahead. After we landed, knowing the worst part of the journey was over I relaxed as the taxi drove us to the port for the boat trip to Funchal. That I could handle. Quoits on deck, drinks handed out by waiters in sparkling whites, the tangy smell of warm sea breezes and a nice bit of supper at the Captain's table. Just the start to a wonderful holiday.

When we arrived our cruiser hadn't turned up yet. The only boat in the harbour was what looked like a floating farm. Yes, this was our luxury cruise liner. Noah's Ark wasn't in it. Chickens, ducks, goats, sheep. Everywhere I looked was some animal or other. Still in sight of land the up-and-down motion of the tub and the overpowering stench had me hanging over the side praying for death. It didn't help that Kenny kindly decided to keep me company, by leaning on the rail munching a bologna sausage and giving a booming commentary on everything moving around us. By the time we docked I felt like a wrung-out dishcloth. All I wanted was a cool hand on my brow and lots of sympathy. But when Barbara started fussing around me Kenny airily told her to 'Leave the miserable sod alone. It's all in his mind.' So with him being an ex-navy man she took his advice and let me suffer on my own.

After that very forgettable start, our holiday quickly went from bad to brilliant. I loved it. Having Barbara by my side for that fortnight, plus not worrying about the phone ringing to drag her off to the other end of the country, I was totally relaxed. By the time we were boarding the plane to come home, my head was buzzing with plans for what I could get into once I was back in the East End. What I didn't know was that Barbara had an idea of her own. Something that would get her husband away from the criminal element and, as it turned out, change his life completely.

6.
My Steamy Life with Barbara

FIVE MINUTES BACK IN the flat, and the phone was ringing itself off the wall. Not even unpacked and Barbara was on the blower for two hours rabbiting on to her agent or some other career mover. Panic stations, they wanted her to go straight into rehearsals for the final run of *Oh What a Lovely War*. So much for a nice cosy bit of domesticity as Mr and Mrs.

When she was at home she could be like any other ordinary cockney housewife, polishing, dusting and singing her head off just like my Mum Nellie. In fact sometimes she reminded me of her, especially Sunday mornings when I didn't get my back off the bed until midday. I'd lie there with my eyes closed, sniffing the roast she'd got in the oven and listening to her as she sung the old songs – I could imagine I was right back in Hindle House. Barbara might say now that I should have stayed there, because all I wanted from a woman was to be mothered. But I don't agree with that.

All right I admit I did expect clean shirts every day, my suit nicely laid out for me – and regular meals. But what I wanted most out of our marriage was nothing to do with mothering – it was the old you know what, and she was more than willing to give me plenty.

I must have been as green as grass when I first met her. Apart from fathering two children, I soon found out that I was a sexual novice. I couldn't believe the inventive acrobatics she kept coming up with, and some of the things – well, I didn't know people got up to those sort of antics. I used to get a niggling touch of the greens, and though I didn't want to know the answer couldn't help myself asking, 'Blimey, Windsor, where did you learn all this stuff?'

She'd just give me one of those Mona Lisa smiles and say, 'Woman's intuition, darling – we're born with it.' Makes me smile now to think of it. But, like I said, I was a bit on the naïve side and couldn't know that she'd had more lessons in the art than I'd had hot pie and mash.

I was a very willing pupil, and that side of things got better and better as the years went on. She was a little ball of fire. Quite often when she got all dolled up for an interview or photo shoot and was looking stunning, I couldn't wait and off would come the clothes. I'd be standing there in nothing but my socks, and she'd say, 'Gawdsake, Ronnie, get them off.' And I'd say, 'When you take that bleeding wig off, then I'll take my socks off,' and we'd fall about laughing.

I made a joke of it, but really I was quite serious about those hairpieces. My June had beautiful 'real' hair. It was long and dark, smelled beautiful and felt lovely when we were having a cuddle. Barbara's was the complete opposite. I loved the rest of her dearly, but burying my nose in that unreal toupee was like making up to a piece of carpet. Mind you, when she was down there using her mouth for her favourite game, and all I could see was a pile of blonde curls, I didn't give a monkey's what was on the top of her head.

Another bit of a turn-off was I'd be doing the business, and she'd be clutching her head and wailing, 'Mind my hair – it took an hour to put on.' I think it's pretty obvious that somewhere along the line maybe Barbara decided to model herself on Dolly Parton, another lady famous for her wigs. On top of that being a good mate of Danny La Rue, perhaps she couldn't help being influenced by his over the top hairpieces. The last time I saw her real hair was back in the early eighties. And without giving any secrets away I've got to say it wasn't in the best of condition. So really I don't think she'd done herself any favours by keeping it unnaturally covered for years and years.

I can't remember any interviews she's ever done

where sex didn't come into the conversation. She couldn't help herself. I often thought that if she hadn't always been so ready to discuss her bum and boobs at the drop of a hat, she might have gained a lot more respect over the years. As far as I was concerned her sex drive practically bordered on nymphomania. Not for her just to lay back, think of England and let the old man have a quickie. She was inventive, playful and aggressive, and giving myself a gee I came up with the goods every time. In fact I doubt very much that since our 22-year marriage broke up, any man has sexually satisfied her in the way I did.

While her male fans were drooling over their own erotic fantasies, yours truly – lucky bastard – was getting the real thing, and I'll guarantee you it was better than anything their fevered minds could have conjured up. Imagine a pert, large-bosomed 'Dick Whittington'. Stark bollock naked except for thigh-length boots and a floppy hat. Well, this was one of the private bedroom matinees Barbara used to put on for me. I'd come home from work, absolutely knackered and ready to fall into bed, and I'd say to Barbara, 'I'm going to turn in, doll, all right?'

She'd give a little smile and say, 'I'll be up myself in a minute', and I'd know she had something planned. Ten minutes later I'd just be dozing off when the bedroom door would open and, costumed up, in would come Rosie from *Fings*. Breaking into song she'd dance all round the bed kicking those lovely legs in the air, leaving me in no doubt that her underwear was missing. I'll tell you what. I woke up pretty sharpish when that little vision high-stepped across the floor.

Whatever part she landed you could bet your life that the character would end up in our bedroom. It was a turn-on for her, and there were no complaints from me. Apart from Rosie I'd get a topless 'Dick Turpin' demanding that I stand and deliver, which I did in about two minutes. Or a Fairy Godmother in lacy suspenders waving her magic wand insisting I 'Rise again, Sir Knighty'. Course I didn't just get her own characters in this sexual parade. She was a brilliant mimic and could take off all the female stars and starlets of the day. I won't mention names, but you'd be amazed at who I rogered the night away with once the light was off.

We might have done it two or three times and I'd be totally shagged out. I'd hear the milkman going up the road, and she'd be whispering, 'You awake, Ronnie?' I'd groan, 'No,' and next minute she'd disappear under the covers to give me an early morning call. If she hadn't been away so often I think her sex drive would've given me a heart attack before I was 40. What a way to go!

Barbara had three obsessions: work, sex and her height. Sticking a pile of bouncy hair on top of her head was one way to gain a few inches, but she had other methods of making her tiny stature less obvious. She'd never stand close to anyone when she was talking to them – she'd hold well back so that she wasn't looking up. Whenever we were invited to showbiz functions or other dos she used to say to me,

'When we get there don't let me get crowded in, especially if I'm surrounded by tall people. I don't want to feel somebody's arse on the back of my head or face some 6'6" actors crotch.' Another thing was she'd never sit on low chairs or sofas at these receptions. You wouldn't believe how may times I'd lifted her up on to high stools in the clubs so she could be of equal height to others.

I remember her doing her nut one night when we went to a club where there was a bit of a cabaret. After a while Barbara took herself off to the ladies and as she was crossing in front of the stage the compère started singing through the microphone 'Hi Ho, Hi Ho,' then he said, 'Where's the other six Babs?' Now she wouldn't show herself up in front of the public, so she laughed it off at the time, but afterwards she went fucking mad at me. I didn't think it was a big deal, but to keep the peace I gave the compère a pull when he went for a leak and made him apologise to Barbara.

I really don't know why she worried all the time about being so small. Surely the proof that she was a lovely little package was evident by all the male fans she had. I must admit there was more than enough of her for me.

A conversation that we had before jetting off to Madeira had sown a seed in her mind. We'd had a drink with Mick Regan, a mutual friend, and afterwards I'd commented that I wouldn't mind getting a bit of work from him because he was obviously doing very well with his betting shops and other interests. Barbara suggested I had a word with him, but I was never very pushy, and anyway you don't go poncing for a bit of charity from friends. She mumbled something about stupid male pride, but we left it there, and it was forgotten. By me anyway.

Once we were back from holiday she slipped in to see Mick and asked him if there was anything going. Instead of thinking she was taking a liberty by leaning on a mate he said, 'You won't believe this. I've just been offered a property, and I had your Ronnie in mind for a bit of business – I'll ring him later.' When she told me what he'd said I thought I would soon be back grafting again, like scaffolding some old gaff he'd just bought. I should have known he wouldn't insult me like that. He picked me up in his motor, and we drove to Charing Cross Road. Pulling up outside number 142, a scruffy run-down looking place, he said, 'There you go, my son. How do you fancy yourself in the nightclub business?' And that's how it all started.

The Artistes and Repertoire Club had gone so far downhill with the previous owner that he had to mug passers by and drag them in to make a living. So with debts up to his eyes he was only too happy for us to shove him a backhander and take over the lease. Mick's deal was that he would run the business side, which was his game anyway, while I would front the place up as host.

Mick was a canny old sod, though. He didn't just want me for my charm, good looks and bit of old chat, he knew I had bundles of associates. Added to Barbara's name and showbiz friends he knew we could get a good return even before we let the punters in. But before punters we were going to need painters and all the rest.

I was so keen to get the club up and running I got kitted out with a pair of overalls and mixed in with the builders. This made me privy to conversations between workmen who obviously had their fingers on the pulse. Like 'The bloke paying for this must be a right arsehole. There ain't no money in clubs,' or 'Prat'll go down the pan in a week. Already 50 of these in the street.'

A month later when I was cramming the night's takings into a carrier bag, I couldn't help thinking, somewhere out there those mugs are sweating their nuts off for thirty a week. Who's the arsehole now? The place was a goldmine from the start. The snappy name above the door must have been like a magnet. Before we'd started renovations I'd said to Mick, 'We've got to get rid of that poxy name Artistes and Repertoire.' He agreed with me and said he thought A & R sounded a lot more trendy, and that's what we went for.

Whether Mick would have pulled me in if Barbara hadn't whispered in his ear I'll never know. But what I did know was a little twist of fate had put this ex-rag and bone man at the top of the tree. I took to the whole scene like a duck to water. Considering I had spent the best part of my adult life propping up the bar in exactly these sort of places, I knew just how to handle it. Except now instead of feeding the golden goose, I was carting away those shiny eggs as fast as they were laid.

Being right next to Denmark Street, London's Tin Pan Alley just off the Charing Cross Road, where all the top stars came to cut records, it was only natural that these people would use my place as a watering hole. I won't even try to list them all, but one bunch of lads I was always pleased to see were the Rolling Stones. Never mind all that drug-taking smashing-the-place-up lark, they were all good as gold. I reckon they were like me and knew when to put a bit of front on. Their fans wanted wild men so that's what they got. Yet in my place, that was members only, they could be themselves nice and comfortable. Sometimes I kick myself for not tucking away their scribbled-on beer mats for the future. The first exploratory notes of 'Satisfaction' or whatever would be a nice little nest egg for me in my old age.

Another group of lads who were just starting in the business treated the club like home from home. Freddie Mercury and his mates. Being a bit East End old fashioned, the skin-tight trousers bit with everything sticking out, and hair half way down the back took a lot of getting used to. But they paid their money, were polite as you like and never caused me a moment's grief.

Not like some of the big names of the time. Harry H. Corbett, one half of *Steptoe & Son*, was a gentleman sober but a complete toss-pot when he'd had too many. Then he wanted to fight everybody in the place. Well, everybody but one. A stern word from Mick Regan, at six foot four, invariably quietened him down until the next time.

Actor Ian Hendry, a rising star at that time in the mid-sixties, never caused any bother other than having to be carried to a taxi at the end of the day. He never knew when to stop. He was working on a film called *The Hill* with Sean Connery, which was set in the desert, most of it at Pinewood. I can only think that all that sand gave him a terrible thirst, because he liked to get his part out of the way in the morning so he could spend the rest of the day in my club.

Dorothy Squires would drop in all the time to drown her sorrows after Roger Moore traded her in for a younger model. Saint he was not. With my record I wasn't in a position to criticize, but all I can say is he left behind a diamond. I loved her. She had a personality that lit up the place whenever she walked in. She could fill any top theatre and name her price, but all I had to say was 'Give us a song, Dot,' and up she'd get and belt out a few numbers. Anyone who dared make a noise while she was performing was soon told, in her ladylike manners, to 'Fucking turn it in'. They did.

Apart from pop stars and TV people there was all Barbara's crowd from the *Carry On*s and all the theatre productions. I can't say they blanked me in the days of following Barbara around to glitzy functions and after-show dos, but some of them used to give me the eye as if they were wondering who this stage-door Johnny was. Now I was the man of the moment, and it felt great.

Running the club took up the best part of my waking day, which gave me no time to brood about what Barbara was up to. Shortly after opening the place the stage production of *Oh What a Lovely War* had taken off to Broadway and my Barbara, the star, with it. We'd hardly had time properly to christen the house we had bought in Aylmer Drive, Stanmore, before she jetted off. Posh, up-market and very desirable. This five-bedroom palace with rolling lawns and its own orchard had everything I could possibly want. Except a bit of company when I came home from work. In the club my ear was bent from 3 pm to 3 am, and I enjoyed every moment in between, but you can't compare company like that to a one-to-one chat with the one you love, and to be honest I was lonely.

On top of that I was worried about a few rumours that were floating around. After our holiday in Madeira where I'd got to know Kenny Williams really well, he made a habit of dropping in for a chat. In the end I think he was closer to me than to Barbara. Before you start having funny thoughts about what sort of mates we were, I'd like to make it clear that though Ken made his living by appearing to be bent as a snide fiver, I never once saw any evidence to back this up. Truth is I think he was so wrapped up in himself and his own brilliant repartee he never had a thought for romantic attachments to either sex. He was a master of the old put-down. Sometimes a word or a haughty look was enough, but occasionally he couldn't help slipping in to his 'carry on' character.

Like the time a young lady approached him while we were talking at the bar. Without so much as a hallo or a kiss my fundamental, she came straight out with 'Is it true you're a homosexual?'

Kenny just looked at her, gave one of his 'Ooers' and said, 'Is that your polite way of asking to see my arse?' Turning his back to her, he dropped his strides round his ankles and waggled his skinny little rump. To the cheers of the other drinkers he did a twirl, pulled up his trousers and carried on our conversation from where he'd left off. Miss Smartypants, outgunned, disappeared into the ladies.

As I was saying, apart from a laugh and a joke over a drink, we did have some serious conversations. And one of these brought me more than a twinge of heartache. Without trying to dig me out or wind me up with idle gossip, he told me with obvious regret that Barbara was having it off with Sid James. I'd suspected Sid for a long time, but on the other hand I had suspected most of the blokes that sniffed round her like dogs on heat.

I hold my hands up, rightly or wrongly I've always had a jealous streak in me. Any man who could honestly say he's never felt that twinge of green-eye must have had a partner he didn't care about. It's human nature. If you feel threatened then you are going to react, and I often did so when I turned up at the studio to pick Barbara up and find Sid all over her. At first I took it all as a bit of a joke, what with him having a face like a sat-on cushion, but it got a bit much all the time, and I gave Barbara a pull. All I got from her was 'This is show business. You don't make a mountain out of a molehill, you just brush it off – it's only a laugh.'

I said, 'It might be a laugh to you, but he's working up to a smack if he doesn't behave.' So she goes up the wall, and we don't talk for a few hours. She must have passed on the message, though, because he always made himself scarce after that whenever I showed.

Now if Kenny was right, they were both taking the piss, and it was much more than a laugh. What was I supposed to be, a fucking saint and keep turning a blind eye? We'd had a row not long before, and that was over her manager Robert Dunn.

My brother Johnny had called round to the house looking for me. Being family it was quite normal for him to walk in, same as he'd expect me to do at his place. So he's gone in, heard Barbara upstairs and walked straight up calling out, 'Only me, love.' He couldn't believe it when there was Dunn, leaning back in a chair, feet up on the dressing table like he owned the place, and Barbara getting dressed.

Johnny's never been one to hide behind polite chit chat, so he asked Barbara, 'What's going on here?' and told the manager, 'Get your dirty feet off Ronnie's furniture.' She's done her nut. 'It's none of your business, and you've no right to speak to my friend like that, or come into my house poking your nose in.' The other fella hasn't turned a hair, just stood up and said, 'I'll say goodnight, nice to meet you, John. Give my regards to Ronnie when you see him' and taken off. A right cool customer, what with Johnny ready to slap him.

When Barbara had cooled down she went all the

other way. Making excuses that they had just come back from a business meeting, and she was just changing into something more casual before going downstairs to talk over the deal. I never did like the intimacy that went on between the show-biz crowd. It was like they had different standards to the rest of us. But I'd got slightly more used to it than Johnny who, when he was telling me about the incident, was more angry than I was.

I didn't make much of it – what was the point? I would only have got her standard reply to any criticism of her behaviour: 'Don't be daft.' Now on top of that I've got Kenny blowing the whistle on Sid James. Perhaps he'd got it wrong. Perhaps I'd got it wrong, and behind all the huggy, touchy nonsense of all those luvvies, it was just as she said – nothing but friendship.

Either way I couldn't do anything about it while Barbara was thousands of miles away. It was bloody hard, though. Specially after leaving the bright lights and noisy company in the club, to come home and sit in that echoing house with no company other than my thoughts. Still, like many times in my past I always found that making money was some sort of consolation. The success of my club had exceeded all expectations. I had hoped for a nice steady wage every week, but the cash that poured over the bar was almost indecent.

Everything I did seemed to take off. One of the better ideas I had was to organize live music in the afternoons. None of the other clubs did this, and it was an instant draw for the punters. First off I brought in any group that could knock out a bit of lively music. But after a while I found that famous rock stars were more than willing to borrow a guitar from one of the band and do an impromptu turn. One thing led to another, and they started bringing in their own instruments when they took a break from recording next door. I was unintentionally giving my customers a floor show, which, if arranged through the agents of these boys, I couldn't have afforded. If I'd stuck a tape recorder on I could have cleaned up in later years.

Success breeds success, and my only business problems were would the floors take the weight of all these eager drinkers, and what to do with the accumulating pile of ready cash. I treated myself to a new Mercedes, tons of jewellery for Barbara, more suits than I could ever wear, and still the money kept coming in. Apart from not paying any taxes on my earnings all this folding stuff was completely kosher. But with plenty to spare I couldn't help myself syphoning some of it off to buy whatever hot goods were on offer. I didn't need the extra, but old habits die hard.

Besides being the most swinging joint in town, behind the scenes it was more like a bring-and-buy salesroom. I'm not saying people were in and out with sacks over their shoulders marked 'swag' like in the cartoons, but certainly deals were carried out over a drink. If the price was right, I bought anything.

Cigarettes, spirits, antiques and at one time a full container load of toilet pans, but there was a market for it all, and nine times out of ten the black-market buyers were sitting at the tables of the A & R. Once word got around that my club was discreet, another type of clientele, worlds away from show biz and pop music, began to drift in on a regular basis.

Faces of the time like the Krays, Richardsons, Frankie Fraser, Alfie Gerrard and so on. If somebody had chucked a bomb in the place on certain nights, organised crime would have been wiped out in a stroke. We had to put up with our fair share of being raided by the law every now and then. But it was never taken very seriously, because I think it suited them to know where they could put their hands on most of the London faces at a moment's notice. Close my club down, and they would be back to square one.

It was comical how conversations took a turn upwards when two fellas with short hair and very shiny black shoes showed up for a casual drink. Suddenly it's all football, the latest cars or the weather. As soon as they pissed off, it was back to business.

One of my regulars, but purely for recreational purposes, was Commander Ken Drury, top man in Scotland Yard. All I can think is that he used my club as a drinker because it was the only place left in town where he could be sure no one would piss in his whisky when he turned his back. This supposed upholder of law and order was one very dodgy bastard, and word was out that he was grafting all the top clubs for his own pension fund. Not only that, he was moonlighting from the fight against pornography and corruption by helping out Jimmy Humphries, the porn king, for a weekly three to four grand backhander. I heard his luck ran out a few years later when he was tumbled, along with half a dozen other top brass, and sent down for eight years.

I thought it was a bloody injustice that he got five years on appeal, and then only served slightly more than I did over that poxy bit of cloth. There were a lot of smiling faces when he was sent to prison, but mine wasn't one of them because I lost a very good paying customer. He never as much as hinted at protection in all the years he used my club. If he had, top dog or not, he would have got the same as Big Boy Ronnie.

You win some you lose some. My partner Mick Regan had been caught up in a bit of bad luck with the law. His cousin was nicked over some deal or other, and Mick was pulled into the frame as well. So he was spending a short spell behind the wall, leaving me to keep things running smoothly. I was sitting at a table, facing the door like I always do, keeping an eye on who comes in and out. Sitting near the gents was Big Boy, and he was having a drink and slowly getting drunker and drunker. When I got a call of nature I headed for the toilets past his table, and he reached out and caught me by the jacket saying, 'What's up? Don't you want to talk to your old pal?' I brushed him off and replied, 'I'm going for a jimmy, I'll talk to you in a minute.'

When I came back I sat down, and he talked about

everything under the sun, finishing up with a bit of old chat about years ago when we knew each other around Clapham. He'd been a bit of a bully then and, if I remembered correctly, had few mates, because most people kept out of his way. Eventually he got to the point. 'Right, Ron, now that Mick's away, I think you might need a bit of help to keep things nice and quiet.' I said, 'Thanks for the offer, mate, but I can manage.' He was grinning like a Cheshire cat. 'No, Ron, what I'm saying is you will have some help. I'm offering my protection.'

I always had an understanding with my staff that when I ask them to send my brother over it was a signal to fetch me a siphon bottle and place it wherever I happened to be. I gave one of the girls a nod – over came the siphon, and I put a little splash of soda water in my drink. I offered some to Big Boy, but he just waved his hand as a no and said, 'I won't fuck about – bottom line is you're going to need my services every week.' They don't call him Big Boy for nothing, so I stood up with a smile on my face, which he took as my agreement. 'Gonna see it my way, then?' 'No,' I said, 'The other way around, you wanker,' and hit him full across the side of the head with the bottle. His eyes rolled up, and I think he was spark out before he fell off the chair. If I hadn't killed him he must have chosen another club, because he never showed up again.

After you have been in the club game for a while, you know exactly when something is going to go off. First sign of that, and I made sure my 'brother' was nice and handy. Considering the percentage of drunks and silly people who came through the door, any violent assaults either way were avoided with as much tact and diplomacy as possible. After all, the club was where people came to relax, they didn't want a pleasant drink to end up in a brawl.

Usually a polite word from the management was all it took to shut up the noisiest table. But every now and then some fridge-size Jack the lad making a nuisance of himself would size me up and tell me to fuck off. Then looking over the top of my head, he'd catch sight of someone like a good pal of mine Eric Mason, casually walking over to see what the bother was. All of a sudden he would be full of apologies, blaming his momentary lapse of manners on too much drink.

Eric was a hard man's hard man. To his friends, and I count myself to be one of that fraternity; he is a lovely guy and a gentleman. If, on the other hand you're against him, God help you. In a now legendary battle with the Richardson gang, he carried on fighting even after suffering half a dozen broken bones. He was only stopped when his punching hand was pinned to his skull by an axe. If you think that's a story of a man who lost a fight, you don't know how many men it took to get him to his knees. He lived through that horrifying incident and went on to fight again. Many of those battles he described to me in great detail, over a drink on the balcony of my home in Spain, the Villa Limonar, while I was in exile there.

That the A & R was used by many of the criminal

element to plan some future heist has never been in question. Where else were they going to get together, but on the safe ground of their favourite drinker? Having said that I have to point out that I was not invited to sit in on every bit of skulduggery they were kicking around. Naturally in the course of mingling I couldn't help overhearing the odd snippet. But in passing, and out of context they meant nothing, or could have meant anything.

Anyway the punters were out for a bit of recreation, more interested in relaxing over a drink than worrying about their day job. Still, as far as the law were concerned, there was implication by association. And it didn't help much when the name A & R dropped into courtroom alibis with alarming regularity.

If the law popped in to verify the whereabouts of certain individuals, I'd swear that I had personally served them myself, even if I hadn't seen them for weeks. I rarely did this by prearrangement, as I wasn't stupid enough to set myself up as alibi incorporated. But if I knew the names of those in need of a bit of friendly back-up, then OK I was willing to swear they were in my club. It was no skin off my nose. Remember, these people were honest villains, so there was no chance at all of me giving some weirdo a ticket to ride.

This is where my rise to infamy began. But why I was marked out from all the other club owners has always puzzled me. There were enough villains about to fill every club in London, so we all took equal shares of the good, bad and downright wicked. Yet I was the one that the law decided to hand out first prize to as Mr Big. I wasn't aware what a hole I was digging for myself by owning a successful club. But, in hindsight, if I'd stuck to the scaffolding game, I might have saved myself a lot of grief in the future.

Forget the criminal aspect, which has been blown out of proportion. My best memories of those days are humorous ones. Like the time actor Ronald Fraser came stumbling in, still pissed from the night before and in a right panic. It seemed he'd gone along to support a charity auction that the Kray Twins had organized. Then in his usual, inebriated state he'd joined in with the spirit of the evening, only realizing next morning that he'd bid for and got a beautiful racehorse donated by Ronnie.

What frightened him more than the thought of where to keep a horse in a London flat was that he didn't have the money to pay for it. 'Seem to be a little overdrawn on the funds, old boy.' Cost me a grand to bail him out of that mess, but he was such a lovely character I couldn't refuse his plea for help. He probably spent ten times that amount in the club anyway. His favourite tipple was what he called a Ronnie Fraser Special. It consisted of two measures of every optic on the shelf, but he could still walk out unaided at the end of the night.

They didn't have to be big stars to make me laugh. One young scallywag was always on the tap. A likeable kid but always skint. Every week was the same: 'Just a couple of quid to see me over the weekend, Ron.' And me, being a soft touch who knew what it was like to be skint, always obliged.

When I saw him come in this particular day my hand was in my pocket before he reached me, only this time I was amazed when he said, 'How much do I owe you? Must be knocking up a bit.' I made a quick mental calculation and came up that he was into me for roughly £280 on the generous side. 'Give me £250, son, and we're square.' He gave me a big smile and said, 'Well, could you make it up to £500 – I'm really down on my luck.' He got it for his bloody nerve. He repaid the whole lot in a lump shortly after, and I knew he'd had a little tickle. I always did with most of the young villains that used my place.

With the older chaps you never knew when they were financially up or down. Whether a caper had come off or gone pear shaped. Though, if it was the latter, they would usually be off the scene for a while. With years behind them they knew how to handle good and bad luck. The youngsters were obvious, though. I'd chuckle to myself when I saw them counting out their small change, then digging deep in their pocket for that elusive shilling. I'd been there often enough. Then all of a sudden they'd come in, suited and booted and buying drinks all round. A quick glance in the paper for some small-time robbery, and, yes, I'd know exactly who had pulled it off. I never risked a thing, and most of the proceeds from their petty crimes were being handed over the bar into my greedy little fingers.

I don't want to blow the old trumpet, but, while I

was very happy to take their hard-earned money for overpriced drinks, when the chips were down I did put something back in. I didn't just drop a few bob here and there. I gave up a lot of my spare time to bring a little bit of cheer to the aways.

Over the years I must have visited hundreds of prisoners, and not once did I get used to walking into those places. The cold atmosphere and grim-faced screws gave me the willies every time. I never failed to get a prickle on the back of my neck when the door clanged behind, caused by the unreasonable fear that somehow they would find a reason not to let me out.

Another little service I provided, free of charge for my customers, when they knew they were due an expense-free holiday, was the use of a very big safe at the back of the club. Anyone who had some item of a valuable, delicate or incriminating nature could deposit it with me knowing it would be well looked after. If they sealed the package well, not only would the contents remain completely private, but they could do their time knowing it was in safer hands than the Bank of England. What was in those packages I never asked and was never tempted to peel back a corner to find out. Some of them had a certain weight that gave me a good suspicion of what they contained, but it was none of my business. I know one thing: the law would have loved to have given that safe a spin.

Though me and my mother-in-law Rosie never reached a stage of falling in each other's arms when we met, for the sake of peace and quiet we had reached a state of amicable truce. If I was passing her door I would pop in for a cup of tea and an enquiry after her health. Trouble was as time went on she always managed to turn the conversation around to children. Namely the lack of me producing half a dozen mini versions of her little girl.

If I'd had a copy of a certain autobiography, published 20 years yet to come, I could have slung it across the table, suggesting that she read for herself her daughter's idea of birth control. But at the time I was equally in the dark as she was. All I could tell her was that we were having some slight problems in that department. Even going so far as to hint mildly that I might be firing blanks just to shut her up.

I had two lovely kids of my own, but on the other hand didn't have or see them at all. So when Barbara told me that she was pregnant, I can't remember now what my reaction was. Though knowing what a bit of a softy I could be, no doubt I was well chuffed that the love we shared was going to be fused into a little person. I'm almost sure that the fact that a baby would keep her at home where I'd know where she was, never crossed my mind.

If there were any celebrations they were pretty short lived, because after a day's filming in *Wurzel Gummidge* or some other show, she came home swathed in bandages 'down there'. Her story was that she had been doing some sort of stunt on a trolley thing, and it had run away with her. When it finally came to a halt by crashing into something she ended up with the gear stick where the sun never shines. I couldn't help but admire how well she took the fact that this nasty accident terminated the pregnancy.

It's almost comical that Peggy Mitchell, the character she plays in *EastEnders*, is a mother who dotes on and idolizes her two sons, Grant and Phil. What Peggy must have had going for her over Barbara was that she hadn't been chasing stardom every waking hour of the day. Barbara had many opportunities to have her own family, because selfish old me still followed some advice I'd picked up in a barber shop when I was a kid – you never want to use a johnny because it's like doing it with a wellie boot on your dick. She refused to take the Pill in case it made her fat, and she couldn't get on with that copper thing women wear. So it was wide open – in a manner of speaking.

EastEnders is quite a good programme. Though being from the East End myself sometimes the characters and situations make me laugh when they're not supposed to. Whichever prison I have been in, without exception, all the boys love it. At Send, I couldn't bear to watch it with Barbara started appearing in it. It was too embarrassing, what with all the others giving it, 'Here's your missus, Ron', or shouting when she blows up, 'Ain't you glad you're well out of it?'

When an East End lad moves up the financial ladder, there is always a point when he's got plenty of spare cash for a house, gold for the missus, and a decent motor – but not enough to buy a villa somewhere in the sun. So what he does is compromise, and fix the family up with a caravan in Southend or Clacton. Me and

Barbara went slightly more up market and bought a chalet bungalow in Seaton, Devon.

My idea of the chalet being perfect for getting away from the pressure, fizzled out very quickly. Because if Barbara wasn't working then she was frightened to leave the phone in case the part of her dreams came up and she missed it. If there had been such things as mobiles in those days our marriage could have been saved a lot of grief. I don't think I was being unreasonable when I asked her to spend some time at home. It wasn't as though I wanted her to give up work altogether, just be more selective, so that she wasn't always busy.

I used to wonder what drove her always to want to be on show. She would do all and everything that was offered. I'm not joking when I say she would have cut the ribbon on the opening of a public toilet if she could have been guaranteed a small audience.

Our arguments always ended up the same – in a blazing row with me shouting, 'Make up your mind, do you want me or your fucking career?' She was well aware of what all the separations were doing to our relationship, so she'd say, 'OK, You're right. I'll only work locally so I can come home every night.' Wonderful. We'd spend a lovely couple of weeks just like any other couple – meals in front of the telly, early nights, friends round for a drink, then the phone would ring, and it was always that offer she could not refuse. 'It's only six weeks in Manchester, and then I really will give up working away.' So we were back to square one again.

One of her ideas to solve the problem was that I should become her manager. That way we could always be together, travelling here and there, her doing the acting and shows, while I looked after the business side. No chance. Anyway there was no way I could walk away from the club scene and certainly not to end up following her around like a dog on a lead, living in the shadow of her success. Then something happened that for a time drew us closer together as tragedy often does. All our petty arguments and my complaints of being on my own were suddenly nothing, as all our lives were ripped apart.

7.
Death of
My David

S O FAR I HAVEN'T SAID much about my sister
Patsy and brother David. The age gap between
us was quite a large one, so while they were
both kids growing up, I was out in the world. Totally
involved with making a living, and not a lot of time to
notice what they were getting up to.

I'm sure Mum must have prayed for a daughter
during every pregnancy. But after four boys in a row
she had probably given up and resigned herself to a
house full of males. She loved her boys, but what
woman doesn't want a girl to share things with. Her

prayers were answered after the war when Patsy was born, and we all loved that little baby to death. Unlike us boys she never got up to mischief, and not once in her life brought any heartache to her Mum.

David, the youngest, turned up in 1949. He got the same attention from us as Patsy had. But being a boy we didn't treat him with the same kid gloves as we had a little girl. Our family was as close as you could ever want. Each of us loved and respected the others but David – because he was the youngest and a sunny laughing boy – was the favourite. He and I were very close because our personalities were alike. On top of that everyone said we looked alike. He grew up with us all looking out for him. Started in the scaffolding game, same as I had done, and was going places.

He met a lovely girl, Barbara, got married, bought a nice house, then, to round off their good life, had a beautiful baby. Over 27 years have past, and I still get choked to think about him; 27 years since I cradled him in my arms as he lay bleeding to death that day in May 1970. I don't really want to relive it all in my mind again, as the memory is very painful. But what happened had such far-reaching consequences for me personally that I can't leave it out.

David had gone to a pub up the Angel one night for a quiet drink with a couple of pals. He was having a laugh and a few beers, when some fella came up and started to dig him out. 'Your brother Johnny took a right liberty with me last week.' David, easy going as he was, said, 'Sorry about that, but whatever Johnny gets up to is nothing to do with me' and goes back to his drink.

The other geezer obviously wanted to make something out of it, so he was poking David in the back saying, 'You fucking tell him, I ain't going to forget.' David was too friendly to go around looking for trouble, but I expect the guy was getting on his nerves so he said, 'I don't tell my brother anything. If you've got a grievance you go and have a word with him. Leave me out of it.' There was going to be trouble whatever David said. As it was going off, Billy Hickson, my brother's stupid mate, swung his fist into the other guy's face as soon as he saw him raise his hand. Then it blew up.

Four blokes came from nowhere and set about David with anything they could lay their hands on. Ashtrays, bottles, if it wasn't screwed down they picked it up and smashed the kid with it. How they stopped short of killing him there and then I'll never know, because when I rushed up to the hospital after I was told about it, he was in a terrible mess. Heavily sedated he didn't know I was there, so as I couldn't bear to sit and look at him I went home.

I took the attack so personally it was eating my insides out, and I couldn't sleep. It was the same for days after, until in the end I had to put myself about and find out who the people involved were. Eventually I was pointed in the direction of the four guys. I caught up with them in one of the clubs, and I was so wild I was ready to take them all on.

I calmed down enough to hear what they had to say for themselves. As they told it, all they saw was Hickson getting stuck into their mate Johnny Isaacs, so thinking David was going to give him some as well dived in to help. 'So,' I said, 'you sided with that scum, and gave my brother the beating of his life?' And looking a bit embarrassed about it they said, 'Yeah, we did. But we didn't know he was related to you at the time.' No, I thought, but Isaacs did, and he could have stopped it.

I went searching for him and found him in his usual drinker. I dragged him outside and beat the shit out of him. David was out of hospital by then and with my knuckles still raw I went round to his house to straighten him out. Lot of old nonsense coming from a rascal like me, but David accepted the telling off as though I was his dad, and if he did think I had a bit of a cheek, all things considered, he never even tried to answer back. He was a nice quiet boy my David.

At that time the circles we all moved in were no girl guides. A wrong move, a slight of some sort or even a nudged glass could end up in violence. So I couldn't bear any real grudge against the four who had hurt my brother. But that Isaacs – I think he knew what he was doing the minute he walked up to the bar. Why I couldn't just forget it and get on with my life I don't know? It gnawed away at me like a cancer, and like a cancer it kept growing, threatening to blow up at any moment.

Don't think that I took thoughts of revenge all on my own. It hit my brothers just as hard, but it seemed that for some reason I became more obsessed with the whole thing than they did. But revenge wasn't the answer, and after talking it over with my brother

Johnny he agreed with me that some contrition from the other side – a promise that nothing like it would happen again – then we could shake hands. David could forget it; we could forget it; the whole thing forgotten – if only.

Us three brothers, – me, Johnny and David – with headcase Hickson tagging along, went up to Leicester Square and into the Latin Quarter nightclub. We expected to find Johnny Isaacs, but he wasn't there and hadn't been seen. By way of a peacemaking gesture, because it might have seemed that we were looking for trouble, the fella who manages the place came over to us, all smiles and his hand out for shaking. Before he reached us Billy Hickson went absolutely crazy. He shouted, 'You fucking bastard,' and went for the governor.

Before he could do any damage I caught Hickson by the throat and flung him against the wall. 'You stupid prick,' I screamed at him, 'he's got nothing to do with this.' To make sure I was getting through I banged his head on the brickwork. I was wasting my time trying to prevent trouble, it kicked off before I'd finished speaking. A bottle smashed on the wall beside me, and in seconds it was like a war zone. Feet, fists and bodies were flying everywhere. Some geezer, about six foot six, leapt in front of me intending to do some damage, but I tiptoed up, nutted him on the chin, and he went down. I side-stepped another punch, swung one of my own and dived out of the way, looking around for David.

When we'd found that Isaacs wasn't in the club he

had gone downstairs to the toilets. Then hearing what was going on he came flying up to help us. As I caught sight of him he was almost at the top of the stairs, and blocking his way was this Italian character, Parelli, who was waving a carving knife around.

I've relived that scene in my mind so many times. As I started towards them with the intention of kicking the Italian down the stairs, David tried to weave past him. Instead he was stopped in his tracks as Parelli plunged the knife twice into his chest. Getting to David's side was like wading through treacle, in nightmarish slow motion. Parelli ran past me in a panic, but all I wanted to do was get to my David and stop the fountain of blood that was spouting from his chest.

I knelt by his side, turned his head towards me and cradled him in my arms. I knew he was dying, but I couldn't stop myself repeating over and over again, 'Are you all right, David? Are you all right?' Inside my head I was praying to a God I'd never troubled before: 'Please don't take him. Please let him live,' and all the time I'm staring into his open eyes for some flicker of recognition. By the time the ambulance came I couldn't see him for tears.

All the way to Charing Cross Hospital, and outside the operating theatre, I offered everything to God above. All my money, everything I owned, my life even. Anything so long as my David lived. But he wasn't listening and my little brother died.

Even now I haven't the words in me to describe my grief. Not just for myself but for all of us. How could Mum and Dad bear a loss like this? And what about his young wife Barbara, and that baby girl Lisa? Never to see him smile again. I just had to get away and be on my own. The police made a half-hearted attempt to stop me, but I forced myself past them and out into the darkness where I could pour out my anguish in tears where I couldn't be seen.

I ran, I walked, then I sat slumped on a bench in the pouring rain hating myself for what I'd done. I'd killed him as sure as if I'd held the knife. It was all down to me and my stupid pride. Why couldn't I have left things as they were? David had got over his beating with no after effects and was ready to carry on with his life, but I wanted to squeeze every last piece out of the business. Not for David, but for myself.

I sat for hours on that bench. Before I left it I swore that I was going to kill Alfredo Zomparelli. It was no idle threat in the heat and despair of the moment, because by then I'd cried myself out. I had no other option. For with him alive the hate inside me would eventually kill me as well. As we laid David to rest in the spring sunshine of 1970 I looked around at all my family and knew our lives would never be the same again.

It wasn't easy, but with the funeral behind me I forced myself back into the club life and put on as normal a front as I could. Nevertheless I spent three fruitless weeks searching every rat hole in London for Parelli. I was just reaching the conclusion that he might have thrown himself in the Thames rather than face what was coming to him, when he suddenly turned up at Heathrow Airport and gave himself up to the police. Apparently he'd been to Italy, where he'd had 21 days to concoct some fairy story. He must have thought he'd got it right, or he wouldn't have shown.

Five months later, in autumn 1970, this tough-guy bouncer for the Latin Quarter and errand boy for retired Soho gang boss Albert Dimes, stood in the dock at the Old Bailey with tears in his eyes. Far from admitting that he'd butchered my David in a cold-blooded attack, the performance he gave for the benefit of judge and jury suggested that my brother had thrown himself twice on to that ten-inch blade.

His story was that he was sitting at a table enjoying a quiet drink and minding his own business when me, David, Johnny and Hickson had walked in and started talking to people in a threatening manner. Then before he could get up and make a polite enquiry as to what the problem was, violence flared, and he was attacked by two men. Frightened for his own safety he ran into the kitchens, grabbed something to defend himself – a razor-sharp carving knife – and dashed back into the fray to calm things down. What happened next, he explained through choking sobs, was that someone rushed towards him. In warding off this attack he raised his hand, and the man collapsed at his feet. It was only then that he realised that he was holding a knife.

Result – four years in prison for manslaughter. That's all my kid brother was worth: 48 poxy months, 36 with good behaviour. Three years less for snuffing out a life than I was to receive 20-odd years later for supposedly getting my hands on a few pound notes. If that wasn't enough of an insult to the memory of a boy who died in such a terrible way, the police made some mileage out of an allegation that David was running some sort of protection racket around the clubs, and that's why he was killed.

Not satisfied with only giving Parelli a mild slap, and trying to blacken David's name, the police then turned their attentions to us. Not long afterwards we found ourselves in the dock, charged with Making an Affray. It was a joke. Desperation on the part of the law to get their hands on the Knights once again. That mad bastard Hickson got 12 months suspended. Johnny and I were acquitted when any witnesses to what went on suddenly suffered amnesia.

With Zomparelli banged up I considered putting the word on the prison grapevine that any con who fancied tipping scalding soup on the rat, or better still cutting his throat in the showers, would be well looked after. But after a bit of thought, I decided to let him sweat it out and catch up with him once the dust had settled.

I served every day of that sentence alongside him. Though by the time he was outside on licence, my passion had cooled. I was still obsessed with killing the scum and avenging my David, but the passing of a couple of years had allowed me to see reason. If spending the rest of my life behind bars could have brought my brother back where he belonged with his wife and baby, I would have strangled the Eyetie with my bare hands in front of the law. As it was I'd come to realise that nothing would be achieved by me wrecking my own life for the sake of 'spur of the moment justice'. If I had run the thought past my old friends Reggie and Ronnie, who were then a few years into a sentence of thirty, I'm sure they would have agreed with me holding back for a while.

Rumour had it that Zomparelli was into some very heavy stuff. One of these was that he was the brains and muscle in a take-over bid to control London's amusement-arcade rackets. Another whisper was that he was a front man for the American Mafia, running the London operation that was not only dealing in top-quality stolen cars but a line in insurance fraud as well. The police took those stories seriously. Going so far as to fly into Britain a top Mafia expert to investigate Parelli's background. He found nothing, and that side of things fizzled out. Well, it would, wouldn't it? The man was nothing.

The London connection for organised crime? I suppose that's why he settled for a two-bit operation running a bucket-shop travel agency in Frith Street. And then when he wasn't busy, which was most of the time, spent all his time hanging out in the Golden Goose amusement arcade in Old Compton Street, just round the corner from my club. Was that bastard trying to rub my nose in it? Any time of day I could have walked round there and stuck a knife in his back. But like I said there is more than one way to skin a cat.

By nature I'm not a violent person. I can handle myself when it's necessary, but I never go looking for trouble. Which might seem a bit at odds with the fact that right then I had made up my mind to murder Parelli within the next week. I'd organised a clean gun, which given the faces I was rubbing shoulders with was like borrowing a fountain pen. I'd established that the Italian was always in the Golden Goose at a certain time and satisfied myself that, with the crowds that got in there, I could be in, do the business and be out in under a minute. All that remained to be done was choose the moment. I wasn't hesitating, I just wanted to be sure the time was right.

It was sod's law that when I could have done with Barbara being away on one of her long trips, it was a time when she was working in London. But that couldn't be helped. It had to be now or that festering cancer of revenge that was eating away inside me would put me in the nuthouse.

Before I made the final decision that would end Zomparelli's life and perhaps change my own, I got into conversation with an old friend, Alfie Gerrard. One thing led to another and before long I'd confided in him that within days I was going to turn executioner. Not the sort of thing you bandy about with any Tom, Dick or Harry, but Alfie was one of your own: completely trustworthy and no stranger to murder himself. One of his most noted was the killing of Frank the 'Mad Axe Man' Mitchell, for which he was never charged. Other than point out the obvious, that I would be the first one in the frame as far as the law were concerned, Alfie didn't say too much about what I intended to do. Perhaps talk of doing away with scum was old hat to the likes of him. As he left the club that night he shook my hand, and his parting words were, 'Don't do anything hasty for a couple of days.'

Early the following evening Alfie's son Nicky came into the club and asked me if we could have a private word. Course we could. Nicky was a chip off the old block and as sound as a pound. The place was pretty quiet, but I took him out the back anyway. The first thing he said was, 'Don't get the hump, but my old man's told me what you're going to do about the bastard who done your brother, and I want to help.'

'Don't worry about it, I trust you both, but, really, I don't need any help,' I told him. Then he said, 'I don't mean help you. I mean I want to do it for you.'

We kicked it around for about an hour until in the end I agreed with his argument that the risks for him were about a hundred times less than they would be for me, given that I'd advertised loudly too often that I wanted to kill Parelli. OK, most people took it that it was just anger talking, but he was right: the law would set out to crucify me, which later on they tried to, and I hadn't done it. I offered to work with him, but he said it would be better if I kept well out of it. And anyway a fella he knew was ready to go with him for reasons of his own.

From what he told me it seemed that some bloke Piggott had been having an affair with Parelli's wife while he was away. In fact she'd moved in with him. Once her husband had done his time she'd thought better of her little indiscretion and gone flying back to the family nest, leaving this Piggott lovesick, pining and ready to kill so he could get his girlfriend back.

I said to Nicky: 'Tell your mate to forget the fucking girl. If he's serious about putting himself up for it and about giving you a hand I'll give you both a grand for your trouble.' We shook hands on the deal, had a drink and that was it. It wasn't necessary for my sanity personally to carry out the deed. As long as it was done I'd be a happy man.

A week later in that September 1974 Zomparelli was shot dead. One bullet in the head and three in the back, while he was playing a game called 'Wild Thing' on a pinball machine in the Golden Goose. I got a phone call breaking the news to me. It was Nicky, and all he said was 'Ronnie, it's done. Are you covered?' I said, 'Don't worry, mate, I've got so many witnesses that I was in the club, there ain't a court big enough to hold them.' And I opened a bottle of champagne, poured myself a glass and held it skywards, saying: 'Rest easy, David. That bastard's paid the price.'

Four years five months. It seemed like a lifetime ago since David had died. Now I felt like a terrible weight had been lifted from my chest, though I'd never forget my little brother. When I picked Barbara up from the theatre, where she was appearing with Sid James, she was shaking like a leaf. She'd heard about the killing on the news in her dressing room and thought of me straight away. The first thing she said as she got into the car was 'Where were you?' I assured her I had been in the club as usual, and it had been a full house. A hundred people could vouch for me. It certainly wouldn't do her peace of mind any good to know about any arrangements I might have made.

Satisfied I wasn't involved she then started to worry about the publicity we'd get, because the papers were bound to drag up everything from the past. I said, 'Oh, that's bloody good. I could get pulled in over this, and all you're worried about is getting some bad press for your fucking career.' She cried and said she hadn't meant it to sound like that, but on the other hand maybe she did.

A couple of days after Nicky Gerrard called into the club again. He didn't make a big fuss or nothing, just said, 'It was a piece of cake, pity he didn't know what was coming.' Simple as that. All squared away nicely. I gave him a nice thick envelope, shook his hand and told him, 'I won't forget what you've done for me and my family.' There was nothing else to say, and he walked away. And, as I thought, that was the end of it.

Because of his gangland-style execution, the newspapers had a field day over the murder, their pages filled with wild speculation. As one of them said, 'It was like Chicago in the 20s had come to the streets of London. That two heavily disguised men could, with impunity, walk into a public place and murder a man in front of a large number of witnesses.' While the papers were exploring every avenue for possible suspects, so were the police. And from a hundred possible combinations they thought the most likely was that I would do very nicely as suspect number one. So when I was pulled into West End Central it came as no surprise at all.

Three hours they held me, banging away with the questions. The main point being that: 'We know you did it, or were involved in some way, so make it easy on yourself and sign a confession.' Do leave it out. I was so confident they had nothing on me I went as far as to agree that I would have liked nothing better than to have been one of the shooters. But, sorry lads, I hadn't been invited to the party. A bit cocky, but it threw them off their stride. And seeing they were getting nothing more out of me called it a day and let me go. At Parelli's inquest in March 1975, the verdict was given that he had been unlawfully killed by person or persons unknown.

That tidy verdict had to be celebrated, so me and Barbara made up our minds to put everything behind us for a couple of weeks and take a holiday in Spain. I didn't have to worry about booking up hotels or accommodation because my sister Patsy and her husband Tony had a villa in Benalmadena, and we were always welcome to drop in any time.

It was beautiful out there. After all my problems the sun, sea and casual lifestyle was just what I needed to relax. It felt like a place I could spend my whole life in. On one of our walks near Patsy's place we came across a building plot for sale. Cut out of the hillside it had breathtaking views of the coastline and seemed like a paradise. I did some mental arithmetic, and it was a bit of a setback to find I was a bit short on what it would take to purchase the site and build a villa. But I couldn't let the idea go so I gave brother Johnny a call to see if he might be interested in going down the middle with me. I got a definite yes on the phone, threw some money at the agent, and three months later was half owner of a newly built and whitewashed Spanish-style villa.

Before the first block was laid, me and Barbara sat on the site having a picnic and trying to decide what this lovely home was going to be called. We giggled and messed about with 'Dun Roming' and 'Ronzanbabs'. Then because it was going to be built under a huge overhanging rock, old clever dick, having a few words of Spanish, hit on the idea of naming it 'Casa Rocca'.

Back in my sister's house that evening I went to the toilet. I'm having a jimmy, and why I never noticed it before I don't know, but staring up at me from the pan in large letters was the word ROCCA. It turned out that every toilet in Spain was christened the same, much like ours here bear the legend SHANKS. The two of us couldn't stop laughing for weeks, but it goes without saying that once the villa was built we named it 'Villa Limonar', after some lemon trees we planted.

Back in dear old Stanmore things between me and Barbara soon reverted to normal. Meaning she was back into swanning all round the country, leaving yours truly, when I wasn't at work, very much on my own. She had really hit the big time. In fact along with the *Carry On* films she was turning into a national institution. There were so many *Carry On*s I lost track of all the titles, though I do remember one called *Carry On Henry*. She did *The Boyfriend* with Twiggy, and even a bit of Shakespeare. The work just kept coming and coming.

I had so much money I didn't know what to do with it, and I'd say to her, 'Please give up working so much – we don't need the cash.' But I knew as well as she did it was nothing to do with finance. She needed an audience like a drowning man needs oxygen. It was all she existed for. She said she loved me but given the choice between the two – career or me – I wouldn't have got a second's thought.

It was all getting me down. Turning to another woman wasn't an option for me so to cheer myself up I used to spend. Some people turn to drink in that sort of situation, or drugs even. Not me. I bought everything that took my fancy. I filled my wardrobe with fancy suits, shirts and shoes – more than I could ever wear. And cars – I changed them like other people changed their socks. I've said I'm not flash, and that's the truth, but I went through a phase, particularly with the motors, of being a right arrogant bastard.

If I ever ran short of the readies, a quick trip to Redbridge, and I'd be back spending again. With the family all grown up and moved out, Mum and Dad had got themselves a little bungalow there, and that's where I banked my stash. I didn't want it in the house, and I couldn't have it in the club so it was the ideal place. Dad had gone to a lot of trouble to make a safe in the back of the larder.

It had wood panelling on the wall, so he'd cut a neat square out, chopped through one skin of the double brickwork and lined the opening. He made a door out of the boards he'd taken off, and when it was screwed back you wouldn't know it was there. It was just like a building society – I had to give him notice of a withdrawal, for the simple reason that he was the only one who was small enough to worm his way through brooms, bottles, tins, boxes, hoover and God knows what else to unscrew the door.

I don't like to mention them both in the same breath, but Dad died, God bless him, shortly after the Parelli business. He was strict when we were kids, but we knew he loved us. In turn we loved and respected him. We'd already lost our Billy. He had a brain tumour, lingered for a while, then passed away. We were all badly affected, and it was a terrible loss. I don't think Dad ever got over losing his sons or the way in which David died.

As if that wasn't enough my first best mate Albert Lennard collapsed with a fatal heart attack. He was only 40. Sid James was next. He died in the only way an old trooper like him could go – on stage in front of an audience. Barbara was distraught, and it upset me as well for, though, I'd never actually put my finger on the rumours, and my own suspicions about what was going on between him and my wife, I liked the man.

When Barbara was at home, or we had a few weeks in the villa, everything was rosy. She was like her old self, funny, loving, attentive. Times like that all my jealous thoughts flew out of the window, and I'd kick myself for causing so many rows over other blokes. Though the way she used to act half the time, a bloke would have to be a saint not to get annoyed every now and then. But she was quite content to let me believe that everything I complained about was in my imagination. It's not difficult to understand how I felt 20 years later, when Barbara wrote a book and spilt out all her infidelities for the world to read.

I was in Wandsworth prison. Just a few months into my sentence one of the screws handed me a package. All the mail is opened before you get it so there's no secret about what letters and parcels you receive. He said, 'Someone's sent you a book written by one of your wives. The little one I think.' As if he didn't know. Barbara's name was right across the front. The kind person who sent it to me was a stranger, and all the enclosed note said was 'You didn't know when you were well off.' What's in the mind of people like that? Do they get some kick out of winding people up who can't do anything about it?

I suppose I should have chucked it in the bin, but with nothing better to do, curiosity got the better of me. And there it was in black and white. Her proud confessions that while I was trying to curb my unfounded jealousy, she was happily being screwed by everyone in sight. OK, a lot of years had passed and I had a new and lovely wife Sue, so you'd think I could just laugh it off, but I couldn't. It made a joke of a part of my life that I had thought was special.

Somewhere along the line I've picked up a reputation for being a bit of a ladies' man. A lot of people might read that book and say, 'Well, good luck to the girl – what's good for the goose' and all that. But I was faithful to Barbara for at least a dozen years. And the simple answer as to why is that I loved her. She made me the loneliest person in the world sometimes, and we had our ups and downs like all couples. But the thought of hurting her, or losing her, for the sake of a quick leg over kept me on the straight and narrow.

I had plenty of offers being in the business I was in. Top club owner, loads of prestige, pots of money, and, let's face it, I wasn't the ugliest bloke in the world. I'd get birds young enough to be my daughter offering it on a plate. Some for the thrill of having it off with what the papers called a 'gangster'. Some because they thought it might help their aspirations to be a film star, and quite a few for no other reason than they fancied me.

I was no monk, and many nights I went home to that big empty house in Aylmer Drive, climbed into an equally empty bed, and laid there in a pool of sweat brought on by an overactive imagination. That's as far as it went. I defy any (probably well married now) young lady to pop out of the woodwork and say, 'Aren't you forgetting that night in 1970?' If I'm big enough to put my hand up to some very dodgy dealings that I've always denied up until now, believe me, if I'd slipped over the side a few times when I shouldn't have, I would be the first to admit it.

* * *

Ignorant of what was going on around me, I put all the upsets and sadness behind me and got on with my life. One thing happened when I was in the A & R as usual one night that gave me a huge lift. It was a surprise that knocked me for six. My partner's brother Brian, who we had on the door, came over to me while I was sitting with a group of people. He told me that there was a kid asking to come in, and he was saying that he was my son! I looked towards the entrance, and there was my Gary, a bit embarrassed, and I should think a bit out of place, smiling over to me. If I hadn't been in company my eyes would have filled up.

I remembered that apart from a fleeting glimpse of a woolly hat, when I'd seen him once from a distance, I'd never had the chance to pick up, kiss or cuddle my little boy in all the years of his infancy. People who have never walked in my shoes might say that the choice had been mine. But true or not, it didn't stop me loving those kids. Years passed and I asked June many many times to let me see them, but she always said no. Understandable – she was happily married and her bloke was a good stepfather, so she didn't want me rocking the apple cart.

I did see them once – June, Lorraine and Gary – when Gary was 12, and we spent a happy day together. It was marvellous – all those lost years swept away as we got to know one another for the first time.

On the business front, always ready to diversify, I'd got my fingers into a few other pies. I'd taken over another club just round the corner, and with some help from French Lou had moved into the very lucrative sidelines of servicing the needs of London's sad and seamy punters. I'd known Lou for years. In fact soon after I opened the club he turned up, ready and willing to supply our future needs in the fine wine and spirits department. At the right price – no questions asked.

Since then he'd come up with the goods as regular as clockwork. And I'd kept my side of the bargain, equally as regularly, by squaring the account with untraceable readies. So between the two of us there was a bond of mutual trust and respect. Apart from his interests in the off-licence business (off as in – off the back of a lorry), he had a very large investment in the porn market. When he found himself a little overextended and a bit short in the cash-flow department, he asked me if I was interested in putting a quick injection of funds into, as he put it, a diamond-white opportunity?

The proposition was that if I came up with £30,000 I could buy into the 'naughties', where profits realised matched that of Colombian drug barons. Except, unlike that disgusting trade, the only people we were likely to kill might be some old judge or vicar who'd got themselves overexcited. I agreed to join forces with him. My only stipulation being that no way did I ever want my name associated with this sleazy enterprise.

Today, that period of time is thought of as the tail

end of the permissive years. But anyone who actually lived through them will remember that there was definitely a social stigma attached to porn, as though everyone involved was a perverted pimp. I have to say, I went along with that way of thinking myself, so I wasn't exactly over the moon about joining the ranks of the low life. But business is business, whatever shape or form it comes in. And I told myself that being a ring master doesn't mean you have to be a performer. I soon found out it was a right performance when I checked out Lou's set-up.

Basically the idea was an 'in the flesh' version of what the butler saw. Around an enclosed stage were about a dozen individual toilet-room size booths. The pervy punter would pay to get inside one of these boxes, where he could spy through a tiny peephole at naked girls as they cavorted within the circle. Just as his temperature or what have you is rising, now you see it now you don't, because down would come a shutter cutting off his view. His sweaty fingers couldn't move fast enough to pump coins in the slot that would reopen the shutter. As if that wasn't enough to dig the money out of their pockets, for an extra five they could have a Polaroid camera passed in so they could take a glossy memento of the girl of the moment, in any pose. All nice and tidy. The punter remained anonymous, and the girls were perfectly safe.

I shouldn't knock them because these deprived, or depraved, souls gave me an income like coming up on the pools every week. But it made my skin crawl to think of what was going on inside those cubicles. Don't think they were all sad old tossers in dirty macs – a lot of our clientele came from way up the social scale. Barristers, top coppers and respectable businessmen. After I checked the place out, that was it, I never went near it again. I was terrified of word getting around that Britain's pocket-size sex symbol wasn't enough to keep Ronnie Knight satisfied.

What started as a little sideline to the peepshows grew so fast that the earnings almost eclipsed what we were taking from those disgusting cubicles: escorting. For a hefty fee any lonely punter who felt a bit spare without a girl on his arm when he visited the night spots could hire one of our attractive girls – all above board and no hanky panky. On the other hand they were both responsible adults, so if they decided to go further than holding hands, well that was entirely their affair.

With all these irons in the fire I was building up a nice little nest egg for the future, not realising that all this unaccounted for cash would one day drive me out of the country when the powers that be decided that it came from an illegal source.

8.
On Trial
for Murder

ON THE HOME FRONT the relationship between me and Barbara was not what you might call ideal. She was away from home so often it couldn't even be said that we were ships in the night, because most nights I spent on my own. I'd given up trying to convince her that there was nothing wrong with our marriage that a bit of time together couldn't put right, but my argument fell on deaf ears, and off she'd go again for a six-month tour of God knows where.

My libido was not designed to be satisfied at

three-monthly intervals. Starving yourself for a week then pigging out on a banquet is not good for your health. I must admit that every time Barbara was home long enough for us to get at it, it was like the first time all over again. Marvellous, rip-roaring, acrobatic, glorious sex. Then as I'd flicked the light off afterwards I'd think, That's your lot for a long time, Ronnie, my son. They say use it or lose it, and I wasn't going to put myself up for that. Yet it wasn't my rampant urges that drew me to a beautiful girl who turned up in the club one afternoon in 1979.

I couldn't help noticing her from a distance as she joked and laughed with her table companions over their lunch. I vaguely knew the publican and his wife who were in the little party, and I'd come across the fella who seemed to be her husband or boyfriend. Tony, his name was – a very successful dealer in the motor trade. I didn't hear what she was saying, but the other three were falling about laughing.

Studying that lovely profile and striking figure I lost myself in my own thoughts and came to with a silly smile on my face to see the publican giving me a nod of recognition. He must have thought I was a right plonker standing there grinning like an idiot. I nodded back and sent a bottle over to their table with my compliments. How slow am I? Just as I'd hoped he invited me over to share the bottle. He introduced me to his friends as 'Ronnie Knight – best club owner in the business and Barbara Windsor's old man', something I was so used to I hardly noticed. 'Tony, the missus and' – I held my breath – 'Susan Haylock'. God she was even more beautiful up close.

She had a gorgeous tawny mane of soft hair that framed her face accentuating a pair of eyes that I felt myself falling into. I was so thrown off balance I'm sure I must have acted like the village idiot as I stammered my way through social small talk. When Tony put a proprietorial arm around her shoulder or touched her hand, I got that old familiar twinge in the pit of my stomach. Too soon for me the lunch-time get-together was over, and they left the club. To them just another day. But I was left shaking with a power of emotion I didn't know I had in me. Almost twice her age at almost 46, and I was like a 16 year old.

When Barbara rang me that evening from some far-flung theatre I was almost annoyed with her for breaking into my thoughts and bringing me down to earth. Without anything to go on, not even the imagined supposition that I'd felt when I met Barbara, my mind was in a turmoil with thoughts of Sue. After a couple of weeks had passed, though, Sue slowly slipped out of my mind as I told myself I had no right to fantasise about a girl who'd shown no interest in me and was already spoken for. I tended to sigh a lot during those few weeks, then everything I'd shoved on the back burner of my mind came flooding back when I arrived late at the club, and there she was, sitting at the bar – alone. Well, not alone, but at least she wasn't with the boyfriend.

As before she was entertaining the friends she was with. Every now and then a burst of laughter would go up, and I'd glance over and catch her looking at me. Each time she coloured up, and I thought perhaps my feelings are not so one-sided. And wasn't it nice to find a woman who could still blush. Someone else might have dived straight in, chatted her up and tried his luck, but somehow I felt that pushiness would get a knock-back from this girl. Not that there was any fear of me pushing myself forward. I was too shy for that. I could handle women who shoved it at me gift wrapped, but when it came to the first move I didn't know where to start. Remember, this fella with a reputation for being a stud about town had only been seriously involved with two women in his life.

Still, we had been introduced, and it was part of my job description to check on my customers, so throwing caution to the wind I sidled down the bar towards her. Far from thinking I was some creep on the make, she greeted me with a lovely smile and a warm hello that made me feel at ease and about ten feet tall. She didn't flirt, she didn't give me the old come-on, and she wasn't all coy like a lot of women when they know just what they're after. She was just friendly, which made it easy for me to talk as though we'd known each other for years.

I told you I was a good listener – well, after a while she just came out with what the score was with Tony. Yes, they had been an item, as they say today, though his being too dependent on the bottle had forced her to walk out on him. The decision wasn't made overnight, but she knew he had reached a point where all the help in the world couldn't prevent him sinking deeper into full blown alcoholism.

Some time later I met Tony, and instead of hating him like I did with most people involved with my women, I got on really well with him. And self-destroying lush or not he must have had a big heart because he asked me to take care of Sue. 'Ronnie, I love her, but if she stays with me I'll drag her down.' If that wasn't selfless I don't know what is.

Thank Christ for good staff. If it had been left to me that afternoon no one would have got served, as my total attention was centred on Sue. My heart sank when I noticed her checking the time, sure that if she walked out without me saying something I might never see her again. I put the moment off until the last minute. She put on her little short jacket and excused herself while she went to the Ladies Room prior to leaving. I broke out in a cold sweat as I rehearsed a speech. That sort of thing didn't come naturally to me at all.

When she came back she didn't sit down, so I stood up and blurted out, 'I've enjoyed your company – how about a meal one evening now you're on your own?' She looked directly into my eyes, and my stomach dropped. 'I'm on my own, but you're not. Why are you considering messing about with me?' I used to lie so easily about the current woman in my life, but I didn't want to start this relationship with deceit. So it was now or never.

I told her I was tired of trying to be in love with a part-time wife. Tired of being on my own. Tired of being gooseberry on nights out with old mates like

Mickey Regan and Freddie Foreman and their wives. And simply tired of not having the warmth of companionship. I swore I didn't want to hurt Barbara. Sue had suffered a lot of hurt herself caused in a different way by Tony, yet she understood what I was saying and accepted my shy offer of a date on those terms.

One dinner date followed another, and in a few weeks we were seeing each other regularly, but very discreetly. Corny it might sound, but I know I fell in love with her as soon as I clapped eyes on her. Kid's stuff, I know. Grown people don't act like that, but in those short weeks I realised I was head over heels – violins playing, hearts and flowers – in love.

You might think you've heard all this before, but this time it really was different. Yes, I loved my first wife June, I thought she was the best girl in the world, but it couldn't survive my growing up and moving into a different world, while she remained the same. My feelings for Barbara were first and foremost based deeply in lust. I thought I loved her and my emotions were very strong, but realising what I felt for Sue made me look back and question what Barbara had really meant to me. Perhaps I'd been confusing sex with someone so stunningly different from anything I'd known, plus a yearning for something I could never really have with the word LOVE. Whatever it was it couldn't compare with the turmoil Sue had brought into my life.

A few close friends hinted that being so young perhaps she was after a sugar daddy, that our casual meeting hadn't been so casual, and she had been putting herself at the front so she could get her hands on my not inconsiderable fortune, which was no secret. I say close friends, because anyone else would definitely have suffered a serious whacking, but it was a question that never troubled me. I had approached her, not the other way round. She had her independence and own money, and on our second meeting had told me she was negotiating to buy her own flat in Mulberry Court, Edgware.

Barbara had been away on one of her long trips when I met Sue, and by the time she returned to Aylmer Drive the damage had been done. I was genuinely pleased to see her, and our lovemaking that night was as good as it had always been. OK, my animal instincts took over. After all, she was still my wife, very attractive, and me and Sue had not reached that stage in our relationship as yet.

Next morning with that side of things drained from my system, the guilt took over. Guilt that somehow I had betrayed Sue, though being a woman of the world I am sure she would have understood. And a worse guilt as I watched Barbara bubbling around the house, cooking breakfast, singing and rabbiting on excitedly about her trip. I thought, you haven't got a clue what's happened to me. She was affectionate and attentive, which made it even worse. How could I hurt her in the worst possible way a woman can be hurt. She did care for me, I was sure of that, and she loved me in her own way, but I was second on her list of priorities. The one and only ruling passion in her life was being a star. She was obsessed, consumed and dominated by nothing else but thoughts of her career. How else could she have risen so high?

I know it was too early to compare the two ladies in my life, but Sue seemed to put me first in her thoughts and actions. Barbara never did that from day one, nor any day in the last 16 or 17 years. So did I do the right thing for once in my life and come clean that what we had was over? No. I kept up a pretence of normality, playing for time, knowing she would be off on her travels again shortly. Something other than cowardice held me back from blowing our marriage out of the water. I didn't know what it was then, but perhaps I'd done a good deed in the past and Him above thought it was about time for pay back. Whatever, I was going to need that little lady more than I could have ever imagined.

Wednesday, 16 January 1980. I was woken up by the barking of some neighbour's dogs. I got out of bed with the intention of shouting abuse from the window, looked out, and it was like a replay of life in the flat. The place was surrounded by the law, dressed to kill. Flak jackets, guns, and bloody great alsatians. Pulling on my trousers I rushed downstairs. Not that I was over keen to face a bit of aggravation but to save the front door. It was over in minutes, and I went quietly. Arrested on suspicion of murdering Alfredo Zomparelli.

What had brought all this on? Five years since it was all done and dusted, and the whole business was back to square one. This was about five o'clock in the morning. I'd had about two hours sleep and was absolutely knackered, so accepted the cuffs in a daze. Barbara was so stunned by the shock of what was happening she didn't kick up a fuss like she always had in the past. But stood crying quietly.

I got nothing out of the coppers on the way to West End Central, and once there not much else but a repeat of the charge before being put in a cell. And there I sat for hours with nothing to do but spin wild theories around in my head. I knew Nicky Gerrard was already in prison, serving time for armed robbery. Could they have turned him? Had the law put the pressure on and forced him to turn grass? No, his dad Alfie would have killed him. What about that Piggott character? A blank again – he had more to lose than I did. And so it went on, round and round and round.

By the time they stuck me in the interview room late in the afternoon I was feeling as low as I could get. The cheese sandwich I had been given at lunch time was wedged in the middle of my chest like a lead weight, and the way I was feeling I didn't know whether to force it up or down.

The tape recorder went on and a smiling inspector said, 'I am showing Mr Knight a photograph of George Bradshaw.' He pushed a photo across to me and asked if I could identify the face in it. My spirits lifted – I'd never seen him in my life before. It showed a fresh-faced kid with short hair like hundreds you see every day. I shoved it back at him and said, 'I don't know him at all.' Instead of being disappointed the inspector's face lit up as though I'd solved the problem instead of causing one. 'That's all for now,' he announced. 'I am terminating this interview.' Interview? It had only taken three minutes before I was back in the cell more puzzled than ever.

Later on Anthony Blok turned up. He was Barbara's solicitor, and she'd gone straight from home to beg him to step in and help me. He was as much in the dark as I was but promised he'd know what the set-up was when we got to court in the morning. His last words were 'Don't worry, I'll get bail sorted out, and you should be home by tomorrow evening.'

My court appearance was just a formality. The judge didn't want to hear a word from me. All that mattered was what the police had to say, and based on that one-sided evidence he remanded me to Brixton prison. Be fair to the man, though, he did give me an alternative – cough up the cash or supply surety of £250,000, and I could walk out there and then. A quarter of a million quid. He was joking me. Did he think I was going to flee the country or something? I didn't know anyone who carried that much spare, so it was in the van and off to my old lodgings. What a place to spend my 46th birthday.

The last time I'd been behind those walls I was a different person. Young, fit and toughened by the life I lived. Now look at me – 20 years of the good life, used to the best food, best clothes, the best money could buy. No way was I equipped to spend any length of time banged up.

Fortunately for me, being a remand prison, Brixton

was just about bearable, but if things got worse I dreaded the prospect of somewhere like Wandsworth. While I sat there twiddling my thumbs in worry and boredom waiting for Anthony Blok to get all the details together, Barbara, bless her lovely heart, was knocking herself out in her efforts to raise my bail. She showed up on my birthday clutching a red rose for me and looking so grey and tired my heart bled for her. We'd had our traumas, and before this happened were on the brink of calling it a day. Now she was solidly behind me fighting for my freedom, no matter how temporary that might be.

Then I thought of Sue, and I didn't feel very proud of myself. Barbara cheered up so much while she was telling me that my brothers Johnny and Jimmy were going to put the bail money up. I didn't have the heart to tell her that Blok had been in earlier and pulled the rug from under my feet.

Before he told me what he knew, he asked me if I'd ever had dealings with a man named George Bradshaw? I asked him if that was the geezer in the photograph I'd been shown, and when he agreed, I swore with honest conviction I didn't know him from Adam. I think he looked a bit relieved at that and went on to tell me what the police had against me. It seemed this villain Bradshaw, with more blaggings, assaults and armed robberies behind him than I've had hot dinners, had turned supergrass, putting the finger on about a hundred fellas he'd worked with over the years. That didn't surprise me, for since Bertie Smalls had sung to the law, he'd started a fashion for grasses to spill everything in a big way.

'You probably know this already,' Anthony said, 'but Bradshaw has just been given life for shooting Zomparelli. In a plea bargain to save himself from perhaps 20 years, he put your name forward as co-conspirator.' Bloody hell, I thought, what's this got to do with me? I've paid out good money to the wrong guys. But to Anthony I said, 'This is a complete frame-up. He's picking names out of the phone book to save his own neck.' 'Well,' he said, 'I don't doubt you're being honest with me, so we should be able to clear this up quite quickly.' Then he got up to leave. As he was picking up his papers he threw in, as a bit of conversation, 'Oh, by the way, he's also mentioned a Nicholas Gerrard as being involved, and Bradshaw also uses an alias of Maxie Piggott.'

Bradshaw and Piggott were the same bloke – I went cold from head to toe. That night I didn't sleep at all as I went through all the possible combinations of what the police might know. His word on its own wasn't enough as I'd never actually met or even seen him. They would have a difficult job proving a case against me.

When Barbara visited next day she'd learnt from Blok as much as I knew. She'd had a word with my brother Johnny who had been arrested as well but released, and he'd given her a message for me. 'Tell Ronnie this Bradshaw is the creep who used to come in the club with Alfie Gerrard.' Now it all fell into place – no wonder Old Bill thought they had me bang to rights. Why else would I deny knowing Bradshaw-

Piggott whatever his fucking name was, unless I was very guilty of something? They knew I knew him because they kept tabs on everyone who walked in the door of the A & R. Those with form anyway.

So that's who I'd been dealing with. Maxie – the bloody Cisco Kid. I took an instant dislike to him the first time I saw him with Alfie. He was a pushy little shit who was always trying to worm his way into our company. I couldn't stand the sight of him so I used to turn my back and give him the cold shoulder. On top of that he was weird looking: beard, goggle-eye specs and a drooping moustache that made me think of that Mexican film cowboy Pancho Villa, except at the time I couldn't remember his name so I called him the Cisco Kid after the bloke he was sidekick to.

How had I been expected to identify that smooth face in the photo when it was nothing like the bloke I knew? They'd dropped me in it. My first two bail applications were not accepted by the police. Johnny and Jimmy's offer was turned down because of their form, and the second for various reasons too boring to go into, but Barbara wouldn't give up. She went to my sister Patsy's husband Tony Chatwell, and he told her he didn't want to be involved. Can you believe that? My own family. He must have forgotten about when his marriage was going through a bad patch, and me and Barbara looked after their kids for weeks to give them time to sort their problems out. And what about the cash hand-outs when he was skint?

Still, some of the offers from outside the family were heart-warming. Like Anna Karen, the lovely girl made up to look awful in that early seventies TV series *On the Buses*. She had nothing but the house she lived in, and without a thought for herself put it on offer as bail. I didn't take it up for the simple reason that when you're looking for getting on to a quarter of a million, it would have been a drop in the ocean. In the end some friends of ours, Harry and Phylis Hewson and their son-in-law, clubbed together and put up £200,000. The remaining £50,000 came from Barbara's manager Robert Dunn. So after two weeks on remand I was released on bail to appear before Lambeth Street Magistrates on 14 July.

Those two weeks in Brixton had seemed like months – a horrible taster of what was to come if Bradshaw got a result. Right at that moment all I wanted to do was get into a nice hot bath and wash the stink of that place off me. Then with a little breather, for the sake of propriety, get round to Sue's as quick as possible.

I'd managed to get a message to her explaining the situation, and though she'd sent me a loving note by return obviously there had been no way for her to see me. I was torn in two. I knew I loved Sue like I'd never loved anyone else, but at the same time I loved Barbara in a different way. We'd been together for so many years she was part of me, and to think of walking away and never seeing her again was difficult to take in; yet I knew it was going to happen sooner or later. Trouble was I didn't hate Barbara or dislike her even – it would have made my life much easier if that was the case.

Our problem was all down to months and months of separation. In the 20 or so years we had been together, without exaggeration you could cut it in half if you added up real time in each other's company. It's funny really, what with my jealousy over the years, but at that time I wished she would come home one day and say, 'Ronnie, I'm sorry, but I've found someone else.' I could have just walked away then with a clear conscience – but life's never like that.

How I got through the next five months without cracking up is a miracle. The mental pressure was terrible. I was worrying about the two women in my life, and yet with a simple 'Guilty' the jury could take me away from both of them until I was 70 years old. Terrifying – no other word for it. Those months toward July went by at a snail's pace. It was a preliminary hearing I was heading for to see if there was a case to answer.

It could go two ways. One I could walk out, or two, have a trial date set for some time in the future. On the day of the hearing I had some lunch with Barbara near the courts, then with a confidence I didn't feel told her to wait for me in the restaurant – 'Shouldn't take too long, doll.'

I wasn't there to plead guilt or innocence, so to be honest I didn't follow all the legal arguments. I just sat praying that it would soon be over. Whatever I thought of the police they were not stupid. They would never have come this far if they didn't think they had a strong case against me. So, whatever I hoped for didn't matter – I was sure it was going to go all the way. So when I heard the judge set a trial date at the Old Bailey for 10 November I wasn't one bit surprised. What did surprise me and knock the wind out of my sails was when he added that he was revoking my bail and remanding me in custody.

Instead of walking out into the bright sunshine as a free man, or still on bail but a temporary free man, I was hustled down the back stairs to wait for the Brixton run. I've said before about that feeling of helplessness and panic that sets in when the door shuts behind you – nothing had changed. I swallowed it, though, and forced myself to make the rounds of the lads who I'd said goodbye to nearly six months earlier. Though we laughed and joked and I said it was good to be back and all that nonsense, it was bloody depressing because a lot of those guys had already done 12 months and some of them 18. And this is just on remand. No sentence yet – just held in case it might be proved they're guilty later on. Whatever happened to innocent until proven?

One good thing about remand was that I was allowed fresh clothes to be brought in, reading material and all kinds of odds and ends that make life tolerable. Top of my list was that meals were allowed in and amongst all the other things she was doing for me, my ministering angel Barbara made sure she cooked the best ever on the biggest plate she could find. And, bless her, when I told her that I was sharing my meal with other less fortunate cons, she packed the roast potatoes on that dish like a pyramid.

When I was first remanded, and before I got bail, as painful as it was Sue and me agreed it wasn't worth the risk for her to try and see me. But back inside and facing months before the trial I would have gone out of my mind if I couldn't see her, so arrangements were made for a good mate to bring her in. It was all done on the hush-hush, so Barbara didn't get wind of what we were up to. I was in enough trouble without her screaming the prison walls down.

I thought my heart would burst the first time Sue walked into the visiting room. And looking at her across the table I felt I could face anything as long as she'd be there at the end of it. That was when we first talked about putting everything behind us and making a new life together in Spain. We had a lot to get through before then, but just taking about it with her made me feel as though we were almost there. One thing we never discussed was what might happen if the verdict went against me. The consequences were too frightening to contemplate.

In Brixton we had the choice of working or not. If you worked you got a couple of pounds to spend in the canteen. If you had the means to survive then obviously you didn't put yourself up for cleaning the toilets or scrubbing the stairs. I was all right for a few bob, so I chose the latter option.

Having a bit to spare I could afford to stock up on the prison currency – cigarettes. I didn't smoke so I could trade them for all sorts – I had so much gear in my cell the screws started to hint that I was in the baron business. But they never got a whisper against me from their grasses because there was nothing going on. What I was doing was helping out those fellas who had nothing. This wasn't to buy friends, nor was it to earn myself points with Him above. I had plenty, and thanked God for it, so I shared – simple as that.

As my trial grew closer I began to worry more and more. I had nightmares about being nailed into a box that had me waking up soaked in sweat. I was still sure they could never find enough honestly to pin involvement in the murder on me, but what if they went about it dishonestly? I wouldn't be the first or the last to go down on perjured evidence from the police.

I had good reason to worry. On the weekend before the trial the prosecution sprung a surprise on my silk, Mr Ivor Richard. They had a witness who could put me smack bang in the middle of the frame. Crafty bastards. They knew that any evidence they intended using against me had to be given to the defence. This is a fair way for the brief to work out a counterargument. So they gave him two days to get his head around it.

Court Number One, the Old Bailey. To kick off the proceedings the prosecution painted a picture of me as king of the underworld; very shady club owner and ruthless mastermind behind not only the cold-blooded murder in question, but also subtle hints that there might be many more in my past. Surely the jury couldn't swallow this obvious character assassination? They made me sound worse than the whole Kray firm put together.

Then they rolled in their star witness. The snivelling Cisco, ready to sing like a canary to save his own neck. No doubt well rehearsed by the police, he told his fascinating story to the jury. On the day of the murder he and Nicky Gerrard met up at a flat in Clerkenwell. From there they went to a theatrical costumier in Soho, where they each bought themselves dark glasses and a false moustache. Then a quick trip to the Golden Goose in Old Compton Street – hang about for a few minutes until they catch sight of Zomparelli, then while tough-guy gangster Bradshaw kept well back, Nicky Gerrard walked up to the Italian and shot him at arm's length. In the confusion amongst the 40 or 50 people on the scene, they calmly walked away and melted into the crowd. Apart from who actually fired the shot, this could have been the truth, but it was the colourful background to all this that was intended to do me some serious damage.

It has to be remembered I didn't even know who Piggott was when Nicky first mentioned him, and my idea was to give him a good drink for something he was going to do anyway. Now, in court, he's making out that I set the whole thing up. I was supposed to have sent Nicky to him to find out if he'd be willing to kill someone for money.

When he reluctantly agreed that he might be up for it, arrangements were made for him to meet me to sort out the details. As though he was an innocent party dragged into the whole thing against his will, he told how I took him to a coffee bar to point out Parelli so there would be no mistake who he was, then back to the A & R, where I handed him a package containing a .38 pistol.

The lying git. He didn't need any reminding of who Parelli was – Bradshaw had been rogering his missus for two years. As for a gun, why would he have needed one from me? Apart from a lifetime of handling shooters, only a few days prior to the murder he'd calmly walked into a scrap yard and shot a guy to teach him a lesson. What did he use then – a water pistol?

The whole point was that all I'd done was take advantage of a situation where the deed was already in the pipeline. OK, I gave him an incentive, but he didn't need that from what Nicky had told me. Be serious. If I'd wanted to set the murder up from scratch, that pimply, 20-year-old Piggott, with a track record as long as your arm, would have been my last choice. If I'd known who he was I wouldn't have paid him to post a letter. Why would I need to? My good friend Alfie Gerrard would have done it for a favour, and very professionally too.

I looked round the court trying to gauge reactions to his speech, and praying they were not swallowing his fairy story. In case the jury had any doubts at all about Bradshaw's credibility, a Chief Superintendent by the name of Wilson got in the dock and gave him a glowing reference that bordered on a citation. Putting aside the fact that his past form included arson, armed robbery, GBH, conspiracy to rob and frequent use of firearms (namely his sawn-off shotgun), 'Tug'

Wilson commended him on his selfless courage in becoming a supergrass and pointing the finger at 105 ruthless criminals.

That he happened to be serving a life sentence for murder and 107 other offences was nothing to do with encouraging him to become a good citizen. He'd seen the error of his lawless lifestyle, wanted to reform, and the only positive way to ease his social conscience was to help the police clear up their backlog of villains who they'd wanted to get their hands on for a long time. I suppose this is where I came into the picture.

At the end of each day I sunk further into despair. No matter what, they were going to put me away for setting up the murder. If this meant whitewashing a full-time robber and murderer to persuade the jury, then so be it. I clung on to the hope that his record might be revealed and go against him. After all, surely they couldn't believe a character like that against me, who only had a tiny bit of form and none of that for violence? It was all going to be down to his word against mine and Nicky Gerrard's.

The prosecution produced their eleventh-hour witness – one Gerald Knight. No relation to me and another one who the law have made a few behind-the-scenes promises to. The line he wanted to throw to the jury was that he'd heard me plotting the murder of Zomparelli. I couldn't believe it. I knew him from years back. Seven years to be precise, and he was nothing but an out and out toerag. Not in Bradshaw's league but a con man and a lying bastard.

He used to come in the club ordering champagne and acting like he was a very successful businessman and entrepreneur. A bit flash, but he struck me as being an honest sort of bloke, so I got sucked in. All I can think is that having plenty of spare cash I let my usually pretty good judgement slip. He came to me with a deal about buying a piece of land. He took me down to the plot and told me we could buy it for £14,000. Seven a piece. He knew some big building company was interested, so if we moved fast we could acquire it under their noses, then sell it to them at treble what we'd laid out. Sounded very sweet so I divvied up my half.

Four weeks went by and nothing was happening so I went after him. He was very apologetic and said the deal had fallen through and as it happens he was on his way round to the club to give me a cheque. I ignored that bit of old crap and said, 'Never mind, I gave you cash, and I'll have the same back, thank you.' He made all kinds of excuses about banks and cash flow, so in the end I took his cheque. It bounced like a kangaroo, and he'd taken it on his toes. Every now and then Barbara would tell me the cheque had come back again, and, getting pissed off about not being able to get my hands around Knight's neck, I told her to chuck it in the bloody bin.

So not only had he done me over the cheque, but he tucked me up over an enterprise we were in together involving the sale of snide Cartier and Rolex watches. This sideline brought in a very nice wage. Being tied up with plenty of other deals to keep me busy, I let my returns build up. No rush. I wasn't that hard up I needed to chase pay days, but I knew it was there waiting. Or I thought it was until he buggered off. Still, it didn't dent the bank balance too much, so after promising myself he'd get a real spanking when he showed up I put it out of my mind.

Now here was the slimy rat helping the law to crucify me. Why was he doing it? He'd done a bit of time abroad for fraud, then come back to England to walk right into another charge for a similar offence. What was it worth? One year to two years? And he's willing to turn grass and get me 20 years for that! As soon as he found he was headed for Brixton, where he knew I was, up went the hand. No way was he risking going down four flights of concrete stairs on his head.

The jury was called to attention to listen to another fairy story. And this one would be a classic. Did he mention our business dealings? Course not – as he told the jury, he barely knew me. The first time we met, he said, was when he was visiting London with his old dad. They saw the A & R club, so he says to his dad, 'Ronnie Knight owns this place, let's pop in and meet him.' They'd come into the club, and, according to him, he had introduced himself to me by making a comment that we had the same name. While we were shaking hands some unnamed guy walked up to the bar. I was supposed to have given him a black look and with a definite show of temper shouted, 'Where the fucking hell have you been? You know I want you to do a murder for me.'

Still on oath Gerald Knight tells the assembled jury that I then excused myself by politely saying to him 'Forgive me, I have a bit of murdering to discuss.' How can you smile in a situation as grave as the one I was in? But, honestly, you wouldn't put lines like that in a farce. Whoever had put together that rubbish must have been an out-of-work scriptwriter for the *Carry On*s. It might have been believable if he'd said he overheard a whispered conversation in a darkened corner – or with a few glasses too many I'd let slip my murderous intent.

As I remember, my conversation with Nicky was very brief. No one was near us at the time, and I'd swear we never used the words murder or shoot. Like I said about Knight, he had an honest face and a plausible manner, and I could see the jury were hanging on to his every word. Everything hinged on him being found credible, and he was making a lovely job of it.

How do you prepare yourself for 20 years behind bars? They might as well book me a room in Broadmoor, because that's where I'd end up. Then a tiny light burst into my gloom. During one of the recesses Barbara came over to me and whispered, 'That cheque – the one from Gerald Knight. I've still got it. I never chuck anything away like that.' Did I hug her to death? No. Even though the thought lit a spark of hope in me I couldn't bear to consider it. 'Leave it out, Barb. Nobody keeps a bit of paper for seven years.'

What tears, panic and frustration went on at home

that night, as I lay sunk in apathy, I didn't know until later, but it seemed Barbara tore the house apart. She screamed and swore at her mother Rose (who lived with us then) if she got in the way of her desperate search. She only found it by chance the following Sunday morning, stuck in the back of the drawer. There was no visiting that day, so I had to wait until the next day before I found out.

God bless my brief – he might have cost fortunes every hour, but he was worth every penny. Now he could discredit that lying git in style. 'Mr Knight,' he said once he got him back in the dock, 'Have you ever had any business dealings with Mr Ronnie Knight?' 'No, sir, definitely not.' 'So he never gave you a sum of money to invest in land or property?' 'No, sir.' 'So then it cannot be true that when the venture did not materialise you gave him a cheque to the value of the money he said he had invested?' 'No, sir, definitely not, sir.'

'Let's think very carefully about this – are you completely sure there was no cheque?' 'I'm sure, sir.' 'Then might I draw your attention to this?' And with that the brief laid the cheque in front of him. You could have cut the tension in the courtroom with a knife. He wasn't smiling now, and watching him squirm gave me such a lift I felt dizzy.

Once he'd gathered his thoughts he started to bluster. 'Oh, yes. That is one of my cheques – I remember losing it in some man's garage under the arches.' He couldn't remember me but hadn't forgotten a piece of paper lost seven years previously. No. He couldn't remember the man's name but did recall that he had died shortly afterwards. And, 'Oh, yes, I do believe the man was involved in forgery of some sort, so he obviously wrote my signature on the cheque.'

I couldn't hold myself back, it was killing me. I shouted out, 'Turn it over. Turn the cheque over,' earning myself a frown from the judge. And there, bold as you like, on the back was his old address and the same signature. Talk about actor? My brief just looked at Gerald Knight, paused only long enough to get everyone's attention, then said to him, 'I think this not only proves beyond doubt that you have carried out business with my client in the past, but it appears to me that you have a financial interest in seeing him put into permanent custody.'

The judge was not happy at having the piss taken out of him. He glared at Knight and said, 'Get him out of my court.' My heart was pumping, surely Mr Justice Wein would call a halt to the case. But he carried on as if nothing of note had rocked Court No. 1. Jesus Christ, what does he know that I don't? Have the police found another grass to step in and win the case for them? Ten months of the worst charge I could get hanging over my head, and still it won't finish. It was a nightmare of endless words. I felt like I was watching the proceedings through smoked glass. I didn't dare listen to the summing-up in case I picked up bad vibes before I'd prepared myself.

Then everything went crystal clear as I watched the jury file out. Five minutes and they were back. Was that all the thought they were going to give a decision affecting my life? No. It was a technicality. They wanted to study some of my previous statements, but the judge turned down their request. How could he do that? A few words of what I'd said might be all that it took to swing the verdict in my favour, but he had the final word, so off they went again, and I was taken downstairs to the prisoners' reception room.

I sat in a puddle of sweat – my nerves stretched to breaking point. If someone had crept up on me right then and shouted, 'Boo,' in my ear, I would have fainted clean away. Two hours of pain no one should be put through. Suddenly I was shaken out of my daze by one of the screws saying, 'Cheer up, Ronnie. If I know anything about juries, and how long they take to make up their mind, you're out of it, mate.'

Was that his sadistic humour? How I got back up those stairs and into the dock I'll never know. My legs had turned to jelly, my stomach to water, and my heart was racing. I couldn't wait for the jury's decision, but sat scanning their faces for a hint or sign that might give me a clue to my fate. Was that a slight wink from that bloke? Surely not. I was imagining things. Was that a little smile on that woman's face, or had she looked at me like that for the past ten days? Then the chosen foreman stood up. This is it, Ronnie. Keep a brave face on it. Don't let the bastards know they've ripped your guts out when they give you life. Life. God help me.

Not Guilty. For a second I wasn't sure if I'd heard the 'Not'. Then Nicky Gerrard, who was in the dock with me, said, 'Thank you, gentlemen. Merry Christmas. You have certainly made mine.'

I looked over at Barbara, and tears were streaming down her face. She cried out, 'My God. Oh, my God. My Ronnie.' I didn't know what to say, I had a lump in my throat that was bigger than an apple. It wouldn't make a decent headline, but I straightened myself up, looked gratefully at the jury who had given me my life back and said, 'Thank you. Thank you all. Justice has been done.' Well, it had. Zomparelli deserved to die, and Nicky Gerrard had earned my eternal gratitude for seeing it was done.

I went back downstairs to get ready for my walk out of the door, and they brought Barbara down to me. We hugged each other, laughing and crying. One of the papers had carried a big story about the case, and in it she was quoted as saying, 'If Ronnie gets sent down, I couldn't live without him.' I was so touched when I read that, I can't tell you how I felt, but I know the guilt was like a knife twisting inside me. Guilt, that while she had stood by me all the way, working a miracle raising my bail, then never missing a visit all the time I was in prison, I was thinking of someone else. Would I ever have the strength to tell her the truth?

9.
Goodbye Barbara, Hello Sue

BARBARA AND ME WALKED out of the Old Bailey like a fairytale prince and princess. Well, that's what the papers had us down as anyway. My old mate Poochie was there to shake my hand and so many reporters you'd have thought we really were royalty. It was no good heading for home because Barbara said the press were practically camping on the doorstep, so we jumped in a motor with Robert Dunn and his wife and took off for the country. Now it was behind me, I could look forward to living again.

Nicky Gerrard got acquitted, same as me, but he

never walked out of the door. He still had a year to serve on his armed-robbery sentence. We kept in touch, and his first letter after the end of the trial said that he was the happiest prisoner in England. Six months later his dad, Alfie, was found dead in the flat he lived in down Brighton way. The inquest said it was drink that killed him, done his liver in or something, but who knows?

He must have had a lot of enemies – over the years he'd put a lot of people in the ground – and some thought he was an evil bastard. Though speak as you find, I found him to be OK. It must have been a blow for Nicky, especially as he was still banged up. I know how hard it is to lose someone when you can't even say a prayer over their grave. Nicky didn't have a lot of time to grieve over his old man. He only tasted a few months of freedom before he was ambushed by some blokes wearing masks and shot and clubbed to death.

I can remember him telling me that he thought he was being followed everywhere he went, but, as we both thought, sometimes the law haven't got anything better to do with their time. It hadn't been the police, though – would have been better if it had been. He just came out of his house in Stamford Hill and got into the big American car he always drove around in when somebody stepped forward and shot him in the stomach through the windscreen. That didn't kill him, and game as anything he managed to get out of the car and stagger down the road. His two attackers followed, and one of them smashed him on the head with so much force the stock of the shotgun, used as a club, shattered in pieces. That wasn't enough, so the other fella shot him at point-blank range. He died on his little girl's eleventh birthday.

Nicky took after his dad and had put himself about a bit. He must have had hundreds of enemies, and I read somewhere that he was 'the most feared man in London'. I don't know about that, but, given such a large choice of potential assassins, who do the law pull in for questioning? Who else but Ronnie Knight.

Same old rigmarole – arrested, given the treatment and subjected to threatening interviews. The first thing the detective said to me was 'Had I heard about Gerrard?' I told him, 'Yes. I read the papers. Terrible shame, wasn't it?' He then said that he thought it was down to me. I told him he had to be joking, but he said it was no joke, who else would want his mouth shut permanently over the murder of Parelli? I said, 'There was nothing for him to keep quiet about. We were not involved, and twelve jurors had put everything straight about that.' He just sneered and said, 'We all know that some juries are silly as arseholes.'

He tried his hardest to get me to say something incriminating about myself, but he could have got the rubber truncheon out, and it wouldn't have made a scrap of difference. I didn't know who had murdered Nicky, or why. What I do know is that it wasn't down to me or anybody I knew. Five hours later they let me go. For weeks I expected to be picked up again for them to have another go at me, so I was relieved when they arrested someone and charged them with the murder. I wasn't pleased that the guy was going to suffer what I had been through when I was on trial, just pleased that now I would be left alone.

Tommy Hole, the fella they charged, was a cousin by marriage to Nicky. He was a wholesaler from Canning Town, and, though he was no angel, no one took the allegation seriously. For Christ's sake, even Nicky's mum stood up and swore that he was innocent. What better reference can you get than that? He went through 12 months of hell before he was acquitted. He should never have been in the dock at all.

Now if there's one thing the law does not like, it's an acquittal. they think they've got it all sewn up, then bang! – back to square one. So one way or another they will get you again; guilty or not, doesn't matter. If they think that you have taken the piss, then your card is marked well and truly.

They got me in the end, and they caught up with Tommy eventually. It took them four years before they could pull him in for armed robbery, for which he got 18 years. Backed up by his own total innocence, he never gave up fighting for justice. I was well pleased to hear that after serving six years his case was forced into review by the campaign group for prisoners' rights Justice, and he got the proper result – freedom.

My own freedom on that cold November day in 1980 was marvellous, and it went by in a daze. As always after a spell away, all I wanted to do was get into my own bath and soak away the months of misery. Barbara was right, Aylmer Drive was like a castle under siege with reporters flashing chequebooks. I've got to take my hat off to her, after all she'd done for me up until then, she did a bit more and cut a great deal with one of the papers for an exclusive worth around £55,000.

On the second day away from a possibly 20-year sentence, Barbara took off on her travels again to start a pantomime season in Blackpool. In the past I would have been gutted, but with Sue on my mind it suited me down to the ground. It was lovely to pick up where we had left off, and I was over the moon that nothing had changed while I had been away.

Other years I'd always dreaded that period. Me and Barbara always managed to spend Christmas day together, but that was it. The rest of the festive season I spent on my own or being gooseberry at parties and New Year celebrations. I'd meet up with old mates and their wives and get tired of them asking, 'On your own again, Ron?' I'd made a joke of it, 'Yeah, got rid of the old ball and chain – I can do what I like.'

The truth was I didn't want to do what I liked. I wanted to be like everyone else and share my life with the woman I loved. With Sue by my side I suddenly realised what a proper married life could be like. Odd, really, considering we were having a top-secret affair. But all the time I was with her, it never felt wrong. It was like we were made for each other.

The way we had to share our time together and conduct ourselves was by no means ideal. Half the time I didn't know if I was coming or going. Lies, excuses and complicated stories about where I'd been all night or why I had to go away for a couple of days. God, what a tangled web it was sometimes. I had a feeling that someone had dropped a few heavy hints to Barbara that some other woman was lurking backstage, but apart from some funny looks and the occasional dig, she never really made anything of it.

A lot of married blokes get complacent and let themselves go. They slop around unshaven, wearing the same shirt for days; why bother, no need to impress the old woman is there? Overnight, they smarten up, dig out the best gear and slip out smelling like an aftershave counter. Result, her indoors catches on that he's over the side in two minutes. Me, I've always looked after myself and taken a pride in my appearance. Didn't matter if I was lounging in front of the telly, or going to one of Barbara's opening nights. I was always smart so I had no fears in that department that she would cotton on to what I was up to during those times she showed herself at home.

Sue had bought and moved into the flat in Edgware that she'd spoken of when I first met her. And as Barbara had recently decided to put Aylmer Drive on the market I thought it would be a nice idea to wangle a move closer to her. Barbara dragged me down to look at a property in, of all places, Windsor. It was a beautiful house, but with my own ideas in the back of my head, I made all kinds of excuses and talked her out of it. So as a stopgap, because the sale was going through of Aylmer Drive, we settled for renting an apartment in Hendon Hall Court – Edgware.

Later on a lot of people with nothing better to talk about, suggested that I set Sue up in a little love nest just around the corner – nice and convenient for randy Knight – but she was living there long before me and Barbara. I loved going round to Sue's flat. She was a wonderful cook and used to prepare cosy suppers just for the two of us. Afterwards we'd enjoy a nice romantic evening, and it would bring home to me just what I'd been missing for so many years.

To be fair to Barbara, she wasn't backward in the kitchen. When she was around she could knock up a meal that was as good as, and sometimes better than, my old Mum's. Difference was, she was rarely around. That's why, when we lived in Stanmore, she hired a male housekeeper and other staff, which for me, from a very ordinary working-class background, made my home seem like a hotel. That sort of thing is all right for the toffs – they just ignore the hired help – but when you're not used to it you feel you should tidy up behind yourself and be on your best behaviour all the time.

The longer Barbara was away, the more difficult our relationship became on her trips home. To be honest, it was a strain. We were becoming strangers. The atmosphere got so bad sometimes, I'd just take off. By the time I came home, she'd be getting ready to disappear again, so we were going round and round in circles.

One weekend I took Sue to a restaurant well away from prying eyes, somewhere in Ruislip. We had a meal and were just having a brandy before leaving when three fellas approached our table. I gave them a nod, as I've said before, what with being in the papers quite a bit I was used to strangers coming up for a chat. One of them said, 'Ronnie Knight?' I said, 'Yeah, that's right,' wondering what was going on. One of the others said, 'Well, you'll know what this is for,' and punched me in the face. I tried to get up and have a go, but the other two pinned me down in my seat, while the same guy gave me another couple of punches to the head.

Then they were all at it. I couldn't move, and they were raining blows at me. Sue was screaming and trying to pull them off, and all I could do was take it. It was all over in minutes, but in that time they made a bloody mess of me. As they walked away one of them turned back and said, 'You was fucking warned.' Bastards! – then the penny dropped. This was over a business deal that hadn't gone the right way for the other side. In this game you win some, you lose some. This one I lost.

Why I didn't stay the night with Sue and get myself presentable I don't know. There must have been some reason why I had to go home, so that's what I did. I must have looked a right state, and Barbara was all over me, fussing about and cleaning me up. Halfway through, the phone rang. She picked it up and all I could hear her saying was 'Who is this? What're you on about? No, you can't.'

When she came off the phone she looked a bit strange, but just said it had been a wrong number.

Later on I found out that Sue had been so worried about the condition I was in that she'd thrown caution to the wind and without thinking of the consequences, had telephoned to see how I was. God help me, the cat was out of the bag. Or was it? Our lives carried on the same as always, and that incident was never mentioned again between Barbara and me.

It gives an insight into Barbara's character that a while after, she sold the story of me being beaten up to a national newspaper. I don't know whether she was after money, publicity or just wanted to dig me out, but she turned it on its head. The way she told it was that I was given a good hiding by some of her adoring fans, who were upset that I was with Sue instead of her after all she'd done for me during the trial. If that isn't an ego and a half I don't know what is.

During our cosy evenings in, or on the long drive to Cambridge to visit her family, Sue and I would talk about our future. As we'd discussed in Brixton prison, I reminded her that the only way I could see an end to our predicament was for us to keep our heads down for a while, pull all the money in that we could and disappear to Spain where my villa was sitting empty. By selling all my interests in the clubs, plus my share of the house sale and the 50 grand from the papers, we could live very happily without any financial worries.

The 'other woman' is always out on a limb, and Sue was no exception. She would ask me if I was sure that that's what I wanted. Or was I like most blokes who wanted their cake and to eat it. Wife at home to run back to, as well as the fun and excitement of a bit on the side. I did my best to reassure her that she was all I would ever want, but sometimes I think she got a bit fed up with my apparent lack of commitment.

I don't want to make it sound like she was nagging me as though she was a wife already, but the way I was stalling, and my indecision about telling Barbara we were finished, must have been a constant pain for her. Of course I couldn't go on indefinitely, complaining that my marriage was a hollow sham and that there was nothing worth saving in our relationship, and then do nothing about it. And the day came when Sue hit the nail on the head. 'You haven't got the bottle to tell her, have you?' She was right, I didn't have. Not after what she'd done for me during the trial. I couldn't hurt her. She had come out of court telling everyone I was her life, so how could I take that away from her?

In more rational moments I told myself that all the touching lines were for public consumption, and that really she would be relieved if I made the first move and gave her an out. After all, the rumours about her were still flying about, so there had to be a bit of a flame with all that smoke. In the end I convinced Sue that I wanted nothing more than to spend the rest of my life with her, but that it would be best for us to keep a low profile while we settled our plans.

It was a shame to give up the clubs, but we were going to need the money, and there was no way I could keep an eye on day-to-day running from the villa in Spain. At that time I had my finger in varied interests all over the place. There was the A & R, my first and most fondly thought of club. Then I'd taken on the Tin Pan Alley round the corner. This was followed up by the eating place of the famous, Mr Kai's, a Chinese restaurant favoured by people like Joan Collins and Twiggy.

The billiard tables had been a good earner while they lasted. If a pub had a corner big enough to take a six by four, we'd shove a table in, then forget about it until pay-out night. 'We' was me and my old pal Freddie Foreman. In 1978, after he'd finished the ten years he got for the business over the McVitie killing with the Kray firm, he was looking around for some legitimate way to earn a few bob. So we got together on the tables.

We had to knock a few heads together every now and again, because it was a lucrative way of earning a couple of grand a week without working and a lot of likely lads were there before us, or thought they could muscle in. Times like that Fred showed why he had the name and the respect that he's got. Eventually the breweries caught on that they were being done over a sideline they could have for themselves, so we were ousted. Though not before Freddie was back on his feet, and I'd packed out the cubbyhole in Mum's larder with a nice pile of readies.

The Hillsdown in Finchley Road was a great success. Even better when, very much behind Barbara's back, I put Sue in to manage the place. And I do mean manage. She ran the place from top to bottom, making sure everything ran smoothly. She wasn't, as Barbara often comments, 'A common little barmaid'. Talk about bleeding snob. When did an honest day's graft behind a bar make any girl common? Considering how Barbara made herself famous it didn't give her a lot of room to knock anyone else.

Sue had a blinding idea to pull the punters in, and I had to commend her on her acute business sense. A pound for any drink on offer, anything from whisky to crème de menthe, all at a quid each. Every club does it now, but then it was very innovative. When I saw how well it was going and told her it was a brilliant idea, she said, 'Not so clever really. I can't add up – a pound at a time I can handle.' She was only joking, she was too shrewd to be otherwise – I think.

Anyway, I set in motion the sale of all my interests, though for the time being decided to hang on to my stake in the naughties. Funny really – 20 years me and Barbara had been together, yet I never felt I could totally confide in her. She knew all about what money I had coming in because I used her account, but as for the 'dirty' money we never discussed where that came from. Not sure why – just seemed easier that way. Me and Sue were together for five minutes by comparison, yet I told her all about the peepshow lark, even though I wasn't too proud of it.

I never had a bank account in my name at any time. Come to think of it, I never paid any tax or insurance stamps either. But that was never a problem because all the legitimate money went into Barbara's bank, through her accountants, Albert Fox Associates. They told me, at some time or other, that because I didn't pay any taxes personally, Barbara would be deducted extra to make up for it. So at least they wouldn't be banging on my door looking for money.

Living the sort of lifestyle I had most of my life, I was never surprised to find the law keeping a close eye on me, so when I found myself being followed it didn't bother me too much at first. I told Sue what was going on, and she laughed. 'Unless you've been up to something you haven't told me about, I think you're getting paranoid with old age.' I might have been knocking on the door of my 50s, but I wasn't that old.

After a few days some instinct told me it wasn't the police following me around, so then I thought back to Nicky Gerrard. He'd got it wrong and ended up with a couple of bullets in him, so I was extra careful. I came out of the club one day, got into my motor and drove off. At the same time a Jaguar pulled out of a side turning and stuck to my bumper like glue. Could have been a coincidence, and perhaps I was seeing too many shadows, but no harm in checking it out. I cut through the back streets and doubled back on myself. When I slowed down, so did the Jag. When I stopped, it slipped into the parked cars 50 yards behind me. I took off at speed, shot down an alley and cut through an empty factory yard. Once out into the main road I gunned the motor and looked in the mirror. Lost him. Whoever it was had definitely been tailing me, but he wasn't too clever, and I'd left him way behind.

Settling back I pointed myself in the direction of Edgware and headed for Sue's flat. Her mum, Margie, had been staying for a few days along with Sally, Sue's sister, and her lovely little baby. I was welcomed in, and it felt great to be part of that nice family. What I didn't know was that my mystery tail was a private detective, hired by Barbara.

He was a clever bastard. I thought I'd lost him, and he let me believe I'd shaken him off, while he'd kept me in his sights all the way to the flat. Clocking my red Honda sticking out of the courtyard, he got straight on to Barbara and blew the whistle. Unaware of all that, I enjoyed a bit of tea with Sue's family before they headed for King's Cross to catch a train back to their home in Cambridge. They picked up their bags, and we stepped out of the front entrance to be confronted by a small female wearing trousers, dark glasses and a scarf round her face.

Here was every man's fantasy turned into every man's nightmare. It was Barbara without the big smile and the bigger giggle. I made some inane remark like 'It's not what you think. We're just going to the station.' Her reaction many years before, when she had found out that I had forgotten to mention a wife and small daughter, was nothing compared with how she blew up. She'd learnt a complete new vocabulary of obscenities in those 20 years and gave me every one of them, some twice. At least she didn't go for me with her nails. I wanted to die of embarrassment.

Everyone within earshot came a bit closer for the show. It was a terrible scene, especially in front of

Sue's mum, who was doing her best to pretend it wasn't happening. Then Barbara went for Sue, and they ended up slapping and pulling each other's hair. I pulled them apart, shouting at Barbara to pack it in and told Sue to jump in her mini and take her mum and sister out of it.

Barbara screamed and swore at them until they were out of sight, then she turned back on me. 'I should bloody well kill you.' She looked as though she meant it, but lucky for me the cab driver who had dropped her off chipped in for his fare. As I paid him off, he said quietly, 'I wouldn't want to be in your bleeding shoes for nothing, mate.' Nor did I, but I had to face it.

We got in my Honda and set off for home, with her sitting in icy silence, red eyed and puffy faced. If anyone had pointed a camera at her then she'd have murdered them. She said, 'We're finished – after this little lot, it's all over.' I didn't answer, but inside I was feeling relieved. Relieved that it was now out in the open, and the responsibility for actually saying the words had been lifted from my shoulders. I wished the present revelation hadn't come out in such a dramatic way. Being naturally reserved and a bit shy, to have my dirty linen scrubbed clean out in the street was one of the most humiliating experiences of my life, yet I only had myself to blame.

I'd had a thousand opportunities to come clean in the privacy of our home, but no. I always thought that tomorrow would be a better time. And if I hadn't got the stomach for that bit of honesty, I could have pulled the plug during one of our many arguments. I could have accused her of playing around with half a dozen blokes and quoted various snide write-ups in the papers. Then, playing the injured party, I could have walked out.

I could have brought up the fact that she was always working away – I could have said I'd had enough of it, which I had anyway, jumped up and down in temper, thrown a tantrum or two and stormed away. Gutless yes, but a lot easier than the more civilised, 'Sorry, Barbara, I love you, but I love someone else even more. Thanks for the 20 years – I'm leaving you.'

All that was immaterial as we drove home with her sniffling into a handkerchief and me gripping the steering wheel until my knuckles went white, waiting for another outburst. When she finally spoke she sounded hurt and dejected. 'Oh, Ronnie,' she said, 'how could you do this to me? After what we've been through, why did you think you had to kick me in the teeth?' That struck home, but having come that far I wasn't going to back off and be the whipped husband.

'What do you bleeding well expect? You spend most of the year in some hotel room, it was bound to happen.' She tried to chip in, but I went on the attack. 'You never gave me a second's thought when you were chasing every bit of work going. I'm only human, I'm not something you can just stick in a cupboard and forget about until it suits you.' I went on and on, pouring out all my frustrations that had built up over the years, and she sat and listened, too stunned to argue back.

By the time we reached home there was nothing left to say. We walked here and there picking up magazines and putting them down unread; straightened up cushions and fiddled with anything that came to hand. Avoiding each other's eyes and keeping enough distance between ourselves so that there wasn't even the chance of brushing sleeves as we passed in our aimless tour of the room. I'd expected a rerun of her previous explosion; the nails, teeth and every swear word she could remember. Instead Barbara was withdrawn and quiet. If Sue had been a quick leg over, a bit on the side or a one-night stand, I could have been suitably chastened, said I was sorry and taken a bit of stick for a week or two before it was all forgotten.

Women have a capacity for forgiveness that is part of their make-up. They know that most men are silly boys who want something they can't have, and when they get it they only enjoy it for a few minutes and are relieved when they get a smack from the wife and are brought back into line. No big deal! Part of life. This was different, though, and I think Barbara knew it.

The hours ticked by, and if she thought that I was going to confess to a mild flirtation and swear it would never happen again, the idea slowly evaporated. Until the tension got too much to bear. I wanted to say something funny, to lighten the scene up, but nothing came. I wanted the phone to ring or somebody to knock on the door – anything to break into that atmosphere. In the end I said, 'I think I should go to the villa for a while.' Without looking at me she said, 'You do that. Pack your bags and just clear off.'

I didn't feel like prolonging the agony by sorting all my gear out, so I said, 'Well, see you then,' and walked out. Perhaps I should have packed. I found out afterwards that my clothes followed me a bit smartish, through the window.

It was a strange feeling driving away with the thought that a part of my life was over. Out of love or not, it gave me a pang of heartache that what had been so wonderful was now completely over. I knew that it had been finished for a long time, but the 'out in the open' finality of it certainly made me think of the better times. The closer I got to Sue's flat the less I thought of the negative side of things and the higher my spirits rose. I couldn't wait to hold her in my arms and tell her that nothing could stop us from achieving our dream.

Considering the verbal – and slightly less physical – battering she'd taken from Miss Windsor, Sue was as chirpy as ever. When she talked about feeling like a stunt woman in *Carry On Girls* I knew she didn't blame me for what she'd gone through. We laughed, kissed and cuddled, and for the rest of the night talked of nothing but jumping on a plane and leaving everything behind us.

First I had to finalise the selling of all my business interests. Mick Regan and myself had sold off the A & R and the Tin Pan, Mr Kai's had also been sold, which only left the Hillsdown and the peepshow. Putting the Hillsdown on the market was less of a problem than I thought. When me and Sue turned up to do a stock check before doing the business, we found four Indian fellas measuring up and jabbering away at each other as though they owned the place. No wonder – they did own it! The bloke who I'd taken in as a silent partner had already sold it for a substantial sum to these fellas for a takeaway or something. My kickback was £40,000, so I had no complaints.

All that needed tidying up after that was the naughties. I gave French Lou a call and told him I was pulling out and going to Spain. He wasn't surprised because he already knew about the situation between Barbara and me. He just said, 'Leave it for a few days, then come and see me.' When I finally called in to his office he handed me a sports holdall and told me, 'Count it if you want, but you've got 60 grand there.' What more could I ask? For well over 12 months my stake had earned me a steady thousand pounds and more a week, and now he'd given me double back. I was well pleased.

He asked me when we were off, and I told him Sue just had a few papers to sign over the sale of her flat, and we were going in a week and a half, two at the most. He said, 'Well, come and see me before you go, and I'll have another little present for you.' Knowing how sentimental these Frenchmen can be, I guaranteed he was having a watch engraved for me: ALL THE BEST FROM LOU or whatever; so you can imagine a week later when we had a meal together, how knocked back I was when he handed me a Selfridges' carrier bag and said, 'Little going-away present for you.' Then he said, 'I'm going to tell you something now.' 'What's that mate?' I asked, expecting a tearful goodbye speech.

'I never mentioned this before, but you'll remember I told you to keep away from the peepshow place? Well, we had a third partner, and he was a high-ranking copper.' I couldn't believe it – me doing business with the law's top brass. 'Why didn't you tell me?' I asked. He threw his hands up like Frenchies do and answered, 'If you'd known you wouldn't have come in on the deal. On top of that the copper didn't want you anywhere near the place. What he said was, "Tell Knighty to keep well away. If my people catch sight of him they'll think if he's involved, the place has got to be worth a spin." ' Would you credit it? Lou wouldn't say no more about this top copper because he was still on board, and as Lou commented, 'Ronnie, what you don't know, nobody can force out of you. That's why you've got such a handsome payday.'

As I was leaving I picked up the plastic bag, and he asked, 'Don't you want to have a look at your present?' 'Look at it? I can hardly lift it. What you stuck in here, a bomb?' I replied. He laughed. 'That's your bonus – £50,000 in notes.' I looked at him and said, 'Are you joking me?' 'No joke, Ronnie. I've already got a third man bought in – that's your whack. You deserve it,' he answered.

I read somewhere that Benny Hill used to walk around with a couple of grand in a bag. What would the papers make of me with that lump swinging from my hand? I didn't hang about, I shot straight down to my Mum's place at Redbridge and stuck it in the hidey-hole. One way or another there was one hell of a lot of dough going through Albert Fox Associates.

I kept a nice healthy bundle back, but all the rest, including my Sue's £40,000 from the sale of her flat, went as usual to Barbara's account through her accountant Albert Fox. He was a proper whizz kid with finance. He put money everywhere to earn the interest – most of it abroad to places like Israel, but I never questioned what he did with mine. He looked after it, and that's all I knew or wanted to know about it.

With Sue by my side, arriving at the Villa Limonar that April 1983 was like coming home. No matter how often I went to the villa it never failed to fill me with pride, and I blessed the day we hired an American architect to design the place. Four enormous bedrooms, a beautiful lounge and a large, fitted kitchen. Outside, beyond the terrace, was a tidy lawn, veg garden and, a must in this climate, a 30-foot swimming pool. The view was breathtaking, and the sun bathed the whole place all day long. Not bad for an East End lad. A long way from Arcola Street and working with the smell of horse's sweat up my nose.

Neither of us were strangers to the Costa. Sue had been there before we got together, and as I'd owned the villa since the mid-seventies, I'd already laid a fair bit of groundwork in getting to know the people in that close-knit society, as well as dipping my beak in a couple of ventures. One was a part share in a bar named Wyns and the other was a stake in a car-hire company with Big Bill. So what with the money I'd invested through Fox's, my own nest egg and three or four hundred a week coming in from those other sources, we could live like a king and queen. I never once missed the old days of being a club owner. It had served its purpose and earned me fortunes. But that was the past, this was a completely new chapter.

Funny, when I think about it. If I'd got commission for every Londoner I'd introduced to the delights of the Costa del Sol, I would have earned fortunes from that as well. You know how it is. You find something that suits you – a car, nice restaurant, even a decent book you've read – you want to share it. It's not enough that you have enjoyed whatever it is. You double your own pleasure when friends say, 'You were right – absolutely brilliant.'

Well, I was like that with Spain. Every time I came back from a trip I couldn't stop talking about it. Anybody who stood still long enough got the works. The complete verbal tour, finishing up with my fanning out snaps like a pack of cards. I'd let friends take a rent-free holiday in the villa, when I was at home in England. They loved it as much as me, so next thing they're buying plots or apartments all along the coast. Happens all the time, no matter where people take their two weeks. As usual, though, this has to take on a sinister aspect when it's applied to me and my mates, but I'll come to that.

Sue loved everything about our new life. The sun, walks in the mountains behind Fuengirola, lazy days on the beautiful beaches and in the evenings romantic barbecues with a couple of bottles of wine, watching the sun disappear into the sea. She told me that she never wanted to leave – ever.

What a contrast to Barbara. I'm not going to start knocking her just because she was old news. She loved the place as much as I did, and before things turned sour we had some wonderful times, which I have fond memories of. But she was always looking to go back to England. She hated being out of touch with her manager, agent and every other Tom, Dick or Harry who might offer her some work.

I used to say to her, 'Don't these people know how to use the fucking phone?' Then she'd be off, wailing that she wouldn't be able to get back fast enough if it was a rush decision. Always terrified in case some other less talented cow got the job that was made for her. Half the time she spoiled things for me, what with her moods and moping around. In the end I'd say, 'I don't know why you don't just pack it in and go home.' Two hours later she'd be jumping on the plane at Malaga airport, and I'd be left kicking my heels.

I might have said this before, but, even if I have, it's worth repeating. Whenever things are all lovely, and I think that my life can't get any better, a fly lands smack in the middle of my ointment. It all started sometime around autumn 1983 when me and Sue were larking about like a couple of kids. I was chasing her around the villa, then when I caught her we had a playful wrestle, screaming and laughing enough to piss the neighbours off. While we were rolling about I felt a sharp stabbing pain in my back that made me cry out.

To cut a long story short I was in agony a lot of the time after that but too frightened to go to the doctor. After my childhood experiences I was no great lover of the medical profession. I might have suspected what I was suffering from, but I didn't want it in black and white.

Sue took it on herself to ring a doctor friend of hers, who advised we return to England to see a specialist immediately. When Sue was out – always the coward – I gave Barbara a call for the first time since I'd walked out of her life that spring. Some young bloke answered and passed me over to her. I wasn't in a position to poke my nose in, so though I wanted to know who he was, I never mentioned him. Nor did she. All I said was 'Are you still paying that health-insurance plan for me?' She said, 'Yes, it's still up to date.' 'Good girl – well, give me the number of it.' She did, and that was that. Twenty years and we're total strangers.

It wasn't as though I was short of a few bob, but as we'd been paying out good dough for years, I thought I might as well get some of it back. I made a few calls and a few days later flew back in October '83 to see an orthopaedic specialist at Harrow Hospital. I got the works. Dozens of X-rays, pulled this way and that, and purple dye injected into my spine. End result? Go under the knife or take my chances on being crippled again. I was warned that the operation to fiddle about with the fourth and fifth vertebrae in my spine would be long, very delicate and not without a certain danger for me. Though having suffered a number of painful attacks, even while attending the hospital, I was past caring.

I told them to go ahead. If I didn't wake up from the anaesthetic, well, I wouldn't know nothing about it, and my agony would be all over. Obviously it was a success, and in weeks I was almost back to my old self. For a couple of months I had to wear a surgical collar, and it drove me bloody mad. It was heavy, it itched, and it half strangled me. Little did I know that something that had happened six months earlier would eventually put something far worse round my neck. And it wouldn't come off as simply as tugging a strip of velcro.

10.
Two Crimes
of the
Century

ON EASTER MONDAY 1983 heavily armed raiders had broken into Security Express headquarters in Shoreditch, overpowered the guards and lifted seven million in cash. When I'd first heard it on the news I was still living with Barbara at Hendon Hall Court. At the time I couldn't help smiling and thinking to myself, Good on you, lads – what a tickle. That had nothing to do with me knowing most of the faces in London nor having mixed with the criminal fraternity most of my life. I saw it as every other ordinary punter did. A fortune in untraceable notes, no one was hurt, and they got clean away. It was stuff that even the most law-abiding dream of.

Come on, how many people imagined finding one of those sacks of money that were scattered all over the place after the Great Train Robbery? What about that manager bloke and his secretary who handed in thousands that they found while taking a short walk in the woods on the way to work? Mugs or what? You could hear ordinary people in pubs and clubs going, 'I'd have kept hold of it. I wouldn't have given it back. It's not like it was some old girl's pension.'

What they would actually have done if presented with the situation is another matter. The point I'm making is that we all like to see somebody get one over on the system. A bit of cheek, a load of nerve, and those guys are set up for life. No one shot. No one with a busted head and the only loser the insurance company, and that's part of the risk they take for getting fortunes in premiums. Lloyds put up a reward for information to the tune of half a million quid, so the raid hadn't bankrupted them.

Today's news is tomorrow's chip wrapping, and the robbery soon got wiped off the pages by whatever else was happening in the world. But it came back to haunt me two years later when my brother Johnny was arrested, picked up on the word of a grass. I was stunned. I didn't know what to do being out in Spain, so I phoned my other brother Jimmy to see if he could shed any light on what was going on. I spoke to my nephew Jimmy Jnr, and he told me that his dad had been nicked as well.

What had happened was the police had been knocking on his door looking for him. He was on holiday at the time at his place in the Algarve. When his son phoned and told him about Old Bill he jumped straight on a plane and returned to England to see what it was all about, and was promptly arrested and charged with receiving money from the robbery. A guilty man would have kept his head down and said, 'Sod it. If you want me, come and get me.' But Jimmy never did, he didn't hang about to sort his story out. Two minutes and he was winging his way back to face the law.

My instinctive reaction was to shoot down to Malaga airport myself and help my family while they were in trouble. Then, I thought, Hang about, stands to reason after my acquittal on the murder that the law will want to get their hands on me, so what better reason? They did it to Tommy Hole after his cousin Nicky was murdered, so I could expect the same treatment, and that wouldn't do anybody any favours, least of all myself. I was completely out of touch and creased up with frustration.

I rang Barbara and asked her to do whatever she could to help them out – even give evidence in their favour if she could. Diamond that she was, she agreed. No time to bear grudges when your family are facing years of incarceration. After all, just because we were no longer together, they were still her family.

On 6 June 1985 Jimmy was sentenced to eight years for handling. Billy Hickson six years. How the fuck he got involved I couldn't imagine in my wildest dreams. And little brother Johnny, the kid we shoved through the fanlight of that cafe, pleaded not guilty but was still handed out 22 years for being the mastermind behind the whole affair.

Result for the law or not I have never accepted Jimmy was involved. He was a very wealthy man, probably worth nearly as much as what was nicked. His interests in the scrap game were so good he even had his own railway, shipping metals up north for smelting. He had a 30-acre leisure complex in Stanmore that Ladbroke had offered him three million for. Ask yourself, why would a bloke in his position and at his age want to get involved in armed robbery and villainy? The case against him was that the police had found ten thousand in his safe, after being tipped off that he'd been given a share. Ten grand. It had to be a joke. He was taking more than that every week from all his enterprises.

I didn't know much about our Johnny. In our personal lives we were very close. The whole family always had been. But when it came down to earning a living, he knew as little about me as I did of him. We didn't live in each other's pockets. You must know how it is yourself. If your family lived hundreds of miles away, you don't give them a blow by blow account of everything you get up to. And if Johnny had been planning and executing one of the boldest robberies ever, why would he confide in anybody – brother or not? After all, there wasn't only himself to think of. There were all the chaps involved. And if it was run on the military lines that it was alleged, then no doubt they were all aware of that army saying, 'Loose talk costs lives'. Or, in their case, certainly freedom.

In case you never got round to reading the acres of newsprint surrounding the job, or have been on a desert island ever since, I'll fill you in on what went down over that Easter weekend in 1983, most of which I pieced together from sources I cannot name. What I would like to stress very strongly is that nothing I know about the robbery came from first-hand experience.

As far as Security Express were concerned, their premises in Curtain Road weren't known as Fort Knox for nothing. It was their HQ and a showpiece for a company that prided itself on handling millions of pounds every day. They thought they had got it sewn up tight with all the latest gadgetry in electronic surveillance. The four-storey building was a fortress with cameras bristling from every angle. It had steel doors, tungsten bars on the windows and surrounding the whole lot a 15-foot high wall. Short of a nuclear attack no one could enter without being invited. That might have been the case for a year or two after the high-tech installations, but nothing lasts for ever, and with cutbacks and lack of maintenance, things were not quite what the firm thought they were.

The idea of robbing the place came about, as many brilliant schemes do, by sheer chance. A relative of one of the chaps worked for Security Express installing security cameras and other electrical bits and pieces. He had married into a family of East End villains, but he was straight as a die himself, wouldn't even nick a bit of cable for a private job. Naturally he talks about his work. How he's pissed off that his overtime has been cut, and the place isn't what it was down to lack of maintenance. He's no fool, so he says nothing that might compromise his firm. However, little titbits he unwittingly gave out in front of his wife's family, which he no doubt thought were of no consequence, were soon picked up by one of the relations.

This fella, giving the impression that he's completely disinterested in the conversation, made a mental note of every little gem concerning Security Express. A bit here, a bit there, they all add up. Security's a shambles – camera blind spots all over the yard, exterior light bulbs blown and not replaced for months.

From those little seeds of information a plan was formed that grew into a full-blown operation. Afterwards, newspaper conjecture had it that the planning stage took 10 to 15 years, that people were planted inside the firm, worked their way up into a position of trust, then opened the gate. God help us! The average villain doesn't want to hang about for 10 minutes once he's got a sniff, let alone 10 years. The way Johnny told it, 17 months observation was the maximum. During that period it was noted that business must have increased. The place was a hive of activity, with extra vans laid on and never a slack moment – except at bank-holiday times.

The hand-picked team had got hold of the keys to a vacant building adjacent to the Express yard. Taking it in turns, and Johnny pulled his weight, every movement was meticulously recorded from November 1981. With a flask, a pack of sandwiches and a pair of binoculars, each man could let himself into the empty property and log the comings and goings of the staff. At some point they marked down movements throughout every hour, every day of the month. Mind-numbing, but the possibility of earning a fortune when they pulled it off made it worthwhile.

All told there were 14 men involved. Every one was important, and each had his part to play. It was no good recruiting the best locksmith in the business if one of the observation team fell asleep on the job. Looking ahead, which is what it was all about, the next move was to note the registration number from the car of the head guard, Greg Consell. Being professionals, the team had no difficulty in tracing his home address through the Swansea licensing department. All they needed after that were some details about his family.

You'd be surprised what people will give away to a friendly stranger or how helpful they are when asked to fill in a survey. 'What dog food do you buy? Lovely. What's his name? Shep, ah, bet the kids love him. How many you got then?' and so on.

This didn't have to be done on the doorstep. Follow a woman to the shops, stick a form under her nose, and she'll spill her life story. Us British are so polite. All this info was written down and stuck alongside a photograph of Consell. Nothing was left to chance.

Letting other long holiday weekends slip by as they checked and double-checked, eventually they were confident that they couldn't be more ready and decided to go for it Easter Monday 1983. After a three-day holiday the place would be overrun with cash. While on the Monday, still being a holiday, security would be at its lowest. Not least because most of the staff would be thinking they'd be better off at home like most other people, and their minds wouldn't be so centred on the job.

In the run-up to that Bank Holiday the team continued to watch from the derelict building on a rota system. Security Express was not only observed from the roof skylight of the derelict building but also at ground level, where different members of the team would casually walk by Security Express's yard to check out what was going on. The gates were timed over and over again as to how long it took one vehicle, two vehicles or a convoy to leave the yard.

The City of London was a ghost town as always over a Sunday. Once the man on the roof gave them an all-clear signal, one by one the rest of the team drifted into the empty building. Once they were inside the nine men settled down for the night. If anything went wrong, the man up top could let them know, and they could be out of the building as quick as they got in. The man in the roof was in an excellent position. He had a clear view of anything entering Worship Street from City Road or from the junctions of Curtain Road, and anything entering Worship Street from the Spitalfields end of Bishopsgate.

The four remaining members of the team were employed as ground workers. Their job was to walk the length of Worship Street as far as Clifton Street, back and then across Curtain Road where it meets Appold Street and sometimes coming from Great Eastern Street and sometimes coming from the Bishopsgate end of Worship Street. All points of the compass were covered. To keep in touch with each other and the lookout they had worked out a set of signals similar to those used by racecourse ticktack men.

Another ploy that had been decided upon was that they would all affect accents when it was necessary to speak, and as most people can do a passable impression of an Irishman that was what they pretended to be. These chaps were not actors by any stretch of the imagination – they were professional villains – so you can imagine in the heat of the moment some of them slipped into their normal 'How's yer father?' One of them could do a lovely Nigel Havers, and the papers made a lot of that afterwards. They just loved the idea that the gang was fronted by some posh 'Raffles' or James Bond type of character – it gave the story a bit extra. Load of cobblers really. They were calling each other Paddy One, Paddy Two and so on to add weight to the pretence they were IRA.

According to Johnny, the tension as they waited in that building was unbearable. The minimum of conversation had to be carried out in a whisper, and that was a strain in itself. By 2 am most of them had dozed off. That's what you call professional. I'd have been climbing the walls.

From what they'd learnt about the set-up in the yard, everything hinged on a single pint of milk. They say it's good for you, but it wouldn't be for Mr Greg Consell. Comical, wasn't it? The key to picking up millions was a pinta costing pence. Normally the main security fella had himself locked safely inside the building. Only way in was by him pressing a door realease. But – and a very big but – when the milkman turned up and left a bottle at the main gate, the guard would leave his post to collect it.

The plan was to be in position to collect him at the same time. By five thirty all the chaps were awake. A quick piss was all any of them could manage, as none of them had eaten anything since Sunday breakfast so that bodily functions could be kept to a minimum. Keyed up, they lounged around the walls of the room while one man watched at the window giving a running commentary on what was happening outside. The minutes ticked by. There had been an overnight frost, and the place was freezing.

At six thirty they all sharpened up as the lookout said, 'That Consell man's just been let in.' Couple of minutes went by. 'Him and the night watchman are talking at the door.' Another wait. 'Right, he's out. Consell's gone back indoors. Let's go.'

As prearranged, each man checked his watch, and those that were going to do the business had a quick look at their new and unused shotguns. Two men were left behind as lookouts, the rest filed down the stairs, round the side and slipped over the perimeter wall. It might have been 15 feet high, but a kid could have climbed it. Once inside, each member took up his hiding place behind several industrial waste bins.

Johnny said that as he stood with his back pressed flat against the bin, his eyes were fixed on the three vans parked opposite him. Each one held a king's ransom in silver coins, just waiting for the turn of a key to deliver them to banks and building societies. The thought occurred to him then and tormented him throughout his prison sentence – why didn't they forget hanging about for hours to collar all those guards, just jump in the vans, drive out and be long gone?

Or why hadn't they thought of only taking the coins in the first place? It would have been safer, and the rewards would have been just as healthy. Half the amount of men could have pulled it off. And the risks always go up with the numbers involved. Bigger the team, bigger the chance of one of them falling down later. It was too late for a change of plan at that stage, so he put those thoughts out of his head, concentrated on what was coming up and waited.

The milkman came whistling up to the gate, put down the pint and walked away. They were all mesmerised by that little blob of white that they could see through the railings. Five minutes crept by. Then ten. Fucking hell. What was going on? Twelve minutes, and there was the guard strolling over to the gate as though he had all the time in the world.

Leaving behind him the main door to the Security Express building wide open.

They captured him and dragged him inside with no fuss at all. He was told to sit at his desk, keep his eyes on the entrance door and keep his mouth shut. Paddy Three crouched under the desk and pressed the barrel of a shotgun tightly into Consell's balls, and even though he must have been terrified, give him his due, he still had the bottle to question what was going on. No violence was used, but again he was told to button his lip.

All the team wore menacing-looking black balaclavas, except Paddy One. He wore a macabre plastic monkey mask, which must have looked frightening in itself – a grinning ape wielding a shotgun. Humour and instant death rolled into one.

While the others familiarised themselves with the layout, and the locksmith secured the keys to the vault, Paddy One put Consell straight. He told him that right at that moment two of the gang were parked two minutes from his front door. If he did anything to cause things to go wrong his family would suffer. Then he instructed him on what he was to do when the rest of the security guards turned up. Before each one came through the glass door, he was quickly to describe whether he was married or single, if he had kids and what their names were and even the names of any pets.

The scene was set. All they had to do was wait for the rest of the security staff to come drifting in. Fortunately they wouldn't all arrive at once.

Traditionally the holiday was an easy shift and also times were pretty elastic as long as the men turned in to oversee a handful of special pick-ups.

The first was expected about 12.45 pm. Four hours to wait and nothing to do but anticipate the action. At 10.15 am all eyes turned towards the telephone as it broke the silence with its insistent ring. Putting his fingers to his lips, the Havers soundalike picked up the receiver and confidently said, 'Security Express. Can I help you?' The others listened to his one-sided conversation, smiling to each other as it dawned on them what he was saying. 'Sorry, sir, we're rather tied up at the moment. I'm afraid not.' He grinned at the others, 'Yes, I've got that, we will make the collection as soon as possible.' With that he said goodbye and put the phone down. As it turned out they didn't take advantage of the pick-up, but it must have been a first where someone rang up and offered a lot of cash to an East End villain for the taking. That bit of cocky light relief eased the tension, and they were all more relaxed after it.

At 11.15 am Paddy Three changed places with Paddy Five. He was more of a bully and would do anything that needed to be done without a second's thought. Consell had one hand tied to the leg of the desk, and the other one they left free so that he could operate the entry button when the time came. Three hours had knocked any confidence and mild bravado out of him. He was convinced he was going to die. So much so that he appealed to Paddy One to allow him to write a last note to his wife and child.

Topping him was never on the cards. But while he couldn't be allowed to know that, at the same time he had to be calmed down in case he couldn't carry out his part in the scheme. Assuring him that he would only be hurt if he didn't cooperate, he was told that if he behaved he wouldn't need to say goodbye to his missus.

At 11.57 am precisely, Greg Consell did as he had been told and named colleague Taffy Jordan. He spilled out personal details as fast as he could, as Taffy buzzed to be let in. To him just another day, and he was completely unaware that Consell had a gun pressed into his belly held by a man under his desk, or that others were hidden behind filing cabinets. As the door slid back, he only had time to say, 'Morning, Greg – a bit parky out,' before being grabbed and blindfolded.

Over his earlier panic, Consell coolly did as he had been told and went through the agonising ordeal of leading his colleagues, who were also friends, into a trap like lambs to the slaughter. He only faltered once when he smiled nervously at security guard Sammy Alcock as he came through the door. Fearing he was trying to signal some unspoken message, he had the gun barrel shoved viciously in his ribs and was told to 'Keep a straight face next time, or I'll blow your fucking brains out.'

As each man walked in he was blindfolded, trussed up and laid on the floor out of sight of the entry door. Alan Grimes was the last to show, and he was given the same treatment. Consell was roughly pushed from his desk and on to the floor, and his hands were tied behind his back. A quick check outside through the windows, and they were ready to open the vaults. The locksmith, armed with the two keys to the vaults, just needed the two security guards who usually operated those keys as they had to be turned in a particular way.

Paddy One spoke to each trussed-up member of staff, asking them to signal if they were key operators. Nobody answered. It seemed like each man had more courage than brains. It was pointed out that they were being extremely foolish in risking their lives for the sake of money that wasn't their own. Still he got no response, so returning to the first guard he dragged him out of the line as if he was a rag doll. Pushing him on to the floor he doused his crotch and legs with lighter fuel. Then shaking a box of matches, he whispered to him, 'Name the two key men or you're going to fucking well roast.' The guard was paralysed with fear. This was all too much for the key men, and they shuffled forward indicating that they were the operators.

Their hands and feet were untied, and they were pulled over to face the vaults. All that remained was to crack the massive safes. The locksmith gave each man a key. Each guard was warned what to expect if the keys were turned the wrong way setting off the alarm. They both indicated one at a time that they fully understood, and, satisfied, the locksmith carefully watched each turn of the keys. In seconds the double doors were swung back revealing a fortune most people could only dream about. Bundles and bundles of cash lying about in full view, each one holding £25,000, and there was about 300 of them.

With time running out each man slipped into action, and it went like well-oiled clockwork. Three transit vans were driven up to the main doors, then using Express' van trolleys, the bundles were loaded on 30 or 40 at a time. As one was run out another was being loaded. Just 30 minutes was all it took to shift £7 million in used notes. I read somewhere that the gang were supposed to have trained in readiness for shifting a load like that. What did they have to practise with? Bags of sugar? Cement? Potatoes? Sounded a bit too much like hard graft for middle-aged villains.

With a warning to the guards still on the floor, that a man would be left outside the door for half an hour – 'So keep your mouths shut' – they got ready to move out. As an afterthought Paddy One told them, 'In case you feel like overdoing what you tell the police and anything goes wrong for us, just remember it will be Greg Consell's family that will take the can back. Think about it.'

At a signal from the lookout in the building next door, one of the gang pressed the button to open the electronically controlled gates and jumped in the last van of the convoy that drove steadily out of the yard and up Curtain Road to disappear without trace. Home and free and not a drop of blood spilled.

The weakest link in the strongest chain is the one that breaks it. The surveillance team and the chaps that carried out the actual robbery were the best, chosen for particular skills or their nerve under pressure. Unfortunately one of the outworkers wasn't all he should have been, and somewhere along the line he was going to break down. When the shit hit the fan Old Bill pulled in four areas of flying-squad detectives, in all close to 200 men.

I don't know why people do it, but the police got about 400 tip-offs with information about the robbery. I can understand it when the crime is violent or against kids and old people – I'd be on the blower myself – but when it's only money, what's the big deal?

Anyway, amongst these phone calls were some pointing the finger at John Horsley, with the result that the law put him under camera surveillance for eight months. Eventually John was pulled in, and once he realised that he was well in it, with photographs showing him associating with two other suspects, Billy Hickson and Terry Perkins, he coughed that, yes, he'd done a favour for Hickson by letting him use his house for storing and counting some of the money. Not only that but he'd also let him store money in his father-in-law's flat near Waltham Abbey. The law shot down to the flat and behind a false wall found £279,000 in notes, and by the marks on the wall soon worked out that the hidey-hole had originally held £400,000.

The last thing that John Horsley said before shutting up completely was that the money had been delivered in a white hire van. Now you might think that being a rascal himself John shouldn't have told the law anything, but he would have been under enormous pressure that day, and it's all credit to him that he said no more; didn't name names and accepted a charge of handling Security Express money. It was reckoned that my Jimmy threatened his family and that's why he never said anymore, but that was rubbish. Truth was John was no grass – unlike Alan Opiola who sung like a canary when he got a tug.

You'd think that the chances of tracing the hire van were nonexistent, but the law checked every hire company in and around London and not only found it but also discovered that Opiola had hired it on 6 April. Two minutes and he was in custody. Does he wipe his mouth and accept the price of the risks he took? No – faced with the threat of a twenty his arsehole went, and the bastard turned grass, or, as the other side put it, turned queen's evidence.

The man was a gofer. While the money was being moved around, counted and shared out, he ran around making cups of tea and fetching takeaways. The biggest job he had to undertake was buying a load of suitcases. So it was an errand boy who blew away what could have been the biggest unsolved robbery of all time. Again it was alleged that him and his family were threatened, so his wife and kid were put in a safe house.

For his part in the robbery he was given a mild three years, to be served in police custody, as opposed to ending up in a mainstream prison, where he would have got what was owing to him. After 18 months he was released, handed a nice new identity and promptly disappeared. Wherever he is he must shit himself every time the postman knocks. And so he should after what he did to my brothers and the others.

Though my John was keen enough to fill me in on what went down that day, he never put his finger on why he got involved in the first place. It wasn't that he wouldn't tell me, he didn't really know himself. He was a shrewd businessman and by no means short of a bob or two. I know if you're up for it, you've got to give it a go, but it cost him everything. Not only 12 years of his life but also his marriage and the most magnificent Bedfordshire country mansion in Wheathamstead that you've ever seen.

What you've got to remember is that a prison sentence doesn't wipe the slate clean. The insurance company that had to foot the bill in squaring up Security Express want their money back, or as much as they can get hold of. So they dig and dig into the background of the convicted person, looking for hidden assets, or anything that might have been bought with the stolen cash.

That was when I found their investigators knocking on my door at the villa. I didn't know whether it was the top half or the bottom half, but one way or another they were going to help themselves to the share they thought Johnny had in the place. That's why Barbara ended up in court swearing on oath that I had bought out Johnny's share from the proceeds of the sale of our house in Stanmore. Thank God everything had been done legally, and I was able to prove it. Otherwise they would have tipped me out on my ear.

The worst thing they did was to confiscate our old mum's bungalow. That lovely lady was well in her 70s and widowed. And those bastards nicked the roof from over her head. What it was, Johnny had bought it for her and Dad, but legally it was still in his name. So it was classed as a recoverable asset. Mum never really understood what was going on. After she lost her home she seemed to go into a shell and wasn't interested in anything or anyone. That business and nothing else started her on the slope towards Parkinson's disease, and ultimately the dream world of Alzheimer's.

What with both my brothers in court, then Barbara showing her face, it stood to reason that Ronnie Knight's name cropped up frequently in the proceedings. In fact the prosecution brought up my name so many times the presiding judge, Richard Lowry, got the right hump with them and openly said in court, 'Why does the name of Ronnie Knight keep recurring. Is he going to be charged?' Then he drew attention to an article in *The Times*, where it was reported that amongst those wanted for questioning over the Security Express and Brinks-Mat robberies were Ronald Knight, John James Mason, John Everett, Clifford Saxe and Frederick Foreman.

Sometimes our justice amazes me. The law can fit you up, stitch you up and fuck you up, and you can't do a thing about it. Then along comes a man like Judge Lowry, and, all credit to him, he was out for impartial justice. Pointing out those articles that could have sown prejudice in the minds of the jurors, on 23 April 1985 he stated, 'There are published errors. Neither Ronnie Knight nor the other four men so mentioned are wanted in respect of these proceedings.' How was that from one of the top men at the Bailey?

The Brinks-Mat job everyone was also putting my name up for at first came six months after the Security Express robbery, and the sheer breathtaking value of gold bullion stolen made Johnny's job pale into small change. Some £25 million was taken from Heathrow Airport in almost copycat style. Only this time, whoever was involved used force that was brutal.

One security guard was stabbed, another whipped with the barrel of a gun, and two were stripped naked, doused in petrol and callously told that only their cooperation would prevent them being barbecued. This little touch, which could have been read in any paper, is what linked the two jobs in everybody's eyes. The gang repeated almost exactly what had taken place on the previous Easter Monday. They terrified the six security guards into opening all the safes and strongrooms. Then inside an hour they shifted nearly 17,000 gold bars, plus many thousand pounds worth of diamonds. Like the Easter caper, they were long gone before the guards managed to shake off their gags and handcuffs, struggle free and raise the alarm. The whole country was shaken by the ruthlessness and audacity of the raiders.

And hundreds of miles away on his mountainside retreat, where I'd gone shortly after the Security Express robbery in March 1983, backwards and forwards as usual, yours truly was as staggered as the average punter. Later on I'd be more than staggered, I'd be bowled over, but right then no one was in the frame, and it was just something else to talk about, and life carried on as sweet as a nut.

11.
Britain's Most Wanted Man

I HAD MOVED PERMANENTLY to Spain with Sue in January 1984. Money was no problem to us there as my various interests were bringing in three to four hundred a week. Nothing like I had been earning as top man on the West End club scene, but then the cost of living was only a fraction of what it used to be. I didn't need yards and yards of expensive suits, which was just as well because I hadn't replaced the lot that Barbara had slung out of the window. I didn't need to. Dressing up in that part of the world meant putting a shirt on over a pair of shorts. Don't think I went all native, I still had a nice line in lightweight mohair, and enough of a more sober nature for trips back to London.

I was 50 years old, and, to be honest, the nightlife was beginning to pall. Gone were the nights of drinking and dancing into the small hours and getting rid of a few hundred notes at the same time. I'd never been a gambler, apart from having a flutter with my freedom when the right offer came up. I didn't smoke, and a drop of wine and the occasional lager were all I wanted. All in all my needs and expenses were comparatively modest.

When I first took an interest in Wyn's Bar it was typical of a lot of small places in Spain: half bar, half shop. Once I got more involved by being on the spot most of the time, me and Sue put our heads together and decided to extend the bar and move the supermarket over the road. In no time we doubled the turnover in both places.

Sue, who was never one for sitting about, made herself busy and earned a bit of pocket money by taking up window dressing. She found she had a right talent for that sort of thing and went all over the place setting up displays and prettying up the shops. I wasn't exactly working myself, unless you count keeping an eye on my investment as work, so I bought a load of tools and got stuck into a bit of do-it-yourself around the villa.

A lot of people have it in their minds that I was exiled from day one. That as soon as I first took off for the sunny shores of the Med with Sue in 1981, I couldn't come back. But Sue and me enjoyed life backwards and forwards for years before that came about. We were both close to our families, so every now and then we'd jump on the plane and do the grand tour. Get together at Johnny's or Jimmy's, over to Redbridge to see Mum and take her out for a treat, and up to Cambridge to see Margie and Bob, the in-laws.

I had more than enough spending cash in Spain, but if some deal came up that needed a bit more than I earned, I used to take advantage of our trips back to London to pop in and see Albert Fox and draw some money out of Barbara's and mine shared account. If I was tied up at the villa for whatever reasons and needed a bit of dough, Sue had authority to draw out whatever we needed.

Albert, ever the professional, always insisted that she produced a letter from me and a photograph of herself, before handing over the cash. Funny, really, a couple of times she went to his office she was told that Barbara had just left minutes before. I used to wonder what would have been said between them if they came face to face. Probably politely ignore each other, because after our break-up had settled down, and I broke the ice telephoning her about the health plan, we used to ring each other up for a chat. Not too often, but enough to say that at that time in the early 1980s there was no real animosity between us.

I wouldn't have changed my Spanish lifestyle for anything. It really was a dream come true. We had the best of both worlds. If I got a bit nostalgic about damp and drizzly days in an East End street, or the sight of familiar surroundings – no problem. The choice was mine to pop home. London wasn't home any more, but I never referred to it as anything else.

Then came the robberies in 1983, the trial, and my brothers being sent away in 1985. I don't want to make light of Jimmy's sentence, which to this day I don't think he deserved, but if you say eight years quickly, it doesn't seem so horrifying. Release a long way off, but you can see the end of it. But 22 for Johnny. It broke my heart. While he was on remand Barbara did for him exactly what she'd done for me in the past. She took him in meals, bit and pieces, and generally did her best to keep his spirits up.

She'd always been close to his wife, Diane, and, funnily enough, looking at the two of them you might have thought they were sisters. Both petite, blonde and lively East Enders. Johnny was a top-rate businessman and knew everything there was to know about the restaurant game. On top of that he knew as much about the pub business, what with being involved in quite a number. In particular The Fox in Hackney, where he was in partnership with our good friend Clifford Saxe.

Why I'm saying this is, when Barbara wanted a bit of unbiased advice, who better to go to for it than my brother. I mentioned some bloke answered the phone when I rang Barbara that first time, well, it turns out he was Stephen Hollings, pretty nifty sort of fella in the chef's department. The two of them had got together, and after a while they thought it might be a shrewd move to combine their talents in taking over a restaurant. Him doing the fancy cuisine that would pull the punters in for miles around and Barbara, with her name and bubbly personality, the perfect hostess.

So what John became, while sweating it out in the Scrubs, was an inexpensive consultant. Those two gained advice that must have been worth thousands of pounds, while Johnny had his mind taken off the terrible ordeal he was facing. Everything was lovely, apart from John's predicament. Him and Diane were really grateful for the effort and kindness Barbara showed to them both. Like I had, they thought she was an angel, and as far as they were concerned, her selfless act cemented an already rock-solid friendship. But when John got his 22, Barbara didn't want to know them anymore. I think it was all too heavy for her, and she didn't want to be seen offering comfort to a convicted robber and his wife.

If she'd explained that to Diane, she might have understood her need to distance herself. But that was too easy. Now, remember, she'd got a new man in her life, and they were talking of marriage. I was set up with my new lady, and, as I said, there was no aggravation between us. Then out of the blue, with all that water under the bridge, she accused Diane of having known that I was having an affair with Sue. She claimed that not only had Di betrayed her by not telling her what was going on but also had condoned it by going out with us for meals. True or not, what did it matter? They never spoke again.

As if she didn't have enough on her plate, it knocked Diane for six, hurting her badly. I wasn't one bit surprised. After that it was all downhill for my sister-in-law. She was hounded by the law, though in a way she couldn't put her finger on. They never approached her at all, but she was followed everywhere. She'd come out of the Scrubs after a visit, and they would tail her to the front door of her home. Anyone she spoke to was picked up for questioning about what they'd discussed. Reporters were hanging from the trees, and the insurance investigators were sniffing around. Inevitably, she had a breakdown, not helped by being advised to apply for a divorce so that she could salvage a few shillings from the wreckage. All the time she kept the worst of what was happening from Johnny. She must have been desperate to talk it out, but she considered how it would affect him so suffered in silence.

Johnny was suffering too. For the first eight years of his sentence, he was on the 'As'. That meant he was escorted everywhere in handcuffs, even out in the exercise yard. When he asked why he was being treated worse than a mass murderer, he was told that his brothers (me and Jimmy) had enough wealth and influence to arrange an escape. Even if it meant dropping into the yard with a helicopter. What did they think the Knight family were? IRA? Mafia?

They each had their own sentence to serve, and they did and came out on the other side. They are together again now and very happy. Though gone are the days of masonic dos, acres of beautiful grounds, priceless possessions and sunglasses to match the colour of their many cars. Now it's working hard for a weekly wage. But after all they went through, they've

got each other, and that's what counts in the end. All
their troubles have been and gone – mine started two
years after the robbery on 3 February 1985.

Someone handed me a copy of the *Observer*
newspaper. Not my usual cup of tea, so I might have
missed the article that was pointed out to me. The
gist of the piece concerned John Palmer, the wealthy
jeweller who, without too much to go on, was
virtually being accused of being the brains behind the
Brinks-Mat robbery. More than accused. While he
was on holiday in the Canaries, the law turned his
home over like a plague of locusts. They attacked his
mansion like ram raiders; digging up his floors and
attacking a 40-foot swimming pool with pneumatic
drills. After causing about £50,000 worth of damage,
they found nothing, and he was cleared of any
involvement.

Bad enough reading about it, but it was the
footnote that sent a shiver up my back. 'Other
Britons wanted in connection are Ronnie Knight ...'
Effin stroll on, I thought, this has got to be a wind-up.
I'd never even met the Palmer fella. Some confusion
might have resulted over another John who the police
also wanted to interview at the time. In fact they flew
out to Miami and dragged him back.

This John – John Fleming – I was well acquainted
with. He was from South London and not only a
regular at the A & R but also a smashing bloke who
never had a bad word for anyone. In fact, like that
razor advert goes, he liked the club so much he

bought it off of me and Mick. After the sale was completed I never saw him again, but a hint of smoke and there had to be a fire, so I was lumped in with him. Strangely, though, never by the Old Bill. They accused me of many things but, unlike the media, never so much as hinted that I might have been the man for the Brinks-Mat job.

That was the beginning, and from then on the media circus set out to create a legend. Cynics might suggest that if I was so innocent why didn't I go back and face my accusers. Sue a few papers for defamation, stand up in court on oath that I had nothing to do with it. What's innocent got to do with anything? If anyone imagines that lack of guilt is any protection, they don't know very much about the system.

First off there was my Jimmy. After what happened to him I was convinced I stood no chance of a fair hearing. Look at Derek Bentley. All right, he wasn't completely innocent – he must have been a rascal to have been on that Croydon warehouse roof in the first place – but he'd given himself up to the police a bit before his mate Christopher Craig shot and killed a copper. Did he get a fair trial? He was hanged anyway.

Even closer to home was what happened to Lenny McLean, stepson of my old business partner Jim Irwin. He was nicked on suspicion of murder, when the bloke he was supposed to have killed had died when the police had hold of him. Make what you like out of that. Lenny was found not guilty, and rightly so, but that didn't compensate for spending 12 months in

the Scrubs with a rec hanging over him. And that's
what I couldn't face again.

If I showed my face in England it was guaranteed
I'd be banged up straight away, while they sorted
through the ins and outs of whether I was to be
believed or not. If we're supposed to be innocent until
proven guilty, why do we have to suffer a degrading
prison term until it is actually proved? Still, that was
never an option I was going to put myself through.
There was no extradition treaty between Britain and
Spain, so I intended to sit tight and see what
happened next.

The headlines continued to roll off the presses.
Don't the papers love a colourful character to knock
up sales! And, like it or not, that's what I was. I
never set out to be Mr Media. I married Barbara
because I thought I loved her, not because of what
she was or became. That alone put me up in lights as
husband of. There was the fact that my clubs were
filled with all those interesting and infamous people.
Then the murder trial. It all added up to a certain
commercial appeal, and they milked it for all it was
worth: KNIGHT ON THE RUN; MOST WANTED MAN; ONE
OF THE FAMOUS FIVE.

So who were these five old lags, supposedly on
the run from justice? We had a lot in common, not
least that we were all from the East End and had
criminal records to our names. We all lived on the
Costa del Sol, and we were well known to each other.

Me? You know all there is to know.

Clifford Saxe? Out of Hackney, formerly the

landlord of The Fox in Kingsland Road, where, according to the law, many notorious crimes were planned, including the Brinks-Mat and Security Express robberies. Me and Cliff went back donkey's years. Right back to when we were raggedy-arsed kids roaming the streets. I got to know him well when we were both employed on the same scaffolding firm, and in better days we used to look back and laugh about how we'd earned a living 50 foot in the air with an icy wind freezing our nuts off. He was a good friend then and still is.

Freddie Foreman? One of the best-known South London gang leaders of the sixties and seventies, a good mate, and I'd never deny it. I've already said we did the billiard tables together, but before that he picked up the title of the 'Mean Machine'. Not to his face, though. It wasn't a joke why they called him mean, and it was nothing to do with putting his hand in his pocket either.

Fred was, and is, a very hard man, with considerable form going right back to the 50s. When I was with Barbara we often went out for meals with him and his wife, Maureen. And when, often as not, she wasn't around, I joined them on my own, and they welcomed me into their company. Since then we've had some good times together, except now I've swopped Barbara for Sue. Regardless of what the law thinks, or what the papers say, we've never done any villainy together. We are the best of mates, but he does what he does, and the same for me.

John Everett is another old pal of Freddie's. And

even 30 years since they went out of business, so to speak, he still has his name prefixed with Kray Twins' Henchman. And finally John James Mason, a former company director, who was cleared of conspiracy in the robbery on the Mayfair branch of the Bank of America. I threw in the James so as not to confuse him with John Mason, who brought down the corrupt porn squad in the 70s when it came out that he had been paying in excess of a grand a week to keep them off his back. Commander Ken Drury, one of my regulars at the A & R, was one of many who ended up inside.

On the face of it I couldn't blame the public for believing what they read in the papers, but if five acquaintances living near each other in sunny retirement suggests a conspiracy to keep away from the law in Britain, why not look at the hundreds of people doing exactly the same thing all around us?

I could understand that it might have seemed extremely suspicious if immediately after the robbery we had all descended on the Spanish coast and started buying property. That wasn't the case though. I had established myself in the villa years and years before anyone thought of turning over Security Express, and, as I've explained, the other chaps followed my example soon after. To even consider that we chose Spain because of its broken-down extradition treaty, credits us with a far-seeing imagination that wasn't in any of us. Anyway, how could anyone know that the treaty might not be put in place overnight? Would have all been for nothing then, wouldn't it?

Whenever the snappers pointed their cameras at me for a world exclusive, I was invariably suited up, sporting a golden tan and raising a glass of champagne to my lips. Being white or blue, the suits gave an impression of filmstar-like living, but I would have looked a bit out of place in a blue pinstripe. Everyone has a nice colour out there, and half the time my glass contained Perrier water. The image, plus the KING OF THE COSTA headlines, did nothing to dispel your average person's idea of me. Where were the cameras when I was scooping dog mess off the lawn at half-seven in the morning, bleary-eyed and with the suggestion of a paunch resting on the top of my shorts? A picture like that might have put the real me more into perspective.

For Johnny's sake I tried to keep my head down as much as possible, knowing that every time another 'Gangster' piece turned up in the news it wouldn't do him any good, or do anything to get him off that 'A' cat. It was all out of my hands. Slack day in the copy room, and out would come the Knight file.

Those 'living in luxury' photographs did nothing to show how the notoriety was affecting me inside. In fact nothing gave away my inner turmoil. There's a picture in my album that was on the front pages all over the country. The one where I'm leaving the Old Bailey after the murder trial. I look like I'm just stepping off a plane àfter six months' holiday in paradise, smiling and completely untouched by what I'd been through. Who says the camera doesn't lie? Inside I was eaten up with the aftermath of pain and fear. So no one, not even Sue, guessed that every time I opened the paper and read another false accusation about myself it was like a knife in the stomach. Not just nerves – a real physical pain.

During the daily run-of-the-mill business I kept a brave face on what I was feeling, but at night, with Sue sleeping soundly beside me dreaming her own dreams, I'd lie awake bathed in sweat. It was like an endless tape running through my head. What if my papers are not in order? What if they get me back? What if? What if? What if? Each thought wrenched at my guts, and I'd curl up in agony. That state of affairs couldn't go on, and it all came to a head one night.

Sue's mum and dad and my own mum, Nellie, were staying with us for a little holiday. Mum wasn't in the best of health, and nor was Bob. So me, Sue and Marge were going out for a meal, leaving the other two behind. That same day I'd heard a whisper that the police were planning to try to apply for extradition again, and though it was a regular threat it turned my stomach upside down.

Just before we were due to leave the villa I cried off, saying I would have an early night. Off went Sue and Marge, and after checking that Mum and Bob were comfortable, I toddled off to bed. A couple of hours later I desperately needed the loo. I put my legs out of the bed, and my head started spinning like a top. Every time I stood up I fell back on the bed. I had to get to the toilet, and the only way was to crawl. On hands and knees I made my way painfully to the bathroom. All the time I was thinking my time had come. They might get me back to England, but it would be in a box.

I never even reached the pedestal. I remembered trying to pull myself up on the bath, then I was out of it. I must have gone down with a bang because the next thing I knew Sue's dad was leaning over me. Game old man that he was, he managed to get up the stairs, despite suffering emphysema and the loss of a leg. What a state I was in. I'd been violently sick, and blood was running out of me like a tap.

I eased myself up with Bob's help, and standing by the bathroom door was my Mum, well into Alzheimer's and trembling with Parkinson's. Bob reassured her that I was all right, then struggled off to phone the restaurant where Sue was. By the time the ambulance got me to hospital I was down to my last spoonful of blood. With an injection on the way, I'd rallied enough to be vaguely aware of what was going on. One, a bloody great ulcer had burst in my stomach, and, two, they were getting ready with the blood-transfusion kit. Luckily I passed out again, and by the time I came to the surgeons had plugged the hole in my stomach and topped me up with nine pints of blood.

With my physical side put to rights, I had to concentrate on the mental side that had put me in that position. I couldn't do much about being what the *Sun* called BRITAIN'S MOST WANTED, but I could change the way it affected me. What's that bit of homespun advice? 'Give me the serenity to accept what I cannot change,' and so on. Unless I gave myself up I couldn't change a thing. So I adopted a new philosophy – Fuck 'em. Enjoy the life I nearly lost.

That might have been one of the reasons that decided me and Sue to tie the knot. Me and Barbara had been divorced for a couple of years, and she'd married young Steve Hollings. Shortly after they took over The Plough in Amersham, Bucks, I gave her a call and said I was genuinely pleased for them both, and she told me she was settled and very happy. Nice happy ending to a life that had seen too many ups and downs. There was no bad feeling between us and no unpleasantness at all.

On Thursday, 6 June 1987 we presented ourselves at Fuengirola Town Hall to do the business. Naturally word was out amongst the press that we were getting married, because we'd had to publish the banns with the British Consulate. They were stuck on the wall for three weeks, so it was obvious it couldn't be kept secret. Joke was, we put down Saturday as the big day so by the time the reporters were running about like headless chickens it was all over.

The town hall, courtroom and nick are all one big complex, and while we were waiting to be called in front of the registrar, the door opened and in walked about a dozen handcuffed prisoners and their escorts. What a picture that would have made. And what about the caption: KNIGHT WHERE HE BELONGS? Or KNIGHT WELCOMES WEDDING GUESTS? The press missed the whole thing, and I think that was about the only time I organised anything without it becoming front-page news.

The ceremony was as simple as we could make it. A few close friends and my old friend Ron Popely, ex-landlord of a Bethnal Green pub, as our best man. The proper knees-up took place a week later at the El Oceano restaurant, cum club and sports centre. Before we got down to the celebrations, we had a short blessing. This was done by the Reverend Matheson, and what annoyed me afterwards was that he came in for a load of stick because of what he did for us. He put them in their place by saying, 'Who am I to turn down a request for God's blessing?'

The reception was marvellous, and the guests had a great time, so I was satisfied that the few pesetas I had left out of ten grand was money well spent for a one-off day. I might have been inviting trouble and speculation in the wrong quarters by inviting Freddie Foreman, Cliffy Saxe and others, but stuff them all – they were my mates, and I wanted them sharing my celebrations. I knew the law had telephoto lenses poking through every door and window, and they would have loved to have snapped me giving any of those chaps a hug – a nice addition to their crime files. But I avoided giving them ammunition by politely blanking my friends when I knew we were overlooked.

It didn't stop the press making a fuss about my choice of guests. And they even went so far as to colour up the occasion by suggesting that train robbers Charlie Wilson and James Hussey were present. Of course they weren't, but it didn't stop them taking pictures of John Ashmore in the mistaken belief he was one of them. John is a straight and respectable businessman, and I'm happy to say he sued the arse off them.

At the end of the day our reception was like anyone else's. A bit more expensive perhaps, but nothing more than good food and good wine amongst wonderful friends. The news media turned it into a garish circus when they told it to the world. And it was all fabrication. The cake was supposed to have been in the shape of Wandsworth prison; I was supposed to have jumped on a table and sung 'Jailhouse Rock'; and according to them I uttered tiny gems at every opportunity like 'It's a fair cop,' or 'This is one sentence I don't mind serving.' Jim Lumley's got a video at home of the whole affair, and it shows that apart from the occasional 'face', it's no better or worse than any other couple's wedding day memories.

My £800 firework display? By the time it was in print the cost had escalated to £10,000. While the ten grand I spent on the whole reception reached in excess of £30,000. Mild stuff from what they usually wrote about me, so I didn't give a toss.

But back home it was giving Barbara the screaming abdabs. At least that's all I could put it down to when she went on the rampage with my character in a series of articles. A story is a story, and then the *Sun* didn't have a clue or care that she was using them to dig me out. God above! she cleaned me.

Her jealousy left no stone unturned. She said I was nasty, underhand, a two-timer and dirty rat. That was just for starters. She hinted darkly that there were things that only she knew of, and that one day they would come out. That while she'd stood up in court and said I was pure white and shining bright, all the time she had been lying to protect a small-time villain, who didn't even pay the mortgage.

Worse was to come. She less than subtly suggested that I would be dragged home within six months and, as though she knew something I didn't, put it across that my time was well and truly up. I was proved right. Eventually she came out with what had started it: 'What makes my blood boil is that he sent £20,000 up in smoke.'

Christ! she put the price up double what the papers had. It all sounded very menacing to me, so I rang her up and asked her what she was trying to do to me. She made light of it. 'It's only a story,' she said. 'Only a story?' I replied. 'What's all that about me being pulled in then?' 'That's them twisting what I said after I made a statement to the police,' she responded. Just what I needed – my ex-missus doing a Gerry Knight on me.

She went on to say that the police had asked her to go to Leman Street station in Aldgate, tell everything, anything at all incriminating, that she knew about me, and that she'd be looked after; given protection when they got me back. I couldn't believe what lengths they'd go to. It was getting out of hand. Now they were sowing seeds in her mind that there was a possibility that I might hurt her.

She went on to say, 'The statement was only a few pages, and most of that was about where you were on the night of the Security Express robbery.' 'Well, you knew where I was,' I said. 'Did you tell them?' She said, 'I told them I couldn't remember – you were always all over the place, I couldn't be sure.' Thanks a bunch.

Not long after the *News of the World* headlined me, stating: THE RUNAWAY PLAYBOY IS THE MASTERMIND BEHIND A SPANISH DRUG-SMUGGLING RING. Next an 'unnamed' senior detective was quoted as saying, 'If we can convince the Spanish authorities that Ronnie Knight is drug trafficking on the Costa del Sol, they may send him back.' It seemed like a fit-up to me. Were the papers cooperating with the police? Fortunately the Spanish police didn't take any notice of the red herring. I was never approached, and the detective failed to crop up again. But once more another nudge, nudge, rumour was tacked on to my name.

I was finding it difficult to stick to my resolution of not letting anything get to me. No matter what I did I couldn't get away from the publicity. Then someone else's problems took my mind off my own for a while. My old friend Siddy Smith was dying of cancer. I hadn't seen him for quite a while, though we'd had some good times together when he and his wife Betty were staying in their villa at Calahorda. Back in the UK, Jim Lumley, our close and old friend, was visiting him every day and generally looking after him. So many years had passed since me, Siddy, Poochie and Jim used to meet up at the salt-beef bar in Stamford Hill, then go round the pubs and clubs, it was a nonstop laugh. I've got to make it clear that like the other two, Jim was a pretty straight guy – I was the rascal. He was no angel, and as a young man was as slippery as anyone from that area, but perhaps he had a different way of looking at things because he saw what I didn't. What starts as a little bit of this and that ends up more serious, as I found out. He wasn't going down that road, so when he and Joy, his wife, started a family he bought himself a house on the outskirts of London and got well away from temptation. Must have worked, because he's never had a day's trouble.

Over the years Jim and Joy came backwards and forwards, treating my place as their own, and I wouldn't have had it any other way. They were a touch of home and kept my spirits up when other visitors from the old country turned up to harass me.

I was cooking some sausages on the barbecue one day when a helicopter flew low overhead, blowing dust and shit everywhere. I looked up and for a minute thought it was two helicopters joined together. It wasn't. It was that big fat bastard Roger Cook, hanging out of the side of it, trying to get a story for his TV show, *The Cook Report*. He had a loud-hailer thing, and he was bellowing in that poncy voice of his, 'Go home, Mr Knight. You are a wanted man.'

What I didn't know was he had a cameraman filming me in the garden. And that little clip he got went into broadcasting history. After that, every time I was in the news, up would come those half a dozen sausages.

I've watched him many times and knew that his

technique was always the same: wind up the victim, and with a bit of luck they'd lose their rag and take a poke at him. Then all he has to do is face the camera like a hurt little hero and, as he thinks, let the piece speak volumes about the 'nasty person' he is unmasking.

When he got round to trying to talk to me at the villa, me and Sue blanked him completely, and all he got was a shot of the dogs, the gates and my orange and lemon trees. Down in the town he went after Clifford Saxe. Being the ex-landlord of a tough East End pub, he'd learnt years before how to handle people who get out of order. He whacked him, and if he hadn't been pulled away he'd have given 'Cookie' a lot more. Thousands of pounds wasted on the hope of getting a world scoop.

It's just as well that I wasn't the crime boss of the Costa, because with the world's press and others on my tail all the time, I never got five minutes' privacy. Since I moved to Spain with Sue, all my supposed notoriety has had pound notes behind it, and it has all been down to the media. Anyone short of a couple of quid only had to pick up the phone, give the news desk a load of old nonsense, and without even bothering to check the truth behind the story, the paper would bung out anything from £50 to £5000.

Look at that fella who wheedled his way into my wedding celebration. I'm too bloody soft. So when he gives me a tale about being a friend of Terry Downes the boxer, who I know quite well, and wouldn't it be nice to have his photo taken with me, like a mug I agreed. Next thing the picture's in the papers, and he's saying he's a cousin of mine. Not only that but he tells them that I often pop home to England in a light aircraft and go to Epsom races and places like that. The papers probably guessed it wasn't true, but it made a good article.

I was the loser every time, because all these little bits added up to give the police and government the right hump. It might not have caused me much aggravation at the time, but one day the law would get its own back. In fact it was likely that a bit of coverage like that gee'd up the British authorities to put pressure on the Spanish police, and me and Sue found ourselves slung into the local jail.

Sue was out, and I was having a nap in the armchair, when the gate bell rang. As usual I ignored it. I didn't need another microphone stuck up my nose. It went on and on, and the dogs were barking, so I peeped out of the window, and there were four *policía* grouped round the gate looking none too happy.

Normally I would have pretended I wasn't in, but a few days previously we'd had a slight problem with our dog RJ, when he'd got overexcited with the local postman. He must have reported it back at the post office, and as a matter of form one of the local coppers had come out to make sure we weren't keeping a dangerous dog. He was quite satisfied, and I thought that was the end of it. Obviously not with those chaps ringing the bell. As I was walking out to open the gate I couldn't help thinking that if I was back home the gate would have been off its hinges by now.

Their English wasn't too brilliant, so while I'm babbling on about RJ with plenty of 'no problemas' they were looking puzzled and kept repeating, 'Pasaporte. Pasaporte.' It was nothing to do with the dog. Something was up. I don't think they grasped what I was saying, but I tried to explain that I couldn't put my hands on my passport at the moment because the 'Señora' deals with all that sort of thing.

They had a quick conflab with their arms flying all over the place, and next thing I'm whisked off to Malaga police station. On the way I was convinced I was going to be put straight on a plane, and breathed a sigh of relief when we turned away from the airport. I was stuck in a room and questioned with some difficulty, as both sides had problems understanding the other.

At home Sue was panicking at my disappearance, until our American neighbours told her I'd been seen being put in a police car. When I saw her walking into the station I thought, great, she's come to get me out. I was wrong – she was coming in to stay.

We were both put in a cell after being thoroughly searched. Sue wasn't too happy about that because they couldn't find any female officers to do the business. After a while Thomas Tuite, the British Consul, showed up and explained that at that moment he didn't know what was going on, but all would be revealed the following morning in court.

Considering the wealth along that Spanish coastline, the cells we spent the night in were like something out of *Midnight Express*. We were separated, but there was nothing to choose between the state of either of them. They were tiny, filthy, and the mattresses and single blankets were encrusted with dirt. The conditions were bad enough, but not knowing if this was the first step to deportation kept me awake all night.

Next morning we were both manacled and led into court to hear the charge against us: illegal aliens. That was it then, all done but the shouting. Some picture I would make at Heathrow when they dragged me off the plane. Unshaven, shorts and tee shirt and looking like I'd slept in a hedge. Welcome home, King of the Costa.

For some reasons the court proceedings were adjourned until the afternoon. At two o-clock, when we were escorted back in, the atmosphere was completely different. There were smiles all round, and we were told we could leave straight away. The police chief who, up until then, looked as though he couldn't wait to have us tortured, was beaming all over his face and asking us to share coffee in his office. I declined as politely as I could, and we were driven home to soak in the bath for about three hours.

Before we got inside the villa, we had to wade through a scrum of reporters and photographers. One cheeky bastard thought it was clever to jump in front of me, smirking like an idiot and saying, 'They let you out to pack for the home trip then, Ronnie?' I knocked him flying over the bonnet of a motor. He'd have got some more if Sue hadn't grabbed my arm and hustled me indoors.

What sorted it in the end I don't know, but it had been a close shave and brought home to me what could happen at any time. I've got to hand it to the Spanish authorities – they didn't usually take a lot of notice of the cobblers the British police spun them. Up until that one little misunderstanding, they always treated me fairly.

Thank God all that nonsense hadn't happened a month earlier in 1992, or it would have spoiled a dream that I'd had for many many years. Just 12 months previously Sue handed me the phone with a quizzical look on her face, mouthing, 'It's a woman for you.' 'Hello,' I said, and this voice replied, 'Is that you, Dad?' I couldn't speak for a minute, so she spoke again thinking the connection was broken. 'Is that my Lorraine?' I asked, and she laughed and said, 'How many other daughters have you got?' We both laughed then, and it broke the ice of all those years of silence. We talked and talked, and the outcome was that she and Jim, the husband I'd never met came out for a holiday the following year.

I was shaking like a leaf as I waited for Lorraine to arrive at Malaga airport. There were a few tears of happiness as we drove back to Villa Limonar. Lorraine loved it there, and I showed her my lemon and orange trees. I pointed out the sights, including Gibraltar, and then took her on a tour of the area. By then me and Sue had opened another club we'd called Knights, so I took her and Jim down there and introduced her to everyone. We were drinking champagne to celebrate, and everybody who came in was saying, 'What's this, Ronnie, your birthday or what?' I'd say, 'No, a hundred times better – this is my daughter and she's come to visit me.' It was a happy time, and I would have given anything other than a prison sentence to have got on the plane with them and gone back to England.

Interludes like that kept me going for months, then just as I'd start feeling a bit down Jim and Joy would turn up to take my mind completely away from my troubles. So what sort of troubles could he have say the people who get up at 6 am and graft their nuts off for a few quid? He's got all that sun, a luxury villa, beautiful wife, and the money comes in without getting his hands dirty. Yeah, I had all that, but I was a prisoner. In a gilded cage perhaps, but just as separated from familiar surroundings as though I was in the Scrubs.

My old mum had deteriorated so much there was no chance of her ever visiting Spain again, and she was being cared for in a nursing home. I couldn't bear to think of it, but it was likely I might never see her again. I couldn't pop in and see my grandchildren when I felt like it, and I couldn't visit my brother in his time of need. On top of that the club was getting me down.

A few years before, in the late eighties, we'd taken over an Indian restaurant called Montaz. We had some Indians running it, but we collected the profits. Right opposite was a club run by a fella named Paco. Me and Sue were always in there, and when we had a good crowd at the restaurant we'd end up taking them all over, so we were doing good business for him.

Sue came in one night and said she'd been talking to Paco; he wanted to give up the club and wondered if we might be interested in taking it over. I told her that the club game was well behind me now, and I didn't fancy it. She kept on about what we could do with the place and how it would be something to occupy ourselves with, so I gave in and went to see him. He said all he wanted from us was a bit of rent, so we did a deal on the spot.

After a good bit of redecorating, new gear and cut glass all over the place, we opened to a packed house. It was in the papers, and people came from everywhere. It went marvellously, so we had a nice legitimate business and were earning a decent honest living. It didn't make for sensational news, so those dirty bastards in the English press had to make our club look like a dive, with stories of fights and drug dealing. The very first night there was a slight brawl in the club next door. Nothing to do with us at all, but there it was in the papers: BLOODY BATTLE AT KNIGHT'S CLUB.

In any club where there is plenty of booze going down you are going to get the occasional upset. One night two blokes, a bit worse for wear, decided to mix it over some past woman trouble. I jumped in to separate them, and somebody put a glass ashtray across my head. I needed a couple of stitches, and that was the end of it. Headlines the next day went: RONNIE KNIGHT STARTS FIGHT IN CLUB AND GETS SMASHED TO PIECES.

Why did I let all that shit get to me? But it did, and I used to wonder if it was worth it. As an earner, it couldn't be bettered, but it was bloody hard work. I was like an entertainer on the stage until the small hours. If you've got a name and you use it to front a place up, same as Barbara at The Plough, you've got to be on the scene – that's what pulls a lot of the punters in. They want to meet the so-called gangster, and I had to be the affable host all the time. It was wearing me out.

I was in my late 50s, and though I wasn't ready for the pipe and slippers, I wasn't the man I used to be. The restaurant would kick out at midnight, and all the late diners would troop over to the club for a nightcap. Lovely business, but all these boys from back home and their wives then wanted to party until breakfast time. It got so that I was saying to Sue I didn't want to go in. Of course she'd say she didn't want to either, but someone has to do it – and we'd end up having a row. Don't forget she was half my age so didn't feel it like I did.

It got to the stage that I wouldn't show myself, and then the staff were saying 'Mr Ronnie, a lot of people came in, but you not there, so they have one drink and go somewhere else.' Sue hears that and goes up the wall about lost trade. I mean, if you're up all night you're completely shagged out all day. What sort of life is that? So I'd be at home, and Sue would be at the club until five or six o'clock in the morning. If she managed to close early, often as not somebody would suggest a party at their place, and off they'd go, and she'd be right behind them. I used to say to myself, 'Ronnie, son, it's getting like the old days with Barbara – always on your own.' It wasn't just that; other things were getting me down. Freddie Foreman had been pulled in by the Spanish police on some wind-up drugs charge. That came to nothing, but they found his passport was forged so they deported him. It took six of them to get him on the plane because he fought every inch of the way, but it was no good, and he ended up being nicked as soon as he landed in England. Result? Nine years for handling Security Express money, plus the dodgy passport. That didn't help my state of mind. Then one of my dogs died, and that just about finished me.

We both loved our dogs; Ellie and RJ were like the kids we never had. They had their own coloured rubber balls and believe it or not they knew exactly which one was theirs. They say dogs are colour blind, but they never got them mixed up.

One morning we went down the town, and we took Ellie with us. One thing she hated was rain, and we were only there five minutes when it pelted down. We did a bit of shopping, started back to the car, and Ellie was missing. We didn't worry too much as, with the rain, she'd probably run home as fast as she could – getting soaked on the way but heading for where she'd be safe. We got home, and she was nowhere to be seen. We both started to panic then. I ran up and down the mountain shouting my head off. I toured all the gardens and asked the neighbours, but there was no sign of her.

The next morning we went up to the top, where they were putting the new road from Marbella to the airport, and had a good look round. Waste of the time really because she never went to that part. Suddenly Sue screamed that from her side of the car she'd seen a dog lying in the road. I told her not to be silly and kept driving. When we got back to the villa I made some excuse and took myself back up to where she'd cried out. I drove up and down until I saw a dark body in the grass. I was frightened to get out of the car, then I told myself there were hundreds of dogs around the place, why did this one have to be mine? With that in mind I got out and crossed over to the furry bundle. I didn't have to look twice – it was my Ellie, and her head was smashed in. I'm not ashamed to say I dropped to my knees beside her, stroked her fur and cried my eyes out.

I put her in the back of the car, dreading Sue's reaction when she found out. It was what I expected. She screamed, 'Why Ellie? Why my Ellie?' and broke down completely. That set me off again, and we both cried. We shed a lot of tears as we buried her on our plot so that she'd always be with us. I had a headstone made, and every week we put flowers on it. She was six years old, and we missed her every single day.

If you think we were over the top sentimentally, all I can say is that you can never have known the pleasure and companionship a dog brings you. I was totally gutted, with that and everything else. I was drinking too much, and the white powder I was taking to give me a lift was turning me into a zombie. Right or wrong cocaine is enjoyed in Spain as a social pleasure. No real secret amongst friends. A little here and there to loosen everybody up. No harm in that, but I was overdoing it, and it was beginning to frighten me. What the hell was I going to do with my life? Daily I was sinking into the downward spiral of becoming a coke addict, a bastard drunk – or both. Then I got a call from an English journalist that cleared my head and told me what I had to do.

12.
Facing the
Music

THE CALL SOME TIME around December 1993 or early '94 didn't come from the journalist first off, it came from Barbara. We'd had a bit of an upset over what she'd said in the papers and about her statement to the police, but time had passed, and we'd got over it and were back talking again. Nothing special, just a chat when I rang her to enquire if I'd hit the jackpot with my premium bonds she still had.

She rang up and said a journalist wanted to come and see me as he had something to offer that might be of interest. Now those people had never given me anything but grief, but as Barbara vouched for him and said it was to do with a lot of money, I agreed that he could come out to the villa. Before the man arrived I spoke to some people and found out he was the guy who had done those articles in the *Sun* with Barbara. By rights I should have blanked him, but you don't whack the monkey if the organ-grinder upsets you, and it sounded like there was good money on the table, whatever his deal was.

He arrived at the villa with his wife, and I treated them both well considering who and what he was. The deal gobsmacked me. If I was prepared to give myself up to the police in England, the paper he was fronting for, the *News of the World*, would sort out all the details, fly me home and, for exclusive rights to my story, hand over £150,000. All I had to do was sign on the dotted line and put my hands out for the cuffs. Heavy stuff. I didn't say yes, and I didn't shut the door on a possible deal. I said I'd have to run it past my Sue and consider all the angles. He understood that, and off they went.

I'll be the first to admit that I've done some silly things in my life. I've done them on the spur of the moment, without thinking, and paid a heavy price. But right then there was no way I was going to put my freedom on the line, even if the reward was almost exactly half of what the law alleged I handled from Security Express.

I needed advice so I turned to a friend of mine, Barrie Tracey. He was a journalist as well, though not one of your knocking-on-doors, digging-the-dirt type.

He had a good business with a news agency in the north of England and another in Malaga. He'd approached me a long time before over some other business, and me and Sue had become good friends with him and his wife Pat.

Tracey said that if I was serious about making a move I should give the deal with the *News of the World* serious consideration by approaching them directly. I still hadn't given the whole thing too much thought, but there was no harm in testing the water, so I told him to go ahead and see what he could come up with. I knew that the *News of the World* wasn't his favourite paper because some years before a deal he had set up with a previous editor went pear-shaped and he decided to sue them. Even afterwards he was still sore about it.

While he sorted the deal out I took myself up to the mountains and tried to weigh everything up in my mind. If me and Sue carried on the way we were going, our relationship was going to go down the pan. Terrible thought, because we both loved each other as much as we'd always done, but circumstances were driving us apart. Added to that I missed my mum badly. She'd always been there for me when I was growing up and all the times I got myself into trouble. And then I missed silly things like salt-beef sandwiches up Stamford Hill; those plates of pie and mash in Cooksie's; and all those clubs, pubs and familiar turnings back home.

I had to get that white stuff out of my nose and straighten myself out. But what would I be letting myself in for? I was innocent of what they wanted to charge me for; I could account for the money I had at the time of the robbery – I'd earned it and never tried to hide it. Most of my cash went to a reputable accountant, Albert Fox. Is that the action of a guilty man? I could account for my movements on the night of the Security Express robbery and had a witness who could vouch for that. As for any statement that Barbara had made, well, what could she say that might hurt me if I had nothing to do with Security Express?

It seemed the only real problem would be whether or not I got bail. I couldn't be found guilty, I was confident of that, but I didn't want to sit in a stinking cell for three to twelve months until I satisfied the court. Back in 1985 I'd written to the Director of Public Prosecutions (DPP) enquiring how I was affected by the Security Express and Brinks-Mat robberies. I mean all these rumours were flying about, but I'd never once been approached by the police. I wrote in July, and on 17 September I received a reply signed by a D. M. Kirk. I've still got the letter, and I quote: 'As far as I know you are not wanted for questioning over the Security Express affair. Nor, to my knowledge, any other matter. There are no plans to interview you in Spain at present.'

How about that from the senior legal assistant? I was so pleased, I wrote thanking Mr Kirk, and he wrote back to me on the 30 September 1985 stating: 'The situation regarding yourself is unusual. The police have never expressed any interest in arresting you, and no warrant is outstanding against you.'

If that didn't put me in the clear I don't know what would, unless it was a conspiracy between the DPP and the police. I go home, they nick me and say, 'April Fool' or something, and I'm away for 22 years like my Johnny. I tried to get those letters published, but the press blanked me. They were more than willing to print any old garbage from the world and his wife, but straight from the horse's mouth, they didn't want to know.

The money being offered now was only important insofar as helping to prove my innocence. Justice doesn't come cheap. For the sake of our future Sue had said she would stand behind any decision I made. She didn't try to influence me one way or another, leaving the final step entirely up to me. The contract from the *News of the World* was lying on the coffee table at home. All I had to do was sign it, pick up the cash and sit back for the ball to start rolling. Either way, as I sat in the sun looking out to sea, I made up my mind to go for broke.

A few days later Barrie Tracey came back suggesting there could be an alternative deal on the table. Not only that, he'd made himself very busy by contacting his solicitor, Henri Brandman, a top man in London, to check out the legal aspects. This was March 1994, and as I'd made my decision I wanted to get it over with. But during the period of the next couple of weeks Tracey kept hedging, making different excuses for not concluding the deal.

He was a good friend. I trusted him and put the delay down to the fact that he was making sure every event was covered for my benefit. Then he told me that the *News of the World* were having second thoughts. A big story had broken, and bearing in mind the *News of the World*, being a Sunday paper, only had one day a week to publish whatever came up, they thought it would be in everybody's best interests to delay my return until July or August. He said they were hedging, but he did not tell me this until he had been in touch with the *Sun* newspaper and Sky television, and their combined deal, though less favourable, might be even better for us in the end.

Some time before I had personally turned down a straight £100,000 from *The Times* newspaper, and there was no way to resurrect it. Also an offer of £25,000 from a bloke by the name of Townsend, the editor of *The Cook Report*. He wanted Roger Cook to interview me and film every step of my return, right up until I walked into a British police station and surrendered myself to the police. The offer was a joke considering the fortunes they spent trying to pin me down before, so I told him where to put it. But where did that leave me?

So, when Tracey said our best option was to go with the *Sun* and Sky I thought, 'Come on, Barrie, you're fucking joking me! The *Sun* paid me and Barbara £55,000 for our story, and that was back in 1981 – 13 years ago.' He told me that, all being well, there would be other side benefits, possibly a film. I asked him how much that lot was worth in cash, but he just said it would all be sorted out later. I told him to go ahead and set it up.

As far as I was aware, Tracey had done everything in his power to smooth the way for me, and a big plus was that I believed he was going to stand bail for me so I wouldn't have to suffer all that carry-on like at the beginning of the murder trial.

When it came together things moved so fast I hardly had time to catch my breath. One minute I was playing with the dogs on the lawn, the next Barrie Tracey was flying in the gate telling me the press had heard what was going on and were converging at the airport before coming up to the villa. He told me to grab a suitcase and jump in the car. Sue was out, so I scribbled a note and left it on the kitchen table. I briefly explained what had happened and told her that she would be picked up, from the Cantina, a little restaurant we owned, and driven to meet me. Then I was whisked away to an exclusive hotel hideaway in Granada.

Two fellas from Sky television drove me there, and when we arrived they told me that as I was on expenses I could order anything I wanted. The best of food and drink, and even expensive suits if I fancied it. I had more serious things on my mind and getting kitted out wasn't one of them, so I didn't take advantage of the offer. I'd regret that in hindsight, like many other things.

Sue was brought to the hotel, and we spent a couple of days preparing ourselves for what was to come. It was bad enough saying goodbye to Sue, but in front of the cameras it was bloody terrible. Still, they were paying for the privilege so I had to swallow it. I managed to hold myself together – they hadn't paid enough to film Ronnie Knight with tears in his eyes, but my Sue couldn't help herself and spent most of her time either laughing or crying, and some of the time both together.

Sitting in the plane looking out of the window and waving to Sue and Pat Tracey as they stood on the tarmac, the thought furthest from my mind was that this would be the last time I would see my beautiful wife for many years. Already I was pre-empting my ordeal, and I don't suppose I had a chance to speak more than half a dozen words to Barrie Tracey on the way home.

As part of the deal Pat Tracey, who was also a journalist, was going to spend a few days with Sue and write up her exclusive story. Only it didn't work out like that. With me gone and not thinking straight, she allowed the *Sun* reporters into the villa. Between drinks and cups of tea she poured her heart out. The *Sun* reporters were no mugs. And one had a tape recorder tucked away, so unknowingly, my naïve Sue gave her story away and lost out.

I've always liked Pat Tracey – and, bless her, I don't want to cause her any grief – but I wish she had been able to make Sue keep her mouth shut. She was an experienced journalist and knew what it was all about, so I wish she could have done something to stop Sue wiping out all that cash.

Half my life seems to be spent finding out bad news after the event. The homeward trip passed too quickly for me, and it seemed like five minutes before I was walking down the steps from the plane at Luton Airport, to be arrested by Inspector Reed McGeorge. Somehow, it had been in my mind that I would have a nice drink on English soil, then leisurely give myself up at the nearest police station. Like with many other things, nobody put me right.

What I hadn't known was that it is the law for a pilot or captain to radio ahead if there is a wanted man or woman on board. Now, according to Mr Kirk from the DPP, there was nothing on me. One tiny detail he forgot to mention was a warrant could be dated at a moment's notice. Mine had been sitting on the shelf all sworn out just waiting for that date to bring it into action. The only difference between what I expected and what happened was that they nicked me before I was ready. So it was no surprise when I was charged with robbery and dishonestly handling a quantity of cash belonging to Security Express and taken to Wormwood Scrubs.

Christ! the place hadn't changed a bit, it was still a stinking hole. Even some of the same screws were there from my last visit back in 1980. One of the cons told me that since I was in before the rules had been changed, and it was no longer allowed for food to be brought in from outside. Still there was no chance of Barbara popping in with big plates of roast potatoes like she had during the murder trial. But what's a few days? Get the bail sorted, and it wouldn't be long before I was out and tucking into one of Joy Lumley's lovely steak dinners. The first of many while I waited for the trial that would clear my name.

Next morning, 3 May, at Bow Street Magistrates' Court, bail was refused, and even if it was granted friends told me that they wouldn't be able to stand bail because they were financially involved with me. Jim Lumley, who was there to support me, went mad. Jim was angry for my sake and said it should have been obvious something like that might happen and should have been taken care of before I left Spain. He looked really pissed off, and he wasn't the one going back to the Scrubs. As Jim was leaving he said, 'Don't get your hopes up, but I'll try to get my head round this at home.' I couldn't help it – my spirits rose because I trusted him.

They'd just about run out of ideas when Joy remembered a conversation we'd all had with some friends of ours – Derek and Betty, a lovely couple I'd known for over 25 years. Derek had once said over dinner, 'If you ever make up your mind to go home, I'll stand bail for you. However much it is.' Knowing Derek to be a decent sort and taking him at his word Sue contacted him. With no arguments, no excuses and definitely no percentage, Derek agreed to help me out.

Four days later Derek turned up at Bow Street Magistrates' Court with a certified cheque which he said I could use for bail. Home and dry for the time being? No, they turned my bail application down flat. What had been the point of letting me think I might get it in the first place if they were not going to accept it? Or had they thought I wouldn't be able to raise that sort of dough? I appealed twice more at Bow Street, then appealed twice to the High Court and once at the Old Bailey. Each time the prosecution, backed by the police, alleged that a major witness, who was married with two young children, had received threatening phone calls. If I was released on bail that family would have to be put into protective custody.

My defence told me that once he got this witness and others into court he could show they were not as squeaky clean as the prosecution made out. If this was the case, those supposed threats could have come from anyone and be nothing whatsoever to do with me. I tended to think that if their background was a bit iffy, a few threats and some arm twisting might make them remember some nonexistent phone call that couldn't be proved one way or another.

Is this what happened with Barbara? Jim had already told me that she'd been back to Leman Street station to make further statements two days after I was arrested. Albert Fox, the accountant, had also made a full statement and had opened up his books and desk diaries for close scrutiny. What was going on? Was Barbara cutting some deal with the law? How else could it be explained that she was going to be a major prosecution witness against me?

We found out later that the two-page statement she'd told me about had suddenly grown into 40 pages. My Sue had a warrant out for her arrest for handling the money she'd collected from Albert Fox. All Sue had done was collect money under my instructions from the accountant. Nothing else. It was all above board – no sneaking into the office under the cloak of darkness. Everything signed and sealed for.

The truth was and is that neither of them is guilty of anything. The point I'm making is that at the time, the police were convinced that the cash came from the Security Express robbery. They wanted me; they wanted my Sue; but they didn't want Barbara.

In case any bits of paper relating to the case were nicked out of my cell and sold to the papers, I was not allowed to keep anything, so I never really got the chance to study all the ins and outs of what was going on. Jim was a diamond though, and every single day he came into the Scrubs and went through all the questions that had been raised by Henri Brandman. Other times Henri came himself, or his assistant Tina, to make a lot of notes.

But to be honest I preferred dealing with Jim. He's a down to earth East Ender, but like a lot of blokes out of that part of London, he's got a bit of a head on his shoulders and an uncomplicated way of looking at things. So he managed to put across the details in plain English.

Never mind his own private life, when he wasn't in the Scrubs he was in Henri's office, and when he wasn't in either, him and Joy were studying all the papers relevant to the case. All for nothing except for our solid friendship. If some of my so-called friends had done what he had, I would never have found myself in that position.

With papers flying backwards and forwards between

prosecution and defence, I was soon aware of the contents of Barbara's statements. She'd already given me a knockback in a *Sunday Mirror* article 12 days after I came home. There was I pleading for bail at Bow Street, and she's earning herself a tidy sum slagging me off. As Derek Jamieson said on his radio programme, he'd 'never known anyone else who could sell the same story over and over again at £20,000 a time'.

Apart from other unpleasantries, Barbara suggested that I had even robbed her some years before. I'm protesting my innocence and facing 20 years, and my ex-wife is telling the world that I'm nothing but a toerag. Not long after the murder trial, we'd been burgled while living at Hendon Court. A load of jewellery was stolen, and a few odds and ends moved about. As I remember it I took it in my stride. No use crying over spilt milk – the job had been done, and there was little I could do about it.

Barbara's story was that when I came home to find the police there after she'd called them I went mad. That I refused to let them take fingerprints; basically that I threw them out. I do know something about the law, even though I picked it up on the wrong side. If someone calls them in and an offence has been committed, they take over the business. Doesn't matter who you are, you don't tell them whether or not to carry out an investigation. So that was rubbish.

Worse than that, Barbara finished the piece by saying in a joking manner, 'Strange how all that jewellery worth £50,000 disappeared at the same time as my husband [Ronnie Knight]. So now he's back in England I won't be going in for expensive jewellery.' Some fucking joke! You don't have to be a genius to work out what she was getting at.

As far as Albert Fox's statement went, it was all very technical, consisting of pages and pages of cross-referenced accounts dealing with every transaction I had ever made through him. Not only that but dates and times of when I telephoned him or called into his office. I had no problem with that as I knew my dealings with him couldn't have been more above board. I'd known him for years, and whenever he asked me where certain sums of cash had originated, as he was entitled to, I always answered openly. To my knowledge he was satisfied and happy to take my business.

Barbara's, on the other hand, was a completely different kettle of fish. Once I had a chance to scan the statement, I found the damning part of it was not so much what she said, but what she didn't say. An actress's trade, stock in hand or main asset, is being able to mimic other characters – but more important than anything else is the ability to remember their lines. Without an above-average memory, they might as well work in a shop. Confronted with Albert Fox's detailed account Barbara, who's been in the business since she was a kid, had major lapses of memory. Questioned about my whereabouts on the night of the robbery, she went blank. And everything else the police asked her brought on a severe case of amnesia.

She did volunteer that she'd never known me to

have a bank account but didn't add, 'But then why should he? He used mine.' She told them that around and up to April 1983 I appeared to be skint. That my usual healthy amount of cash had dried up. If that was the case, who was paying her very expensive [£5000] life insurances, when she couldn't? Albert's statement for that period states: 'From my records I can see no other source of income for Barbara Windsor other than Mr Knight.'

Now, remember, we were husband and wife. Bills had to be paid and everything for daily life had to be bought. We must have been a bloody odd couple if we never talked about what sort of money we had in our shared account. We shared it, but it was in her name only, and she told the police she didn't have a clue what was in it.

Asked about her paying in the sum of £25,000 cash, she said she knew nothing about it. And added that in fact she had never seen such a large sum of cash in all her life. Asked about a cash payment of £8000, she had no memory of this but could only guess it was from me towards some jewellery I was buying for her. Nice little present. How could she forget that? Back then £8000 was more than many people earned for a year's work. Later on she amended her statement to say the £8000 might have been for repairs or alterations to jewellery her mother had left her and the purchase of a car.

It went on and on. Questioned about sums of money, each time her answer was the same: 'I have no knowledge of this money.' Every page was signed by her and witnessed by Detective Sergeant Wraith. If DS Wraith thought she was taking the piss I'll never know. But come on!

This was one very shrewd lady with a sharp business sense and her finger on every penny that came near her. She'd grown up in the cut-throat world of show business and could scan a contract in two minutes, then remember every clause, right down to the last half per cent. She wouldn't even sign an autograph without checking the paper first, yet she was quite happy to tell the law that she blindly put her name to anything that Albert Fox stuck under her nose because she trusted him.

She could remember every word to songs learnt at her mother's knee. And don't forget this was the woman who remembered a seven-year-old rubber cheque that helped to convince the jury that I was innocent of being involved in the murder.

Barbara may have forgotten, but I went to Hendon Court Hall on the night of the robbery, and I had a witness to that visit. I often gave clothes that I was tired of to Wayne, the caretaker of the flats. I'm talking expensive gear and most of it nearly new. Trouble was half the time I spoke more about giving him bits and pieces than actually doing it, because with so much going on in my head it wasn't until I bumped into him that I would remember my promise, or it would be in the boot of my car, and I'd clean forget. So I said to him, 'Don't be embarrassed to remind me next time you see me.' And that's what happened on the night.

I was walking into Hendon Court at about 11.30 and met the caretaker at the main door. As soon as I saw him I knew I'd done it again, so I took the coat off my back and handed it to him. He was well pleased, and so he should have been – that coat was top quality and had cost me a fortune. We said goodnight, and I went into the flat to Barbara. And stayed all night.

The only drawback to the caretaker proving I was at the flat that night, and at the same time giving Barbara's memory a nudge, was that Henri Brandman couldn't find him to serve a subpoena. The last time he was seen was when him and his wife, Jean, worked at Barbara and Stephen's restaurant, The Plough. When news leaked out that I was on my way back they then disappeared. Why? Where? Draw your own conclusions.

My other witness, Graham Roberts, was another one employed by Barbara. She first took him on as a housekeeper and chauffeur when we lived at Aylmer Drive. He was a nice fella with a bit of a feminine side to him, and whether it was down to that I don't know, but Barbara often acted bitchy with him. What she didn't realize was that he was a better friend to me than he ever was to her. He was another one like Kenny Williams when it came to marking my card. He was always running her around so knew what was going on. 'She's having it off, Ronnie,' he used to say. And he filled me in on plenty of other stuff.

I'd banked on him being able to square up many things once he got into court, but it wasn't to be. After I was arrested he was one of the first to send me his best wishes, though apologising that his ill health would prevent him visiting. When Henri Brandman went to interview him he found that while I had been in Spain Graham had been fitted with a pacemaker, and medical advice suggested his serious condition ruled him out from giving evidence as an Old Bailey ordeal could prove fatal.

Two witnesses down, but even then I was still confident that Barbara would be forced to tell the whole truth. One way or another her whole statement was completely negative – almost scripted to put me in a bad light. But I would have my day in court.

Acting for me were two of the finest barristers in the country: Richard Ferguson and Trevor Burke; I knew that they couldn't wait to get Barbara on the stand. All I needed was the chance to put my side of the story, then all the years of speculation and rumour could be settled once and for all.

My counsel told me many times that it would be very difficult for a jury to be sworn in due to the fact of the unprecedented amount of publicity I had received over the years. How could anyone remain unbiased after constantly reading about the accusations against me for 12 years? My newspaper cuttings filled a suitcase, and the television coverage was vast. In fact, during one of the attempts to have me expelled from Spain, I was on every peak-time news broadcast for three days.

In what I thought was a pathetic attempt to nullify this mountain of publicity, the judge slapped a ban on the news media. This meant that nothing could be reported concerning myself or the case for at least three days for fear of prejudicing my trial. The way I looked at it was that it wouldn't matter if they never mentioned me for a year, it still couldn't wipe out what had been said before. But I suppose there was some legal angle – and he was the guvnor.

One Thursday in October 1994 I was glancing through the *Sun* newspaper and read a small piece about Barbara that said she was going to make her debut in *EastEnders* the following month. I can remember thinking good luck to her, but it was a pity she hadn't got a job like that when we were together; at least she would have come home every night. Then I turned to page five, and there, in glorious colour, were two photographs of me in my cell, and an inset photo of me and Sue in Spain.

What Henri had said flashed before my mind; 'The press cannot publish anything concerning you before your trial – the matter is *sub judice*.' Well, that was out the window for a start. I couldn't take it in. How could it have happened? It must have been one of the screws earning himself a few bob, as it was unlikely a con would be wandering round with a camera in his hand.

Not realising the full importance of the piece at that moment I just thought, so much for the press ban, and got on with what I was doing. Which was mainly signing autographs. Can you believe it? It seemed like every con in the Scrubs had a copy of the *Sun*, and the cheeky bastards were lining up for me to write my name across the pictures.

About an hour later I was brought up in front of the Governor. He was livid and asked me what I knew about the article and pictures. I told him it was as much a surprise to me as it was to him. He seemed sympathetic to my protests and said he would get to the bottom of it, but I'm not so sure he didn't think I really had something to do with taking those photographs. I put in an immediate request to see Henri Brandman, but the Governor told me he'd already contacted him and sent me back to my cell.

When Henri turned up in the afternoon he didn't look too happy. He said that far from being just another bit of publicity, like I thought it was, it would have far-reaching and damaging implications for me. He also said that this was the first time ever that a prisoner had been photographed in his cell and the picture sold to a national newspaper. Like the Governor, he asked me if I was involved. I gave him an emphatic No! and told him I was fed up about it. He said he would write a formal letter to the Governor asking for an investigation and then wait for the results.

For a week or so I carried on my daily prison life in blissful ignorance of what was going on behind the scenes. Then Jim Lumley brought a bombshell with him on a visit. Because of our friendship and the way he'd worked tirelessly between me and my defence, they thought it best if he explained the situation I was just about to find out about. I remember that day clearly. As he walked into the visiting room I knew something was up. Every day for seven months we'd sat face to face with just a table between us. Usually he kept my spirits up with a laugh and a joke but not this time.

'Sorry, mate, there's no easy way to say this. There is a problem. They know who took the photos in the cell. Like we suspected it was one of the warders. He brought the camera in, done the business, then smuggled it out and handed the film over to a third party who sold it on to the *Sun*. And he's prepared to go in to the witness box on oath and say you paid him to do it.

'It seems this warder had a second job on the side – moonlighting at Hammersmith Palais as a bouncer-cum-doorman. He'd been under observation by a team of drug-squad detectives and was caught red-handed selling ecstasy tablets. He was nicked and taken in for questioning. I don't know what went on in the station, but at the end of the day he's done a trade with the law and put you up as get-out.

'What this means to you is that, from the point of view of the law you deliberately set out to break the no-publicity ban in an effort to prevent a jury being sworn in that could honestly say they hadn't heard of you. In a nutshell the law are saying you tried to pervert the course of justice, and that carries a 12-year sentence.'

Worse was to come. Jim told me that a deal with the prosecution had been discussed. If I pleaded guilty to handling money from Security Express, the charge of taking part in the robbery would stand, but perverting the course of justice would be dropped. 'Ron, this is the worst day's work I have ever had to do,' Jim said. 'Don't go up in the air, but I've been asked to put it to you that you consider very carefully your defence's proposal.'

My first reaction was to go up in the air. 'No fucking way, Jim! I'm not holding my hands up. They can bring who they fucking well like into the box, but I'm never going to plead guilty to anything!' As he was leaving Jim said, 'Just give it some thought, mate. Henri will be in to see you soon.'

My defence had assured me right from the beginning that with lack of evidence there was little chance of me being convicted of taking part in the robbery. As for the handling charge they said there was a fifty-fifty chance of discrediting the two witnesses against me. Particularly Barbara, whose statements showed that her memory came and went. As Jim pointed out, by bringing in the perverting charge, one way or another they were going to make sure that my forthcoming trial gave them the result they were looking for. Unlike the murder trial and its happy ending. Every time in the past when I'd pulled a flanker on the law, it had strengthened their resolve to get me one way or another, and that day had arrived.

An incident I didn't think much of at the time, though it upset Sue, was when Barbara came over to Spain during the time I was considering giving myself up. Back when she first put the reporter on to me with an offer from the *News of the World*. Like I've said, I left it in the air for a while so she was probably wondering what was going on. Having been through a major woman's operation, she came over to Spain to recover at the home of her friend Gina, which was not very far from us. Before she'd left England, my friend Poochie, who still kept in touch with her, had asked her to pass on a birthday present to me of £200 cash. She phoned me after arriving, and I popped over to Gina's place to say hello.

We chatted, and it was all quite friendly. She asked me what my plans were and all other kinds of stuff, which I put down to general conversation. It wasn't until I found out about her cooperation and statements to the police that the whole thing took on a more sinister aspect. Only then did Sue's comments when I got home that day, come back to me.

'Ask yourself, Ronnie, she'd said, 'with all her money and the whole world to choose from, why did she decide to convalesce five minutes away from you? And that money. She could have had it delivered, she didn't have to meet you personally unless she's up to something.'

No way would I plead guilty to handling. I came back voluntarily to clear my name, with the firm belief, based on my innocence, that I could answer every accusation. If I allowed the law to gag me I would never get a chance to explain where my small fortune came from at the time of the robbery. Nor would Barbara have to climb into the dock and justify her statements. To plead guilty would go against my nature. I never considered it all the times I really was guilty. To do it when I was innocent wasn't on the cards. Henri Brandman came in to see me and warned me of the very serious risk I faced, telling me to give the matter some serious thought. I told him I would make a decision, tell Jim on the coming Sunday, and he would pass the message on.

It was a sad-looking three that discussed my fate on that Sunday. Jim and Joy both came to see me, and they were clearly upset. They couldn't make up my mind for me, but were obviously aware of the hopelessness of my situation. Joy pointed out that my brother Jimmy had pleaded not guilty to the handling charge, and he'd got eight years. Freddie Foreman had gone for a not guilty on the same charge and had received nine years. Trevor Burke had told Joy and Jim that, taking into consideration that I had come back and given myself up, I would be saving the state the expense of a lengthy trial, therefore in his opinion I should expect a sentence of between six and seven years.

Seven years is a very long time, but when weighed against the possibility of twelve years, it certainly did look the easier option. I was shaking like that time I met Lorraine at Malaga airport. God, that seemed a long time ago. I stood up, counted to ten, kissed Joy, shook hands with Jim and said, 'Let's get it over, mate. Tell Henri I'll plead guilty to the handling.'

After that it was all downhill. As I watched the two of them disappear down the long visiting room, there was no turning round with waves and smiles like every other time. I went back to my cell and pondered on what it would all mean. How would Sue understand what I'd done? In her last letter she'd told me that she had the local builders in putting up new balustrades and generally tidying the villa in readiness for my homecoming. She said she was already planning the biggest party the Costa had ever seen. Poor girl, she would have to put that on hold for half a dozen years.

And what about the public? All those years of protesting my innocence and resisting deportation. What would they think? That it was just so much bullshit, and the law had been right all along. They wouldn't know of what forced me to put my hand up, they'd just read my 'Guilty' in the papers and accept that I must have done it. The sighs of relief from the police would be like a gale-force wind, and what about Barbara? Would she be relieved that I was going to be banged up without a full trial?

My day in court that was going to be so momentous and perhaps even make legal history was short and to the point. With a stroke of a pen Judge Gordon sentenced me to seven years in prison for handling £314,813 of Security Express money. The old sod wasn't going to miss the chance of having a dig at me. He looked over his glasses and said, 'I think you know more of this robbery than you are prepared to say.' Then added, 'It is my opinion that you handled a robber's share.'

Small consolation at the time, but he didn't make a compensation order against me on behalf of Security Express. They would have to chase this themselves, and there was no question in my mind other than that they would. Not only did I face imprisonment – at the end of it I could look forward to bankruptcy.

With finances in mind I asked Jim to arrange a meet with Barrie Tracey so that I could find out what the situation was. Like I'd thought earlier, he wasn't slow off the mark and was already knocking on the door about further deals. When we met up, he went into great detail over what other stories would be about. Jim and me listened to all this with patience, but to be honest I wasn't too interested, and in the end I said, 'That all sounds great, but what I want to talk about is how much you're holding for me in the bank.'

'As you know,' he said, 'I had to take the only deal that was on offer, and that was £50,000 from the *Sun* and Sky; a proposed deal for Sue was refused by the lawyers.' I stopped him there. 'Hang on,' I said, 'I thought that was separate from my deal.' 'It was,' he said, 'but she lost it when she volunteered her story regarding your return. I know my wife Pat was with her, but Sue never left off talking, and there was no way of shutting her up.'

'Yeah,' I said, 'and what about the rest?' 'I paid a huge sum to Sue. Then there were your bail appeals. And pre-legal aid costs which came to £10,500, and then your legal aid contributions were £6500, plus another £3000 for accountant's fees you weren't covered for and you got the balance as agreed.'

'OK, that covers one payment.' So I thought, 'Fucking good, innit? I come back for almost nothing. I get seven years. I'm facing bankruptcy, and nothing in the pot to square it.' I was so gutted I didn't want to discuss it any further. I was beginning to look a right mug for entertaining the idea of coming back.

As to how I came to be in this position, what had really happened? A month or so prior to my trial Trevor Burke went for a contempt of court action against the *Sun*. And also to extend the present order to cover no photographs to be taken of me in the prison environment. Nothing came of the contempt, and why should it? Thanks to British justice the law got the result they were after. As for the extension of the order, the judge said it wasn't in his powers to make orders concerning what went on inside prison walls. Nor did he have the power to order the Governor of Wormwood Scrubs to set up an enquiry as to who really took the photographs. You scratch my back, I'll scratch yours.

Everything about my case from the moment I left for Spain with my Sue, right up until I got seven years was rotten. Nothing but lies and corruption, and I ended up paying the price. How about a bit of justice for me, Roger Cook? You're the knight in shining armour battling for the truth. You scaled mountainsides, hung from a helicopter and ran yourself ragged all round the Costa in your efforts to get something against me. Why not do the same again, but this time on my behalf?

I've nothing to fear. Find my missing witness. Talk to anyone you like about my money. Talk to the prison warder who took the photographs. Have a quick word with Barbara Windsor. And if you don't find enough intrigue to keep your viewers on the edge of their seats, then I don't know what will.

Failing that, the truth will never come out in the open, because once the judge's gavel came down on my seven years, the media's circus was over, and Ronnie Knight was history.

13.
Approaching
Parole

AFTER THE VERDICT I was sent back to the
Scrubs. Not only to consider how the hell I
was going to get through the best part of
seven years, but how to face the devastating news
that once I'd paid my debt to society I was to be
stripped clean of every possession. With no choice
I'd put my name to handling £314,813. Henri
Brandman told me that Kennedys, the lawyers
acting for Security Express, were already planning
an action to recover this money, and were seeking
damages and interest that could amount to half a
million. Unless I could show some satisfactory effort
to pay back this money, it was guaranteed they

would make me bankrupt and seize all my assets.

If Barrie Tracey had negotiated a good deal for me, I should have had at least a hundred grand in the bank. All right, it's a long way off half a million, but making some gesture might have just swung their final decision to be lenient. As it was I only had my villa, and to lose that would just about finish me. It was never a flash second residence. It was my dream come true. My only consolation was that any civil-court action could take years, so I had to put the thoughts of it out of my head and concentrate on being strong for my forthcoming ordeal behind bars.

What with digging up memories – good and bad – writing this book has been painful at times. Normally we keep our sadnesses buried deep. We know they are there, but the edges are off the pain. Yet I've had to think deeply about friends and family and resurrect thoughts that give me grief. Mum and Dad, my brothers Billy and David, and two good mates – Albert and Siddy. Bless them, they're all gone, and I miss them all.

My marriages to June and Barbara: we had our ups and downs, but a lot of nice memories too. While I was in prison I thought of my Sue and how it would be when I finally walked out of those gates. Despite those nasty bastards who wrote anonymously from Spain telling tales about my Sue being on the town every night, I never let them get to me. My strong belief in what we had took the sting out of every letter.

Now I'm free, I'll be on licence until near enough the year 2002. If I break my parole during that time I can be put back inside to finish my full seven. I will be under the supervision of a probation officer, and unless they show some compassion for my situation, I'll not be allowed to leave the country. Problem! I haven't been able to return to my wife, and as she still has a warrant outstanding against her for handling monies from Security Express, she can't come to England.

All I can hope for is that any ensuing publicity about the anomaly of Barbara being free as a national institution on *EastEnders*, while my Sue is a wanted criminal, will bring the matter to a head. In my view, they're either both guilty – or they're both innocent. I'm not blaming Barbara for all this. It's down to the law.

One really fantastic bit of news I've had lately is that my friends, working together, have saved me from the bankruptcy that would have meant losing my home. A conversation with my mate Johnny Lloyd about the situation I was facing reminded him that his wife, Jean, had once had a similar problem, which was all squared away to her advantage by a chap by the name of Terry Bell. Jim Lumley got in touch with Jean, and she gave him the details of what she'd been through and put him on to Bell.

Terry Bell's a professional negotiator and Managing Director of Crown Central One International. What he explained to Jim was that if a sensible amount of money could be found, he would act as a go-between in talks with Kennedys, to stave off the threat of bankruptcy. This is where two lovely people came back into the picture. Derek and Betty who had put up my bail money. Jim contacted them, explained my situation, and, without hesitation, they offered to buy my villa at its market value of £110,000. Armed with that amount of cash Terry Bell approached Kennedys' lawyers, and there must be a god in heaven because they accepted this in full settlement of my debt to them.

The whole business is over, and all threats of me being made insolvent are in the past. I have squared my debt to society. I've settled with Security Express and can start with a clean slate. But have I lost my home? No. That's the beauty of what Derek and Betty have done for me. They bought the villa, but for my sake not their own. And they want me to live there until such time as I am back in the position of buying it back from them. Whether it takes five years or twenty.

During the last few months in prison, I felt I could face my future with a clear mind. I was looking forward to my first day out. Day release is the system's way of easing you back into society. I had to stay within a certain radius of the prison, but between 9.30 am and 6.30 pm I was a completely free man.

I was also looking forward to being able to sink into obscurity to enjoy the rest of my life with Sue.

And when I was still in prison and I really did believe that's how life would turn out once I was released. And to tell you the truth, the thought of getting back to Spain and my wife Sue kept me going during my four years behind the door. But how many relationships can survive when two people are separated by a thousand miles and the contact is by phone or letter? I'm not saying it can't happen, but obviously our feelings for each other were not as strong as I'd imagined. I really did love Sue and told myself her feelings for me would stay the same, but as the time between letters got longer and longer I just had to accept that whatever was between us was over. When you're inside there's not much else to do but think and I'd be lying if I said it didn't hurt. But I've never been one for worrying about something I couldn't change, so I kept my thoughts to myself and got on with finishing my time.

Things got easier for me when I reached the point where I was trusted enough to be sent out for daily work in the community. I loved every minute of it and it took my mind off what had gone wrong in my marriage. What they had me doing was tidying up the gardens around old people's bungalows and I had a great time. The old girls loved having this bit of a rascal pottering about and they all looked after me like mothers. 'Little bit of dinner here Ronnie.' 'Got a cream bun to go with your cup of tea.' They spoiled me rotten.

By now I'd accepted the way things were between Sue and me and come to terms with the fact that as far as I was concerned, love and romance were right out the window. That is until I met Diane. I wasn't looking for anyone, but isn't that always the way? Life's plodding along, then out of the blue – bang – everything's turned on its head and that's just what happened one Saturday when I was staying with friends on my day home release.

This nice young girl turned up with her children and I think my mate Poochie must have noticed I was a bit taken by her, because the following Saturday he invited Diane to join us for my birthday celebration in a restaurant in Leicester Square. The rest, as they say, is history.

Back inside Send open prison, I began to phone her every day. No thoughts of romance or nothing, she was just someone nice to talk to. But slowly our relationship got stronger and stronger until we were making plans to make what we felt for each other permanent. This didn't happen overnight and we didn't rush into it without a lot of thought. It wasn't just our feelings we had to consider but those of her three children, Jessica, Hannah and William. As it turned out they took to me quite naturally and I love the three of them like they were my own.

When I finally walked out of those prison gates, I knew exactly where I wanted to be and that was with Diane and the kids. My lifestyle now is the complete opposite of what it was in the old days and I don't regret the change one bit. Peace of mind, that's what it's all about and I've certainly got that with my new family. We have a lovely, ordinary life which is a lot quieter but normal. We love going to good restaurants with the children, but every now and then we treat ourselves to a nice romantic meal on our own at a favourite restaurant.

This is all I want: No more ducking and diving; no more dodgy deals – just a good quiet life with Diane and the children.

Falling back on a past that's all behind me, I spend my days now writing crime fiction novels. And believe me that's the closest I will ever get to those days that got me known as 'Britain's Most Wanted'.